"Mark McKergow's book provides a complete and e
development of Solution Focused practice, summari
knowledge in the field and looks at possible changes and advances in this part
of the therapy world. I know of no clearer record of its history and the conse-
quential events."

Dr Alasdair Macdonald, *retired consultant psychiatrist
and freelance researcher, author of Solution Focused Therapy:
Theory, Research & Practice*

"A fascinating account of the past, present and future of SFBT that inspires us
solution-focused practitioners to 'stretch our world' to notice key developments
and invites others to 'stretch their world' to regard SFBT as a viable approach!"
Peter Sundman, *Taitoba Institute, Helsinki, Finland*

"My coaching school and I have been waiting for this book! Finally, we can
read about the most recent developments in Solution Focused thinking and
practice, and all in a nutshell! I would recommend this book to anyone who
would like to understand Solution Focus in order to enhance their Solution
Focused work."

Kirsten Dierolf, *MCC, Owner and Founder of SolutionsAcademy,
ICF accredited coach training school, Germany*

"What Mark McKergow achieves with this book is quite phenomenal. Beyond
an enthralling history of the development of Solution Focus practice, it offers
new insights in the philosophy of therapy as such. This work will be an instant
classic and a reference for everybody who aspires to be an effective, efficient
and respectful coach and therapist."

Anton Stellamans, *Il Faro, Belgium*

"Mark McKergow takes the reader through the story of Solution Focused practice from its conception and early formative influences through the dilemmas
and developments that led to the effective, efficient, ethical and elegant form of
the practice that is most widely taught and used today. The book is invaluable
not only for how to do good SF practice, but also about what happens when
we do, why it works, and how we can explain this convincingly and powerfully
to others. It is also a really great read!"

Suzi Curtis, *Clinical Psychologist, Accreditation Lead for the UK
Association for Solution Focused Practice*

"This book provides a beautifully straightforward, comprehensive overview of
the current state-of-the-art of solution-focused brief therapy and where it sits
in the larger therapeutic landscape. Excitingly, it goes the extra mile by exploring how we can make sense of the effectiveness of this special kind of therapy
through the lens of the avant-garde enactivist movement in philosophy and

cognitive science. It is a full package that serves as an exciting starting point for looking afresh at how we might better enhance mental health and wellbeing, effectively and efficiently."

Daniel D. Hutto, *Senior Professor of Philosophical Psychology, Head of the School of Liberal Arts, University of Wollongong, Australia*

"Mark McKergow offers fresh and exciting insights on the evolving practice of Solution Focus Brief Therapy in this new book… by looking back at its genesis and emergence as a distinct and new kind of treatment; analysing its present principles and aesthetic, before building a new paradigm, which explores the question of how we continue to 'stretch the world' for our clients and practitioners. Turning these complex problems into solutions speaks loudly to my instincts as a coach and improviser. Exploring Mark's new insights, ideas and methods will become the bedrock of my work with individuals and groups for years to come."

Andrew Paine, *Life Coach*

"I can think of no other book that extends the classic canon of the development of Solution Focused practice as well as this one. The world has been awaiting a description of next steps in the continuous, and unstoppable, development of the practice. Mark has been at the centre of it all, but also pleasantly looking beyond its horizons. This book captures the twists and turns that have been evident for quite some time, both viewable from a far and from its midst. It is an amazing achievement."

Jonas Wells, *Coordination manager of South Dalarna Coordination Agency & chair of the Swedish Association of Solution-Focused Practitioners*

The Next Generation of Solution Focused Practice

The Next Generation of Solution Focused Practice shows how practitioners help create change by 'stretching the world' of their clients.

The book brings new ideas from enactive cognition which show how skilled attention on the client and their words is important both practically and conceptually. It provides both a summary of the development of Solution Focused Brief Therapy (SFBT) over time and how the latest developments form a newly coherent form of practice based on developing descriptions. The author has structured the book using simple and easy to understand metaphors to paint a rich, creative, and visual picture of therapy for the reader, which makes it an accessible read.

This book will be of interest to a wide range of SF practitioners internationally, as well as to those involved in coaching, counselling, family therapy, education, social work, healthcare and organisational change.

Dr Mark McKergow is Director at the Centre for Solutions Focus at Work in Edinburgh, Scotland. He is the author of six books including *The Solutions Focus* (with Paul Z Jackson) and *Hosting Generative Change* (BMI, 2020). Mark sits on the editorial boards of the *Journal of Solution Focused Practice* and the *Journal of Systemic Therapies*, and is a leading light in the SOLWorld community of organisational SF practitioners. He also plays jazz, clarinet and saxophone.

The Next Generation of Solution Focused Practice

Stretching the World for New Opportunities and Progress

Mark McKergow

Routledge
Taylor & Francis Group

LONDON AND NEW YORK

First published 2021
by Routledge
2 Park Square, Milton Park, Abingdon, Oxon OX14 4RN

and by Routledge
52 Vanderbilt Avenue, New York, NY 10017

Routledge is an imprint of the Taylor & Francis Group, an informa business

© 2021 Mark McKergow

British Library Cataloguing-in-Publication Data
A catalogue record for this book is available from the British Library

Library of Congress Cataloging-in-Publication Data
A catalog record for this book has been requested

ISBN: 978-0-367-42885-3 (hbk)
ISBN: 978-0-367-42883-9 (pbk)
ISBN: 978-0-367-85571-0 (ebk)

Typeset in Bembo
by Apex CoVantage, LLC

Paperback cover image by Emily Allchurch

Contents

Acknowledgements

This book draws on close to 30 years of work, learning and exploration. There are many people to thank. First I heartily acknowledge Steve de Shazer and Insoo Kim Berg who led the development of Solution Focused (SF) practice in its first iterations and opened the doors for what has come next. I was thrilled to know them and work with them. Among their colleagues I particularly thank Gale Miller, 'researcher of SF practitioners', for his encouragement and fellowship over the years.

I discovered SF through an encounter with James Wilk at an AMED seminar in London when I collapsed on a hot day wearing a woollen suit and he had to call in paramedics. I have a great deal to thank him for in pointing me in the direction of brief therapy. When I discovered SF work it was with colleagues who formed the Bristol Solutions Group: Harry Norman, John Henden, Jenny Clarke, Paul Z Jackson, Kate Hart, Ron Banks and later Alasdair Macdonald. I worked for a long time with Paul Z Jackson in writing *The Solutions Focus*, the first SF coaching and organisational change book, and learned a lot about writing along the way.

Over the years I have worked with so many people that it is impossible to mention them all here. Chris Iveson, Evan George and Harvey Ratner at BRIEF in London have been generous with trainings, connections, co-operation and allowing the use of their offices for meetings. Matthias Varga von Kibed and Insa Sparrer of the SySt Institute in Munich have offered immense encouragement and delightful Wittgensteinian conversations. My colleagues at SFWork over the years helped in devising new ways in applying SF ideas: Roy Marriott (Shakyakumara), Antoinette Oglethorpe, Bruce Woodings and Steve Onyett. Stanus Cloete and Sofie Geisler travelled many miles many times to be with us. Eva Persson and (the much missed) Björn Johansson invited Jenny and me to work with in Karlstad many times and started the Karlstad group, which has turned out to be an influential step in many ways.

The organisers and participants of SOLWorld conferences and events (the long list is at solworld.org), European Brief Therapy Association and UK Association for Solution Focused Practice conferences have always created great settings for mutual learning and sharing. My fellow InterAction journal editors have always been important sounding blocks for new work: Kirsten Dierolf (who also gave me access to her archive of SF papers and articles), Carey Glass and Anton Stellamans. I received a great deal of help on Wittgenstein and enactivism from Dan Hutto, Daniele Moyal-Sharrock and others in the Philosophy Department at the University of Hertfordshire, where I was privileged to be a Visiting Research Fellow from 2013–2017, and also the British Wittgenstein Society.

Many people have helped me to get the historical aspects of this book into shape; Brian Cade, Wendel Ray, Harry Korman, Guy Shennan and Alasdair Macdonald were generous with their time. Steve Flatt helped me understand the state of therapy provision in the UK. Ben Cross, Tara Gretton and Chris Iveson provided key input to the practical chapters. I thank Janet Bavelas, Sara Smock Jordan, Peter De Jong and Harry Korman for giving permission for their microanalysis table to be reproduced in Chapter 7.

The book was improved enormously with input from readers including Jonas Wells, Suzi Curtis, Peter Sundman, Andrew Paine, Leigh Jones, Sofie Geisler and Anton Stellamans. I am excited that artist Emily Allchurch produced the cover illustration in her own style and featuring her work.

And, in the end, none of this would have been possible without Jenny Clarke – my colleague, fellow traveller, so-whatness monitor, first and sternest editor and my wife. Thank you for everything Jenny.

Chapter 1

Introduction

Change is happening all the time ... the simple way to change is to notice useful change and amplify it.

American futurist Buckminster Fuller wrote: 'You never change things by fighting the existing reality. To change something, build a new model that makes the existing model obsolete' (Sieden, 2011, p. 358). This book sets out to show how, in the world of mental illness and personal change, there is already such a new model. It doesn't rely on diagnosis. It doesn't rely on a conventional therapeutic alliance between practitioner and client. It appears to be effective across cultures, class and social hierarchies. It has been extensively researched, though sometimes not in ways which satisfy the old model. And, in the latest evolutions, it complements a new picture of mental wellbeing based on the integrative paradigm of enactive cognition. It is the next generation of Solution Focused Brief Therapy (SFBT) and, more broadly, Solution Focused (SF) practice.

SFBT has had an interesting and distinctive evolution. Arriving as a distinct form of practice in the late 1980s, it has in many ways seen a meteoric rise. From roots in the interactional brief and family therapy tradition, the approach has found enthusiastic adoption in myriad fields including social work, education, coaching, organisational development and public service. It is in use around the world, with more and more national associations appearing every year. The results and research are very positive – successful outcomes for most clients are built consistently and rapidly, with long-term sustainability and customer satisfaction. This huge international impact from tiny beginnings in a maverick therapy project in Milwaukee, Wisconsin is in many ways a runaway success.

And yet ... SFBT has operated, and continues to operate, largely outside the mainstream of mental health work. Other practices such as Cognitive Behavioural Therapy (CBT) are often presented as a default choice by providers, while older traditions rooted in the work of Sigmund Freud and Carl Gustav Jung still hold considerable sway in some circles. In some ways this is not surprising – new ideas have always had to struggle against the forces of conservatism to gain a foothold. There are few sightings of SFBT in academic settings (with a few honourable and growing exceptions), perhaps because it has been practitioner-led and empirically developed.

It seems to me that the lack of headway for SFBT in the 'establishment' (as opposed to with individual practitioners) is more fundamental than this. Bluntly, SFBT challenges some fundamental assumptions in the field of mental health. To take it seriously would be to undermine many decades of established wisdom. SFBT practitioners have been eloquent in *showing* what we do, but less convincing in being able to *talk about* what we do (as opposed to how we do it) to other professionals, academics and service commissioners.

The purpose of this book is therefore threefold:

- To bring together developments in the field of SFBT and of SF practice more generally over the past three decades into a coherent starting point for the next generation of practitioners and researchers
- To connect this emerging practice with the emerging theory of enactive cognition, a field rich in possibilities which resonates well with theoretical positions taken by SFBT co-founder Steve de Shazer and others, and
- To combine these two positions to show how SFBT, particularly in the latest developments, 'stretches the world' of the client – giving a theory of change, a look at why SFBT might be effective, and ultimately a new view on how we look at mental illness which is applicable across the board – providing a potential new agenda for practitioners and researchers alike.

We will look at established practices in new ways, gain novel understandings of how they work, how they contribute to effectiveness and how they might be further developed in future.

A bold ambition

This is, I admit, a bold ambition. It is no less bold than the ambition of Steve de Shazer, Insoo Kim Berg and others when set up their Brief Family Therapy Centre (BFTC) in Milwaukee, Wisconsin in 1978. Not long before her death, Insoo told me (and the audience at the SOLWorld 2006 conference in Vienna, Austria) that their original impetus had been to further develop Brief Therapy methods, as a response to the long-term therapy methods which still held sway at that time.

Now, in the 21st century, that struggle against long-term therapy (at least in its 20-years-on-the-couch form) seems to be largely won. People are more interested in efficiency, resources are limited, there is increased awareness of the need for informed choice and involvement for patients and clients rather than simply handing all power to the all-knowing professional. However, some of the assumptions of long-term therapy still hold considerable sway. Longer treatments must be 'better'. Rapid progress is to be distrusted as a 'flight to health'. Expectations of progress are 'putting pressure on the client', and so on.

In this book I will be presenting a view of how we as humans operate which shows how such assumptions are misguided. We are now in a position to reshape not just practice but the very paradigm of what it means to live well. The practice can be subtle, and there will be some fine distinctions to be made. They will make better sense, however, in this framework of 'stretching the world'.

A tradition of outsider perspectives

de Shazer and Berg were both 'outsiders' in their chosen field. de Shazer was a professional saxophonist with a fine arts degree and a master's in social work before he found his place as a therapist. Berg trained in pharmacy studies in South Korea before getting bachelor and master's degrees in science in the USA. They chose to work with colleagues from a variety of fields – 'philosophers, educators, sociologists, physicians, linguists, even engineers, along with usual mental health professionals' as Insoo recalled (Berg, 2007).

I too am an outsider in the world of brief therapy, albeit one with a long-standing interest. My original doctorate was in nuclear physics, and my first job was at a nuclear power plant. (I now say, half-jokingly, that I am a 'recovering physicist' – an allusion to the famous Alcoholics Anonymous phrase. It is only half a joke though – I am still a committed scientist too.) By strange coincidence, I too played the saxophone at professional level for a while. Working with people as a management consultant, trainer, coach and facilitator, I have spent the best part of three decades working with SF therapists and practitioners learning, writing, teaching, developing, experimenting and arguing about it. Perhaps it is easier for an outsider to see what's happening, and what else might happen.

Why is SFBT so interesting?

Why have I, this recovering-physicist management consultant outsider, spent so much time learning, using and sharing SFBT-related methods? What makes this field so worthy of interest and exploration? I like to sum it up in five headings:

- Effective
- Efficient
- Ethical and respectful
- Energising
- Elegant

Effective

The first question is, naturally, 'does it work?'. The answer is a resounding yes, with the caveat that in the field of therapy and human relations nothing seems to 'work' all the time. Readers will no doubt be aware of the common factors research from Bruce Wampold and others (for example, Wampold & Imel, 2015) which suggests that the specific techniques and models used by the practitioner only have a small effect on overall outcomes; more important are factors common to effective therapy including alliance, empathy, expectations and cultural adaptation (all of which appear strongly in SF practice). From this perspective, most therapies are effective in the range of 60–70% of cases.

In recent years there has been a shift towards looking at the effectiveness of individual practitioners rather than models. Scott Miller has long been an advocate of this approach (see Miller, Hubble & Chow, 2020), making use of brief client questionnaires, focused reflections and assessments to help practitioners keep track of their own results. This is laudable, a welcome progression from traditional views like the model being more important than the client, and 'the longer the treatment the better'.

SFBT, as part of the brief therapy tradition, has always been interested in outcomes. Steve de Shazer and Insoo Kim Berg kept records from the start, and also carried out follow-ups on clients. Over the past 30 years a large evidence base has grown, catalogued for much of that time by psychiatrist Dr Alasdair Macdonald (Macdonald, 2011, 2017). By 2017 the list had grown to include ten meta-analyses; seven systematic reviews; 325 relevant outcome studies, including 143 randomised controlled trials showing benefit from solution-focused approaches, with 92 showing benefit over existing treatments. Of 100 comparison studies found, 71 favoured SFBT. Effectiveness data was also available from over 9000 cases with a success rate exceeding 60%; requiring an average of 3–6.5 sessions of therapy time.

This looks to me like an impressive track record. It is deemed somewhat less impressive by some in the academic world (and indeed in the medical field) who point to the lack of psychiatric diagnoses in most of this work. As SFBT is not a diagnostic approach, this 'lack' is in fact a boon. It's like early research on air travel being discounted because the number and size of the horses used was not recorded (the horses being historically normal to transport, but irrelevant). Some of this research comes from areas such as nursing and occupational therapy, which have historically been regarded as 'lower class' by doctors and scientists. For whatever reason, these results have not led to breakthrough interest in SFBT by the academic world. I hope to offer new routes to mutual interest and co-operation.

Efficient

Efficiency is surely the great ignored parameter in therapy studies. Decades of intensive work has gone into attempting to measure the effectiveness both of talking therapies in general and of specific modes of such practice. By contrast hardly any effort has been given to how quickly these methods work. This may be because of a clash of priorities; half a century ago it might be a badge of honour for both practitioner and client that the issues being dealt with were so complex that years of treatment were necessary. There is an important differ-ence, of course, between such lengthy treatment being really necessary (needed, with no alternative) and being applied anyway in a kind of mutually agreed complicity by people who are both very comfortable to carry on, with at least one of them earning good money to do so. I will return to the ethics of such situations in the next section.

SFBT, by contrast, has always been part of a wider brief therapy tradition. This is so little known to the public that I am sometimes understood to be talk-ing about 'grief therapy' at first hearing. As we will see in the next chapters, it links back to the Brief Therapy project at the Mental Research Institute, Palo Alto, started in the 1960s (see Weakland, Fisch, Watzlawick & Bodin, 1974). This kind of work has always held efficiency as a hallmark – it's not satisfac-tory that clients simply get better, they should preferably get better quickly. This meant, broadly, single figures of sessions. This is not to be confused with a 'brief' psychodynamic therapy tradition, which works in terms of some 50 sessions. (SFBT, like other interactional brief therapies, is not time limited – the expectation of progress within a few sessions is a norm, not a rule.)

In a world where most therapies are viewed as being effective, it is puzzling why relative efficiencies are not of wider interest. There are strong ethical, practical and societal reasons for preferring treatments to be brief. We do not have the right to waste our clients' time. We certainly do not have the right to waste our clients' time while charging them money for the privilege. As long as they are effective, shorter treatments are preferable to clients (who can get back on with their lives), their families (who don't have to worry as much or for as long), their workplaces (who get back to having productive staff) and those who have to pay (be that the clients themselves, insurance companies, national schemes or whatever).

Ethical and respectful

Of course, practitioners of all talking therapies would say that their work is ethi-cal and respectful – even those tiny minority of practices which deliberately set out to discomfort the client (for example Farrelly & Brandsma, 1989) would say they are doing it in the client's long-term interest.

Many of these practices, however, revolve around practitioners forming a view of what their clients need to do, and then having them do it. Moreover, the practitioners will have their own special language about their clients' dis-orders and problems, which they will use to interpret the client's situation. In some cases they may even insist that the client learns to speak in their way, so as to show they, the client, have really 'understood' what's going on.

With SFBT the ethical stance is more straightforward. We work with clients towards their *own* best hopes, goals and desired outcomes as described by them, and we do it using their *own* language as the starting point. There is no need for elaborate interpretations of dreams, revelations of unconscious thoughts, establishment of root causes, working through of negative emotions – all of these from an SFBT perspective are the practitioner privileging their own understanding over the client's understanding of themselves.

We seek instead to privilege the client's experience of their own lives, their networks of support and most of all their language. The words chosen by the client matter, and we will seek to use them as starting points rather than substituting our own (perhaps more technical and professionally impressive) language. As we will see as this book unfolds, the practitioner's role is not one of clever interpretation, it is more like a physiotherapist exercising muscles which were always there but have been neglected for a while.

In practice this means listening very hard to the client and the words they are using, and the cultivation of a slightly detached position where we are interested in the client's progress but do not feel primarily responsible for it. The client will succeed through their own efforts – and while we are there to help, our work is in supporting the client, not doing the work for them. This looks somewhat like a 'coaching' role, and the success of SF in the coaching field is surely not coincidental.

The client sets the agenda, taking account of their own contexts and lives (including the legitimate interests of others). Their words lead the process. As practitioners we will be very interested in what they are hoping for from their lives, what's working for them and how they are making progress already in what may be very difficult and challenging situations. This is usually experienced as a respectful relationship – partly because of the centrality of the client, and partly because, being interested in efficiency, we are not hoping or expecting that it will be a long-term relationship. We don't want to take over the client's life (unlike some mental health settings where 'we'll always be there for you' can quickly turn into 'you'll never get rid of us').

Energising

The focus of SFBT dialogues is about the client's hopes for the work and for their lives, what is working for them (particularly in connection with their hopes), and in particular the tiny signs that will indicate progress to them. This takes place in a very open and encouraging atmosphere, where the client will have plenty of time to think and to adjust and refine their ideas. It is solution focused, not solution forced.

It seems that this twin focus on what people want and what's working for them brings with it a useful energising effect. Clients begin to look up, begin to relax, begin to engage, get involved in the conversation ... and it's a natural part of the process. In SFBT we don't 'build rapport' before starting the work; whatever connection is to be built comes as part of starting the work in this open and client-focused way. The general link between positive emotions and wider scope of attention, creativity and openness to new possibilities has been supported by research in the field of positive psychology (for example Fredrickson, 2009).

Some people look at SFBT in action and see a very 'positive' process. Many experienced practitioners would dispute this; they would say that the focus is not primarily on positivity but rather on usefulness for the client – what would be useful from the work, what is useful that's happening now, and so on. I would say that the apparent positivity is a side effect of a close focus on what clients want and what they see as useful rather than a goal in its own right. And if clients say it's positive and we are taking their words seriously, then who are we to argue?

There has been a little explicit work on comparing the impact of problem-focused and solution-focused questions. Tony Grant (2012) looked at this in a coaching context and found that SF questions produced significantly increased positive affect (emotional state), decreased negative affect, and increased self-efficacy. Remember this is in a coaching context where action is deliberately sought; in the context of long-term problem focused therapy, it seems by contrast that tears and negative emotion have become seen as success.

Another important effect of this energising practice is for the practitioners, who in turn appear to suffer less from burn-out. Medina and Beyebach (2014), for example, show that working with strengths-based beliefs and engaging in SFBT training both decrease burn-out, while workers working with deficit-based beliefs show increased burnout. This study also showed that changing practice in the direction of becoming more collaborative, 'leading families from one step behind', and of working in a more trans-disciplinary way with team members and other colleagues (all encouraged from an SFBT perspective) predicted lower burnout.

Elegant

The idea of 'doing more with less' was in the minds of Steve de Shazer, Insoo Kim Berg and their colleagues from the start. This was not only in terms of efficient practice but also in terms of discarding parts of their practice which didn't make a useful difference. de Shazer wrote approvingly about Ockham's Razor (for example de Shazer, 1985), the widely known principle named after 14th-century philosopher William of Ockham, which states that 'entities should not be multiplied without necessity' – in other words, don't assume more than you need to. Remove unnecessary hypotheses from consideration.

As part of their development of brief therapy, de Shazer, Berg and colleagues always sought to experiment to simplify their work and their thinking. This was, in many ways, a parallel to William of Ockham's own efforts to debunk the scholastic school of philosophy which sought ever-more-complex models, with the most complex clearly being the cleverest and therefore the closest to the truth. As psychology, psychiatry and other fields expanded in the 20th century, a similar 'rush to the complicated' seemed to be taking place, with expert clinicians lining up to prognosticate, the number of approved diagnoses in the DSM exploding and a dizzying array of 'mental' phenomena being called upon to explain clients' suffering.

de Shazer and Berg, taking their lead from their mentors and teachers at the Mental Research Institute, Palo Alto, set out to counter this rush by valuing simplicity of practice along with efficiency and effectiveness. In so doing, they helped the brief therapy tradition to step away from the received wisdom of Freud and Jung with its hydraulic assumptions, and instead focus on actual dialogue between actual people – which is surely the engine of talking therapy.

As we will see, this practice steps way from conventional mentalistic language and instead focuses on interactions – the interactions between the client and their surroundings including other people, which are the subject of interactions between practitioner and client. What may or may not be going on 'in the client's head' is left unremarked (which is not to say that there is nothing going on there, but it doesn't make much sense to talk about it). The cause of the client's problem is usually left on the side, along with ideas that the client is somehow a helpless passenger at the mercy of their feelings, their brains, their emotions, their backgrounds or their childhoods.

Rather the client is seen first as an active agent in their own lives, someone who has fallen into an unfortunate rut and is perhaps seeking a way forward to a more fulfilling life for themselves and those around them. This is then actively explored as a basis for the work, which is carried on in 'person grammar' (see for example Harré, 1997) – who does what with whom? – rather than any other explanatory or causal terminology. This is a disciplined practice which is somewhat outside our everyday conversational norms; this book will both help you practise it and understand why it's important.

The five headings in this section are important, at least to me. I am not an adherent of solution-focused work on any old grounds. If anyone can show me a practice which achieves all five of these things better, faster or more thoroughly, I'll go and do it. There have been some interesting developments in recent years which might point to interesting new possibilities, such as the Open Dialogue work of Jaarko Seikkula (Seikkula & Olsen, 2003). Until then, I'm sticking with exploring SF-related work.

About this book

In the coming chapters we will examine new developments both in the way SFBT is coming to be practised around the word and in the growing field of enactive cognition. The enactive paradigm offers a way not only to look afresh at how SFBT might work but also how this apparently simple practice might be a successful way to tackle mental illness – a term ripe for re-examination and redefinition. We will approach the meat of the book from two sides, like a pincer movement; developments in the practice without a theory, and developments in theory which can inform practice.

The focus of this pincer is that SFBT 'stretches the world of the client'. This is a change not to what the client does, but to what the client sees as open to them. (The client will very probably do different things as a result of the process – that's up to them.) This world-stretching is a co-operative endeavour between client and practitioner, though the client will do most of the heavy lifting. This way of seeing SFBT has a very satisfying coherence with the philosophy of Ludwig Wittgenstein, whose work so fascinated Steve de Shazer in his later years. It is also the subject of recent interest and developments from a new generation of philosophers and cognitive scientists. The word 'stretching' is carefully chosen rather than 'transforming' or 'rebuilding' – the impact of the process is somewhat uncertain to start with and may require reinforcement later. It is more akin to gardening than engineering.

The first part of the book looks at the development of SFBT from roots in the 1950s and 1960s to its appearance as a distinct practice in the late 1980s and subsequent spread around the world and into many other fields.

The second part examines developments in the 21st century which have led to a next generation of SF work with distinctive features and priorities. These developments have often been put forward modestly by their originators, keen to stress continuity with the past, which has led to clear and not-always-acknowledged differences in practice. I think that we have reached a point where another new form of practice has emerged. These chapters include both the foundations of a novel view of mental health/illness from enactive cognition, and a new assessment of the role of the practitioner in this form of talking therapy building on recent developments from microanalysis of therapy conversations. This new take moves away from seeing theory as a distraction from focusing on the client towards a theory which *requires* close client focus.

The third part looks in detail at the practice of next-generation SFBT through this world-stretching lens. The chapters are based on an art gallery metaphor for SF practice, starting in the Ticket Office and progressing into galleries about future, past and present experiences. The client exits through the Gift Shop, where they may pause to collect something to remember the conversation. We will also look at follow-up sessions. This is a robust framework which can help us remember what's important as we work with real-life clients and situations. It is also very flexible and can be expanded in various ways to suit different practices.

In each of these chapters we will examine actual therapeutic dialogues and show how some rather small contributions from the practitioner can play key roles in helping the client to stretch their world. These dialogues are taken from everyday practice and are therefore not perfect – no actual exchange attains 100% precision, partly as we are dealing with real people usually in challenging situations who are tentatively building new possibilities for themselves, and partly because these exchanges (like all real conversations) are improvised and are therefore experimental and constructive in their own right. However, they form a rich vein of learning and allow the mess of actual practice to come together with a novel and clear theoretical viewpoint.

The final part of the book brings this all together and looks at SFBT in a different way, as an aesthetic; what do we think is beautiful? All along, SF practitioners have viewed certain kinds of event as positive and cheer worthy – such as clients sharing power and control, therapy being completed quickly, small differences being important – which are at odds with much conventional therapeutic practice. The relative lack of impact of SF outside a certain sphere is, I contend, not a matter of research, evidence or practice; it is misunderstood because of these aesthetic differences. By laying out this SF aesthetic clearly, I hope to at least build some form of basis for dialogue with those of other persuasions.

Key points

- This book seeks to re-examine Solution Focused Brief Therapy (SFBT) practices some 30 years after it arrived.
- We will connect SFBT, particularly these new developments which are already visible, to the developing field of enactive cognition, to see how SFBT 'stretches the world' of the client.
- SFBT is a field worthy of a lifetime's study and practice because it is unusually:

  - Effective
  - Efficient
  - Ethical and respectful
  - Energising
  - Elegant

- The book is in four parts – the development of SFBT in practice and theory, a detailed look at the next generation of SFBT practice based on new theory developments and an examination of each phase of an SF session with reference to an art gallery metaphor. The book concludes with a look at SF work in aesthetic terms.

References

Berg, I. K. (2007). For students only: Originally published on the BFTC website, referred to in Brian Cade's obituary of Steve de Shazer and Insoo Kim Berg. Retrieved from www.counselingsoft.jp/workshop3.html

de Shazer, S. (1985). *Keys to Solution in Brief Therapy*. New York, NY: W. W. Norton.

Farrelly, F., & Brandsma, J. M. (1989). *Provocative Therapy*. Capitola, CA: Meta Publications.

Fredrickson, B. (2009). *Positivity: Groundbreaking Research Reveals How to Embrace the Hidden Strength of Positive Emotions, Overcome Negativity, and Thrive*. New York, NY: Crown Publishers/Random House.

Grant, A. M. (2012). Making positive change: A randomized study comparing solution-focused vs. problem-focused coaching questions. *Journal of Systemic Therapies, 31*(2), 21–35.

Harré, R. (1997). *The Singular Self: An Introduction to the Psychology of Personhood*. New York: Sage Publications.

Macdonald, A. J. (2011). *Solution-Focused Therapy: Theory, Research & Practice* (2nd ed.). London: Sage Publications.

Macdonald, A. J. (2017). *SFBT Evaluation List*. Retrieved from https://solutionsdoc.co.uk/sfbt-evaluation-list/

Medina, A., & Beyebach, M. (2014). The impact of solution-focused training on professionals' beliefs, practices and burnout of child protection workers in Tenerife Island. *Child Care in Practice, 20*(1), 7–36. doi:10.1080/13575279.2013.847058

Miller, S. D., Hubble, M. A., & Chow, D. (2020). *Better Results: Using Deliberate Practice to Improve Therapeutic Effectiveness*. Washington, DC: American Psychological Association.

Seikkula, J., & Olsen, M. E. (2003). The open dialogue approach to acute psychosis: Its poetics and micropolitics. *Family Process, 42*(3), 403–418.

Sieden, L. S. (2011). *A Fuller View: Buckminster Fuller's Vision of Hope and Abundance for All*. Nederland, CO: Divine Arts Media.

Wampold, B. E., & Imel, Z. E. (2015). *The Great Psychotherapy Debate: The Evidence for What Makes Psychotherapy Work* (2nd ed.). Abingdon, UK: Routledge/Taylor & Francis Group.

Weakland, J. H., Fisch, R., Watzlawick, P., & Bodin, A. (1974). Brief therapy: Focused problem resolution. *Family Process, 13*(2), 141–168.

Development of Solution Focused Brief Therapy

Chapter 2

Roots of Solution Focused Brief Therapy

The interactional view

This chapter gives an overview of the roots of Solution Focused Brief Therapy (SFBT) from origins in Gregory Bateson's work on communication and Milton Erickson's work in hypnotherapy, via the Mental Research Institute (MRI) in Palo Alto. It will help us to see how these things develop in time; facets of theory and practice get carried over from one phase to the next and can sometimes end more like traditions than active choices.

There are also some common elements across the whole field of interactional brief therapy. It is instructive to remember these elements and see how they are built upon in the later versions of these practices. The founding principles of a field often continue to be relevant even when they are not very visible. In the world of art, both abstract expressionist Jackson Pollock and pop-art meister Andy Warhol started by learning to draw people and things around them, in the good old-fashioned way, with pencil in a notebook. It is easy to miss this foundation in the glamour and intrigue of their very different canons of work, but it's there. Likewise, a surprising amount of what we do now and might do in the future is presaged in these early developments. My purpose in putting this story together here is both to give credit where it's due, and also to point to the appearance decades ago of elements of current and future solution focused (SF) practice.

Gregory Bateson, Milton Erickson and the Bateson Research Project

The evolution of interactional brief therapy models can be said to 'officially' start at the Mental Research Institute (MRI), Palo Alto, in the 1960s. However, nothing emerges from thin air and the way in which the MRI's protagonists arrived at that point is itself worth recounting. There are some truly revolutionary developments in this story, some of which are still resounding today.

Gregory Bateson

Gregory Bateson (1904–1980), English anthropologist, social scientist, linguist, semiotician and cyberneticist is a figure who can still divide the brief therapy world. Some view him as one of the great-grandfathers of SFBT, others view him as a confusing writer who seemed to baffle as much as enlighten. There is some truth in both positions. Nobody would dispute Bateson's role in bringing together the main players in the development of brief therapy, and some of his own original insights are still visible in SF work today.

Bateson's father William was a distinguished biologist who carried out early work on heredity and biological variation, actually coining the word 'genetics' along the way. Like his father, Gregory read Biology at St John's College, Cambridge. Unlike his father, he then got interested in the workings of social rather than biological systems and turned to anthropology. After various expeditions to study indigenous cultures in New Guinea he realised the importance both of the world-view of the observer (which was inseparably bound up in their observations) and of circular causality in human relations.

Bateson observed that men danced more when women were watching their performance, which in turn spurred the men on to even greater levels of exhibition. This realisation takes communication away from simple message-transmission concepts (A communicates X to B) into circular, looping and self-referential modes (A does X, which encourages B to do Y, which in turns makes A do more X/less X/something different). This simple insight later developed into the MRI's 'Interactional View' of human relations.

Bateson married fellow anthropologist Margaret Mead in 1936. Together they travelled to Bali to study, in part, how children were reared and integrated into society in that culture. There are long-standing claims that Mead in particular was hoaxed by the locals and misled, but the results of this work are less important for us than the way Bateson approached it. Up to that point in anthropology, photography was used to illustrate the work – a few dozen pictures might be taken during a project for use in the final report. Bateson, however, took some 25,000 photographs. These were not illustrations of the project – they *were* the project. Even though this particular work was never formally written up, the shift to documenting events as they happened is another key element in the development of the brief therapy approach.

One of Bateson's interests in the 1930s was 'schismogenesis' – literally, the creation of division. Inventing this concept to account for behaviour he observed in New Guinea, Bateson defined schismogenesis as 'a process of differentiation in the norms of individual behaviour resulting from cumulative interaction between individuals' (Bateson, 1936, p. 175). In these processes, forms of circular communication are observed to escalate, with initially small differences growing into vast chasms of divergence. Intriguingly, these processes were not originally intended by either party – they emerged from a whole series of logical steps from both sides.

During the Second World War, Bateson worked for the US Office of Strategic Services, putting his ideas into practice in designing communications to confuse and mislead the enemy. Bateson, along with Margaret Mead and a handful of others, participated in an invitation-only meeting in May 1942 organised by the Joseph Macy Jr. Foundation on the topic of Cerebral Inhibition. This meeting has been referred to as the 'coalescence of cybernetics' by the American Society for Cybernetics (ASC, 2020). There were two presentations on the agenda: Conditioned Reflex introduced by psychologist Howard Liddell, and Hypnotism introduced by hypnotherapist Milton Erickson. For our purposes here, the connection between Bateson and Erickson is fundamental. Let us now turn to this fascinating and individual character, another key player in the story.

Milton Erickson

Milton H Erickson (1901–1980) was a psychiatrist and psychologist who specialised in hypnosis. Growing up in a farming family in rural Wisconsin, the young Erickson suffered from dyslexia, colour blindness and polio, all of which he learned to overcome in some ways by using spontaneous autohypnotic 'creative moments' (Erickson & Rossi, 1977). Having studied for medical and psychology degrees concurrently, Erickson developed his distinctive practice of therapy on a largely self-taught basis and practised alone for much of his life. He was, as we will see, 'discovered' by Bateson and others who became interested in his work, and these contacts propelled him into a wider public sphere. Erickson's polio, which he had initially learned to overcome, returned in his fifties. He overcame it again using similar autohypnotic methods but was forced to use a wheelchair and suffered chronic pain. This only added to the drama and magnetism of his appearances, rather like Stephen Hawking in a later era.

Erickson's practice is hard to define succinctly. Indeed, this may be why it has intrigued so many clever people for so long. Using a variable combination of hypnotic trance, indirect language and suggestion, metaphor, paradoxical tasks and building on his clients' own experiences and abilities, Erickson seemed to have a way of arriving at simple but unexpected ways of helping his clients to overcome their problems. He worked not from a deficit perspective (focusing on what clients could not do) but rather from the perspective of utilising whatever abilities, strengths and resources they could summon up. Indeed, his own early experiences of overcoming paralysis were based on the realisation that he could make tiny but self-initiated movements which he could repeat and learn to expand.

Erickson wrote extensively about his work, usually with collaborators including Ernest Rossi; his collected works run to 16 volumes, still in print from the Erickson Foundation. This body of work has fascinated many over the decades, with much effort expended on trying to figure out precisely how Erickson worked and what he did that was so successful. Bill O'Hanlon, later one of the early pioneers of working in a solution-focused way, became Erickson's gardener in order to get closer and spend time with him (Norman, 1994). O'Hanlon later went on to produce his own collection of Erickson's cases (O'Hanlon, 1987). Steve de Shazer was also fascinated by Erickson's work, and talked to me about spending ages trying to categorise the cases by the type of intervention used. The trouble was that however he did it, there was always a large miscellaneous pile left over that didn't fit into any category!

As we shall see, Bateson's connection with Erickson extended to organising his MRI colleagues to visit the therapist a couple of times a year to watch, learn, and ask questions. His influence grew even wider with his engagement with Neuro Linguistic Programming (NLP) co-developers Richard Bandler and John Grinder (who were also introduced to each other by Bateson). They attempted to model Erickson's style of indirect communication and influence. Bill O'Hanlon says that Erickson was very alienated from the NLP world towards the end of his life – 'Bandler and Grinder spent four days with me and they thought they got my technique in a nutshell ... what they got was a nutshell!' (Norman, 1994). A whole school of Ericksonians still exists today.

Before and after his death, there has been a widespread tendency to view Erickson as some kind of genius persona, the character referred to by Steve de Shazer as 'Erickson-the-clever' (de Shazer, 1994, p. 33). His style, a huge influence in brief and strategic therapies over the years, has proved hard to replicate, but there are key elements that have survived several iterations of practice and are still visible in SF work. Erickson's interest in what people could do (as opposed to what they couldn't) has grown into an ever-wider interest in strengths and resources. Erickson once famously engaged a patient who identified as Jesus Christ to help him build some bookcases, on the grounds that he had experience of carpentry (Gordon & Meyers-Anderson, 1981, p. 43). He was not interested in pathology but was very keen to get people doing things and actively engaged in their own treatment. His way of asking questions which are loaded with presupposition of awareness, ability and possibility remains to this day. His 'crystal ball technique', a method of pseudo-orientation in time (Cooper & Erickson, 1954) was discussed and refined by Steve de Shazer (1985) and may have sown the seeds for the miracle question so familiar to us.

This is leaping ahead in our story. The scene returns to New York City after the Second World War.

The Bateson Research Project

After the Second World War, Bateson became a key player in the emerging science of cybernetics, studying information, feedback and control in mechanical and organic contexts. During the latter part of the 1940s, two similar but separate schools of research developed: cybernetics and general systems theory. Both schools were interested in the kind of looping self-referential patterns noticed by Bateson before the war, with this interest now driven by the practical potential offered by the novel electronic control systems, computers which were appearing as well as a broader and more abstract interest in the propagation of information. General systems theory, led by Ludwig von Bertalanffy, took a high level and overarching view of the potentials and possibilities of such systems. Cybernetics, led by Norbert Wiener, Warren McCulloch and others, focused on the restraints which prevent such systems moving outside a particular operating zone. Psychiatrist Carlos Sluzki has observed that these two traditions grew up 'as if not knowing each other, both disciplines evolved with such amazing similarities that the distinction between them seemed to be retained primarily for territorial reasons' (Sluzki, 1985, p. 26).

Bateson played a leading role in the cybernetics camp, joining the series of Macy conferences chaired by Warren McCulloch. These events aimed to consider the 'general workings of the human mind' from a multidisciplinary standpoint (ASC, 2020a), unusual for the time. Topics included information theory, reflexivity, self-regulation, neural networks, learning and the beginnings of what was to become cognitive science, and how all this might apply to group processes. Bateson's elder daughter Mary Catherine recalls this period with Norbert Wiener, the 'father of cybernetics', visiting frequently, 'smoking smelly cigarettes, pouring out his latest idea … without being much interested in the response' (Bateson, 1984). It is worth noting the appearance of this perceived parallel between electronic control systems, the emerging computer paradigm of the age, and the supposed working of the human mind – a parallel which persists to this day in many circles (and which I shall be rejecting later in this book).

One day Bateson was puzzling over an equation sent to him by McCulloch when the phone rang, and the slightly nervous young man on the line introduced himself as John Weakland, a student of cultural anthropology who was interested in Bateson's work. On hearing that Weakland was formerly an engineer, Bateson interrupted him, said 'Come right over' and solicited his help in understanding McCulloch's equation (Ray, 1999). This began a relationship which would have a profound effect on the social sciences, and on groups, families and organisations into the 21st century, with Weakland playing a central role in the Bateson project, the Mental Research Institute, its Brief Therapy Center and being a mentor, supervisor and friend to Steve de Shazer right up to Weakland's death nearly 40 years later.

Bateson proposed a research project examining how disrupted, confused and paradoxical communication might give rise to some of the patterns of behaviour called 'mental illness'. In 1952, he raised a grant from the Rockefeller Foundation and, over a celebratory dinner at Peter's Back Yard restaurant in Greenwich Village, offered Weakland a job on the project (Weakland, in Ray & de Shazer, 1999, p. 4).

Weakland moved to the West Coast with Bateson, and they set up shop in the Veteran's Hospital at Menlo Park, California. Bateson had also recruited Jay Haley and William Fry, and together they examined paradoxes of abstraction in human communication. It was varied work: they introduced the novel practice of taping interviews with schizophrenics at the hospital (extending Bateson's anthropological documentation methods) and studied their conversational patterns. They were all interested in film criticism and compared notes on Chinese, German and American movies. They even went to the zoo and observed animals communicating. Bateson was always interested in seeing things at high levels of abstraction, and it is no surprise that he was interested to go beyond the bounds of merely human communication.

Milton Erickson visited, contributing in his down-to-earth style. Bateson also recruited Don Jackson, a psychiatrist who had previously studied with Harry Stack Sullivan. Sullivan's role in these developments is sometimes over-shadowed, and it is good to spotlight it here. Having trained as a psychoanalyst in the 1920s, Sullivan became interested in the role played by interpersonal relationships, and introduced the idea that these dynamics rather than the inner urges favoured by Sigmund Freud, played a crucial role in his patients' experience. Sullivan coined the expression 'problems in living' as a way to talk about what was otherwise referred to as 'mental illness', drawing attention to the practitioner's prime aim of helping their patient live better. It is still, of course, visible in SF work in our interest in peoples' everyday lives.

The work of the Bateson communication project can be seen as culminating in the famous 'double bind' paper, *Toward A Theory of Schizophrenia* (Bateson, Jackson, Haley & Weakland, 1956). Reading it today, the contents of this paper are less relevant than its aim. The authors seek to show how schizophrenia, then a somewhat poorly defined and widely diagnosed condition, could result from a series of communication paradoxes which put the sufferer into an impossible logical place from which there could be no progress, return or escape. The resulting disordered behaviour might be seen as a sane response to an insane situation. While the details of this analysis, misunderstood by many as a quest to identify the 'binder' and the victim, have not stood the test of time, the more important result was to launch the next stage of our story: working with mental illness and therapies in terms of interactional patterns and systems.

Bateson himself gradually stood back from this work and moved his attention onto other things including the intimate cybernetic connections between mind, information, environment and consciousness. He died in 1980. Brian Cade (2007) recalls John Weakland saying that the project team had trouble understanding Bateson much of the time, but his role in raising money, connecting them with Erickson and encouraging them to follow through on their ideas was important. We now have a chance to see a little of what inspired them in Nora Bateson's film *An Ecology Of Mind* (Bateson, 2010). Bateson's younger daughter produced a fascinating story about her father's life and work, including footage of him speaking at conferences in the 1970s. While Bateson's writing was uncompromising, his podium style is delightfully engaging, witty, erudite, thought-provoking and rather mischievous. No wonder he had so much influence over so many.

The Mental Research Institute, family therapy and the Brief Therapy Center

In late 1958, the Mental Research Institute was founded in Palo Alto, California. Don Jackson was instrumental: he secured funding, assembled a Board of Directors and a group of research associates, and was the first Director. Jules

Riskin MD was Assistant Director, Virginia Satir was head of training and John Weakland and Jay Haley became research associates. For a time they shared premises with the Bateson Project. Bateson himself was never a formally a member although he participated frequently, and his (third) wife Lois was an MRI research associate (Ray, n.d.). They were later joined by Paul Watzlawick, Richard Fisch, Janet Bavelas, Lynn Hoffman, Lynn Segal and others. The group developed the ideas of family therapy and delivered the first federally funded trainings in the topic, the manuals for which morphed into the classic book *Conjoint Family Therapy* (Satir, 1964).

The term 'conjoint' here means that the patient is seen along with their family, the therapist working with the whole group or 'system'. From an interactional perspective, the patient's problems should be seen in the context of, and as constituted by, their interactions with those around them, typically their family. The family is seen together, so that their stories can be heard but more importantly their interactions can be observed. It is these interactions, visible in the here and now of the therapy room, which are of most interest to the therapy team. The dynamic and responses between family members are assumed be playing a part in maintaining the problem; it is these patterns of behaviour which the therapy team is seeking to identify and interrupt, in order to allow new behaviours to develop. In order to see these patterns more clearly, most of the team observe the therapy session from behind a one-way mirror, through which they can see the family, but the family can't see them.

Of course at least one of the therapy team has to be in the room with the family, to engage, ask questions, offer reflections, make interventions and so on. The usual arrangement was that the team were able to contact the therapist by telephone and ask them to ask certain questions, make certain interventions. Towards the end of the session the therapist would usually leave the room to consult with the team behind the mirror. A discussion ensued out of sight of the family before the therapist returned to deliver some kind of summary of the session together with a task for the family to tackle before the next session. These discussions sometimes continued after the family had left.

The family therapy of the 1960s and 1970s was thoroughly interventionist, with the practitioners seeing themselves as devising tasks to break patterns of interaction, confuse the family into new behaviours and sometimes be less than truthful with the clients about the conversations behind the mirror. However, there are some elements here which will already be familiar to SF practitioners today – the focus on what's happening here and now (as opposed to some putative cause or pathology in the past), the break, the end-of-session message. Family therapy continues today and has evolved into a less tricky and more collaborative stance.

The Brief Therapy Center

The Brief Therapy Center was formed within the MRI in 1966, led by Dick Fisch and including John Weakland and Paul Watzlawick. The group had a profound influence on practice and developed important ideas, models and techniques. It is not really clear, however, what led them to take this step. It seems to MRI archivist Wendel Ray (n.d.) that they were keen to explore family therapy with individuals. One of the key assumptions of conjoint family therapy was that the whole family should attend; this was not always possible in practice. Was it possible to work with some members of the family/system and through them influence change on a wider scale?

Don Jackson would surely have played a greater role had he not died in 1968 aged just 48. Weakland observed at the time:

> The most basic contribution Jackson made was to be among the first to see things in terms of what people are doing between each other in the present, rather than get stuck on the idea that behavior just depends on something that comes from the inside and has no relationship to the world people live in.
>
> (Weakland, n.d.)

Another driver behind the Brief Therapy Center was explicitly to work on practice that was efficient as well as effective. The group had been part of the development of Jay Haley's book *Strategies of Psychotherapy* (Haley, 1963), itself highly influenced by Milton Erickson's work. They were keen to expand on Haley's ideas, in particular to focus on the client's presenting complaint and stick with it rather than going in search of putative 'deeper' or 'underlying' causes. Haley had left MRI in the mid-1960s and went on to be a leading developer of Strategic Family Therapy in the 1970s.

At about this time Paul Watzlawick started work on a key text in this interactional revolution – *Pragmatics of Human Communication* (Watzlawick, Bavelas & Jackson, 1967). This book set a new standard and methodology for looking at *actual* communication (taken from actual conversations) rather than starting from a more abstract linguistic basis. Janet Bavelas, who worked on the book as a graduate student, is to this day examining therapies and other conversational approaches by closely examining what is said and done (including all the pauses, ums, ers, interruptions, and so on) to learn more about how language is actually used in work with clients. Her work on microanalysis has thrown up some fascinating signposts, which we will visit later on. At this point it's useful to notice the tradition of using actual dialogues for research and learning, an extension of the Bateson project's style and used by the MRI, BFTC and SF workers to this day, and indeed in this book.

Taking the format of family therapy, the Brief Therapy Center team set to with experimenting on working with individuals and couples, with a self-imposed limit of ten sessions of treatment. The team behind the mirror, the incessant recording and documenting, the openness to 'trying whatever we could think of that was legal and ethical regardless of whether it was conventional' (Weakland, quoted in Cade, 2007, p. 39) were all part of the experiment.

By the early to mid-1970s the group had evolved an approach which was defined, usable and teachable – the first true interactional Brief Therapy, also known as MRI model Brief Therapy or Problem-Solving Brief Therapy. This was set out in the classic paper *Brief Therapy: Focused Problem Resolution* (Weakland, Fisch, Watzlawick & Bodin, 1974), operating from within the framework of first and second order change as proposed in *Change: Principles of Problem Formation and Problem Resolution* (Watzlawick, Weakland & Fisch, 1974). A wider view of the research came in *The Interactional View* (Watzlawick & Weakland, 1977) and culminated in *The Tactics of Change* (Fisch, Weakland & Segal, 1982).

MRI model Brief Therapy

As can be seen from the titles of the MRI's key publications from earlier, MRI model Brief Therapy is primarily concerned with the resolution of problems. Problems, in this approach, are distinct from difficulties. A difficulty is 'an undesirable state of affairs which can be resolved by some common-sense action' (Watzlawick, Weakland & Fisch, 1974, p. 38). So for example, the room is too hot, and someone opens a window. This requires no special skills in problem solving, can be resolved by a first-order change (within the system) and is a frequent experience in everyday life.

People don't come to therapy with mere difficulties, however. For the MRI team, a problem arises when a difficulty is mishandled and persists, producing a situation which is deadlocked, knotted or an impasse. The problem situation is being held in place, unwittingly, by the actions that the family are trying to take to resolve it! A vicious circle has been created, where 'more of the same' leads to 'yet more of the same'. As the problem is the result of continued misapplication of the wrong attempted solution, the therapist's job is to have them stop doing that and do something else. Once they have found what works, they simply need to do more of it. This leads to the three key principles of MRI model Brief Therapy (quoted in de Shazer & Berg, 1991):

1   If it ain't broke, don't fix it.
2   Stop doing what doesn't work and do something different.
3   Once you know what works, do more of it.

The first of these principles is a reminder to stick with the client's presenting complaint, not to be too clever and try to turn it into something else or see something else lurking behind/beneath. It's not up to you to see what might be broken or not.

The second principle is central to MRI Brief Therapy – the idea that this problem pattern is being maintained by something the client and/or those around them are doing in the present. This in itself is a key breakthrough from earlier ideas about psychotherapy which held that the persistent problems were a chronic manifestation of something that had happened in the past (which therefore had to somehow be addressed). A change to what was happening in the present would therefore be sufficient to move things along.

However, this was a hard task; if the client was doing what they thought was common-sense, they first had to be disabused of this notion and stop doing what seemed the right thing. The end-of-session message therefore turned into a 'sales job', where the client had to somehow be convinced to at least try out what was being recommended by the therapist and team. These tasks could be behavioural (do this rather than that), paradoxical (for example, do more of what seems to cause the problem), go slow (when the client seems to be trying too hard, or not at all) or utilising relationships with others (focusing on what a key third party might do or not do).

The third principle – once you know what works, do more of it – was what happened once the problem-maintaining pattern had been interrupted and more useful behaviours had started to appear. These patterns would in turn be discussed and investigated and the client would be instructed to expand what seemed to be helping. The MRI's original work measured 97 cases and found successful outcomes in 40% of those along with significant improvements in another 32% (Weakland, Fisch, Watzlawick & Bodin, 1974). The authors noted that this was generally comparable to results reported for various forms of longer-term treatment.

All this was carried out in a similar setting to family therapy – a practitioner in a room with the client(s), the team watching through a one-way mirror (or later on closed circuit TV), the end-of-session break for consultation between practitioner and team followed by the delivery of the message and task to the clients. The MRI team were very keen on recording these sessions on tape, another link back to Bateson's practice. When I visited MRI for an intensive training course in 1994, I found the place stuffed to the rafters with tapes, some clearly decades old. Sitting down to learn (and to eat pizza) with Paul Watzlawick, Dick Fisch and others was a memorable experience.

The MRI Brief Therapy Center continued after the deaths of the founding members with Karin Schlanger taking over as Director on the retirement of Dick Fisch in 2007. The decision to vacate the historic premises at 555 Middlefield Road, Palo Alto in 2019, the scene of so much great work over the years, has at least paused the Brief Therapy Center's direct work with clients, but there are plans to continue and expand with offices in South America.

Key foundational ideas that are still with us

Looking at MRI Brief Therapy today (still practised by followers around the world), there are some aspects which look strange to the eyes of the SF practitioner. The focus on the problem, the interest in 'more of the same' holding the problem in place, the tasks to break the problem pattern all look foreign to us. However, there are many aspects of this work which are still alive and well in contemporary SF work (some of them almost as traditions rather than as conscious choices). These include:

- Taking a non-pathological approach to the work, with no attempt at defining or treating a general illness/condition rather than the specific client(s) in their own context
- Avoiding the question 'why?' which tends to lead to an 'individualistic, voluntaristic, and rationalistic conception of human behavior, rather than one focused on systems of interaction and influence' (Weakland, Fisch, Watzlawick & Bodin, 1974, pp. 150–151)
- Not seeking 'insight' for the client but rather engaging the client in behavioural changes
- Regarding brief treatment not as merely 'first aid' or second-best but capable of providing lasting change
- Taking the client's ideas seriously from the start and sticking with them
- A keen interest in specific, concrete, interactional details from the client
- 'Thinking small' in terms of the details of the complaint and potential courses of action
- The idea that a change now, here in the present, is sufficient to move things along
- Utilising client idiosyncrasies, resources and context in the work (inspired by Milton Erickson)
- Taking a 'one-down' position of apparent ignorance or confusion (and inviting the client to clarify the situation themselves) rather than 'coming on strong'
- Terminating treatment by agreement with the client, frequently before the ten session limit, with an option on the client leaving further sessions 'in the bank' if needed.

The year 1974 is significant in this story for another reason beyond the publication of the classic works *Change* and *Focused Problem Resolution*. It was also the year in which one Steve de Shazer published his first paper, 'On getting unstuck: some change-initiating tactics for getting the family moving' (de Shazer, 1974). de Shazer was already thinking and working along similar lines. It is the story of Steve de Shazer, Insoo Kim Berg and the development of Solution Focused Brief Therapy to which we now turn in the next chapter.

Key points

- Gregory Bateson's interest in communication and reflexive systems is a key starting point for this tradition, as is his desire to record and document everyday events.

- Milton Erickson's therapeutic work is another key starting point, bringing his focus on the specifics of the client and their context, strengths and abilities to the fore.
- The Bateson Research Project drew key players including John Weakland, Don D Jackson and Jay Haley together and provided a starting point for the development of what became the interactional view of communication and therapy.
- The Mental Research Institute, Palo Alto, sprang from the Bateson project and was key in the development of both conjoint family therapy and brief therapy.
- The MRI Brief Therapy Center developed the first interactional brief therapy approaches, aspects of which are still with us today in Solution-Focused practice.

References

ASC. (2020). *The Coalescence of Cybernetics*. Retrieved from www.asc-cybernetics.org/foundations/history2.htm

ASC. (2020a). *Summary of the Macy Conferences*. Retrieved from www.asc-cybernetics.org/foundations/history/MacySummary.htm

Bateson, G. (1936). *Naven: A Survey of the Problems Suggested by a Composite Picture of the Culture of a New Guinea Tribe Drawn from Three Points of View*. Cambridge: Cambridge University Press.

Bateson, G., Jackson, D. D., Haley, J., & Weakland, J. (1956). Toward a theory of schizophrenia. *Behavioral Science*, 1(4), 251–254.

Bateson, M. C. (1984). *With a Daughter's Eye*. New York, NY: William Morrow.

Bateson, N. (Producer & Director). (2010). *An Ecology of Mind: A Daughter's Portrait of Gregory Bateson* [Motion Picture]. Chico, CA: Impact Media Group.

Cade, B. (2007). A history of the brief solution-focused approach. In T. S. Nelson & F. N. Thomas (Eds.), *Handbook of Solution-Focused Brief Therapy: Clinical Applications* (pp. 25–63). Binghamton, NY: Haworth Press.

Cooper, L., & Erickson, M. H. (1954). *Time Distortion in Hypnosis: An Experimental and Clinical Investigation* (2nd ed.). Baltimore, MD: Williams and Wilkins.

de Shazer, S. (1974). On getting unstuck: Some change-initiating tactics for getting the family moving. *Family Therapy*, 1(1), 19–26.

de Shazer, S. (1985). *Keys to Solution in Brief Therapy*. New York, NY: W. W. Norton.

de Shazer, S. (1994). *Words Were Originally Magic*. New York, NY: W. W. Norton.

de Shazer, S., & Berg, I. K. (1991). The brief therapy tradition. In J. H. Weakland & W. Ray (Eds.), *Propagations: Thirty Years of Influence from the Mental Research Institute*. New York, NY: Haworth.

Erickson, M. H., & Rossi, E. (1977, July). Autohypnotic experiences of Milton H. Erickson. *The American Journal of Clinical Hypnosis*, 20, 36–54.

Fisch, R., Weakland, J., & Segal, L. (1982). *The Tactics of Change: Doing Therapy Briefly*. San Francisco, CA: Jossey-Bass.

Gordon, D., & Meyers-Anderson, M. (1981). *Phoenix: Therapeutic Patterns of Milton H. Erickson*. Cupertino, CA: Meta Publications.

Haley, J. (1963). *Strategies of Psychotherapy*. New York, NY: Grune and Stratton.

Norman, H. (1994). "If you meet Bill O'Hanlon on the road ... kill his metaphors!": An interview with Bill O'Hanlon, *Rapport, 24*, 62–64.

O'Hanlon, W. H. (1987). *Taproots: Underlying Principles of Milton Erickson's Therapy and Hypnosis*. New York, NY: W. W. Norton.

Ray, W. A. (1999). Introduction. In W. A. Ray & S. de Shazer (Eds.), *Evolving Brief Therapies: In Honor of John H Weakland*. Iowa City, IA: Geist and Russell.

Ray, W. A. (n.d.). *The MRI*. Don Jackson Memorial Website. Retrieved from https://web.archive.org/web/20070609080835/www.mri.org/dondjackson/mri.htm

Ray, W. A., & de Shazer, S. (Eds.). (1999). *Evolving Brief Therapies: In Honor of John H Weakland*. Iowa City, IA: Geist and Russell.

Satir, V. (1964). *Conjoint Family Therapy: A Guide to Theory and Technique*. Palo Alto, CA: Science and Behavior Books.

Sluzki, C. (1985, May–June). A Minimal Map of Cybernetics. *Family Therapy Networker, 9*.

Watzlawick, P., Bavelas, J. B., & Jackson, D. (1967). *Pragmatics of Human Communication: A Study of Interactional Patterns, Pathologies and Paradoxes*. New York, NY: W. W. Norton.

Watzlawick, P., & Weakland, J. H. (Eds.). (1977). *The Interactional View: Studies at the Mental Research Institute Palo Alto 1965–1974*. New York, NY: W. W. Norton.

Watzlawick, P., Weakland, J. H., & Fisch, R. (1974). *Change: Principles of Problem Formation and Problem Resolution*. New York, NY: W. W. Norton.

Weakland, J. H. (n.d.). *Quotes from MFT Leaders*. On the archived Don D Jackson memorial website. Retrieved from https://web.archive.org/web/20070609081013/www.mri.org/dondjackson/quotes.htm

Weakland, J. H., Fisch, R., Watzlawick, P., & Bodin, A. (1974). Brief therapy: Focused problem resolution. *Family Process, 13*(2), 141–168.

Chapter 3

Steve de Shazer, Insoo Kim Berg and Solution Focused Brief Therapy

This chapter traces the arrival of Solution Focused Brief Therapy (SFBT) and its development at the Brief Family Therapy Center, Milwaukee, led by Steve de Shazer and Insoo Kim Berg along with their colleagues and fellow travellers. de Shazer was keen on the idea of SFBT as a rumour (Miller & de Shazer, 1998) and would probably resist the idea of a definitive account of this story. I hope to present a version of the 'rumour' which acknowledges as many of the key participants as possible, as well as charting the appearance and development of key ideas and practices.

There has been no biography of de Shazer and Berg published as I write. This chapter will, I hope, serve until something more complete appears. The relationship between these two very different yet complementary characters plays a large role in the way SFBT has developed; having two role models rather than one offers more in the way of possibility to those seeking to learn and develop their own styles of work. The collection *Encounters with Steve de Shazer and Insoo Kim Berg* (Vogt, Wolf, Sundman & Dreesen, 2015) offers a grand variety of perspectives and experiences from those who studied and worked with them.

Steve de Shazer and Insoo Kim Berg

Steve de Shazer

Steve Darwin de Shazer was born in Milwaukee, Wisconsin on 25 June 1940 to an electrical engineer father and opera singer mother. The family had German roots which de Shazer enjoyed in various ways, from reading philosophical tracts in the original German language to a keen interest in beer and home-brewing. The opportunity to taste beer brewed to medieval recipes helped Harry Norman, Jenny Clarke and me to get a rare interview with him (published as Norman, McKergow & Clarke, 1997). He was also a keen cook, enjoying German food in Milwaukee which he said was more traditional than that then obtainable in Germany, and a lifelong supporter of the Milwaukee Brewers baseball team.

The young de Shazer pursued varied interests including the visual arts, receiving a Bachelor of Fine Arts degree in 1964 from the University of Wisconsin Milwaukee (UWM). He was also a professional musician; Yvonne Dolan (2005) notes that he was classically trained and active on the jazz scene as a saxophonist. He told me of an occasion in New York when he literally bumped into tenor sax star Paul Gonsalves on a corner, causing Gonsalves to drop and damage his saxophone. de Shazer was carrying his own saxophone which he lent to Gonsalves, the latter already being late for a Duke Ellington band rehearsal; the two of them went on to the rehearsal where de Shazer enjoyed listening to this great ensemble (McKergow, 2015).

de Shazer first became interested in social work and family therapy in 1969 (de Shazer et al., 1986). He recalled discovering Jay Haley's 1963 book *Strategies of Psychotherapy* (Haley, 1963), apparently somewhat at random:

> Until I read this book, as far as I can remember, I had never heard the term, 'psychotherapy'. Certainly, this was the first book on the topic that I read. I enjoyed it more than any other 'professional book'" I'd read in philosophy, art history, architecture, or sociology. So, I went to the library and looked at its neighbours, I was shocked. I was unable to finish any of the others I tried to read.
>
> (Cade, 2007a, pp. 42–43)

de Shazer went on to discover the work of Milton Erickson through Haley, which he also found clear and well-written. He was on the road to a career in brief therapy, awarded a Master of Science in Social Work from UWM in 1971. Not backward in coming forward with his ideas, de Shazer published his first academic paper 'On Getting Unstuck' in the very first issue of the journal *Family Therapy* in 1974 (de Shazer, 1974). His address is given as 1133 Socorro Avenue, Sunnyvale California – just a few miles from the Mental Research Institute (MRI) in Palo Alto.

De Shazer and the MRI

The connection between the MRI group and Steve de Shazer has been a matter of some uncertainty over the years. Steve asserted strongly that he didn't train there, even if he somehow ended up with John Weakland as a lifelong friend, supervisor and mentor. Weakland states that de Shazer was in contact with MRI and its work from 1972, when he took one of their early brief therapy workshops (Weakland & Fisch, 1992). Whatever, de Shazer was certainly living and working in that part of the San Francisco Bay area, and engaged in similar work. His next publication the following year, 'Brief Therapy: Two's Company' (de Shazer, 1975) shows him to be working at Family Service of the Mid-Peninsula, Palo Alto.

These initial papers reveal the young-ish de Shazer to be a forward-looking family therapist already interested in making matters as brief as possible. *On Getting Unstuck* is about the therapist tossing a 'hunch' into the mix with the family early on, which is observed to act 'as a kind of land-mine to break up the pattern in which the family is locked' (p. 20), irrespective of whether the hunch is correct or not. 'Two's Company', a more substantial piece which de Shazer thought enough of to mention it in the classic 1986 paper announcing the arrival of SFBT, is about using a triad view of the family to become more aware of the potential for new alliances among the family: two onto the odd one out.

The paper mentions an intervention of the type popular at the time in these circles, which is worth quoting here partly because it's delightful (at least to me, and apparently to the clients) and partly to show the kind of tasks which might be devised. The family were mother, daughter and father. The mother and daughter were fighting over the daughter's carrying on with undesirable friends, shoplifting, lying and so on. The parents were ganging up on the daughter, and the daughter and mother had long silences where they refused to speak with the father ending up carrying messages between them.

de Shazer was keen that the family find a novel way to show their anger towards each other. He wrote:

> I suggested that we might devise a simple way for them to show this anger toward each other without either yelling or silence. However, I said, I doubted if they would be able to accept a simple solution to what seemed to them a complex problem. Mrs. D said that she was willing to try anything short of shooting someone. I asked Mr. D if he would be willing to serve as middle man, and he agreed. I gave him pen and paper to write down the instructions: when they got home, both Laura and Mrs. D were to make large signs to hang around their necks saying, 'I'm angry', and they were to put these on when they next got angry with each other. Then they were to get two squirt guns and a couple of gallons of water, and mother and daughter were to have an old-fashioned Western-style duel. Mr. D was to judge the winner, in addition to keeping them supplied with water. They agreed to try this instead of silence next time they became angry.
>
> (de Shazer, 1975, pp. 91–92)

To modern SF practitioners this sounds extraordinary – a contrived scene. But in creating this intervention de Shazer was listening carefully to the family, to their language and metaphors, and seeking to help them as rapidly as possible. In the paper, de Shazer recounts how the family carried out such fights, until the mother and daughter came to a point where the mother offered to take the daughter out for a pizza to talk things over, and only hold the duel if they couldn't agree. At this point they stopped therapy, saying that the 'silly solution' had worked well, and they were delighted with the results.

In the conclusions to 'Two's Company', de Shazer notes that designing interventions that work quickly is challenging and that the therapist must listen to the clues given by the family. The therapist must present the task in a way the family can accept. His final words in the paper are:

> The therapist must talk the family's language to be heard.
>
> (p. 92)

The preoccupations revealed by de Shazer in these two papers – the desire to move things along rapidly, the seeking of clues in what the family is saying, the need to talk the family's language – will not change radically over the next 30 years. The practice that lead in this direction will change, quite dramatically. However, the underpinning of de Shazer's work in the interactional view from the MRI, the utilisation of the client's abilities from Erickson, the detailed awareness of language he is now developing, will all play important roles in what happens next. And then he meets Insoo Kim Berg.

Insoo Kim Berg

Insoo Kim was born in Seoul, Korea on 25 July 1934. She was the second of five children. Her family was in the business of manufacturing pharmaceuticals and Insoo studied pharmacy at Ewha Women's University in Seoul. She moved to the United States in 1957 with her first husband, Charles H Berg (born 9 August 1930), and their daughter Sarah was born in 1958.

Insoo had enrolled at the UWM to continue her pharmacy studies but discovered that the local norm was that students studied what interested them rather than what their parents laid down. She recalled (Yalom & Rubin, 2003) realising how, with her parents thousands of miles away in Korea and having no idea what she was up to, she could do the same thing. Doing lab work on white rats was losing its appeal, so she switched to social work without telling her family and obtained bachelor and postgraduate (MSSW) degrees.

Continuing her post graduate professional development and becoming interested in psychotherapy, Insoo trained at the Family Institute of Chicago/Center for Family Studies (graduating in 1974) and also at the Menninger Institute in Topeka, Kansas. Insoo recalled (in Yalom & Rubin, 2003) how one of the requirements of the family therapy programme was to keep the family in therapy for a year! She did it, although not quite knowing how or indeed why; this was very far from a brief therapy process.

Much later, she said that she was attracted to the ethos of brief approaches in response to such experiences. She was using a psychoanalytical approach with clients who were not interested in 'insight', they wanted the problem out of the way. It seemed like a bad fit for both her and the client families. She recalled the beginning of the end of her work with psychoanalysis during her time at the Menninger Institute working with a group of American Vietnam veterans (Yalom & Rubin, 2003). 'Week after week ... they tell horrible stories. About how they themselves killed women and children, how their buddies next to them had their heads torn off, and that kind of stuff'. In the end she taped a session, took it to her psychoanalytic supervisor at Menninger and asked for his help. His response? 'What is your counter-transference issue?'

Insoo recalled being furious. She was asking for help and all of a sudden it was *her* fault. The supervisor continued, 'These are veterans, these are people who shot and killed your kind of people'. Insoo said,

> I was just absolutely floored. Never expected something like that. To turn my plea for help, to turn it around and suddenly it became my problem, that it was my countertransference issue. I thought, 'You ass. My kind of people – I'm Korean! These are Vietnamese! You dumb ass'. I thought, that's it. That was the beginning of my end with psychoanalysis.
>
> (Quoted in Yalom & Rubin, 2003)

The late 1960s and early 1970s were exciting times in the development of family therapy and Insoo, like Steve, was soon attracted to the work of Jay Haley. She soon connected Haley's work with the MRI and started visiting Palo Alto to train and be supervised by John Weakland.

It is around this time, of course, that Insoo met Steve de Shazer. The circumstances of this meeting are not totally clear. Brian Cade (2007b) writes that Weakland suggested that she go and see this de Shazer guy who had 'hung his shingle up down the road' and was doing some interesting work. Insoo herself said the afternoons were free and she asked Weakland who else she might visit in the area to learn more. Wendel Ray thinks Weakland's wife Anna may have had a hand in it, as a matchmaker. After all, de Shazer and Berg both had roots in Milwaukee (Berg was working for Milwaukee Family Services by this time), and they were both interested in working briefly with families. Cade understood that she didn't like him at first. Jim Derks, a colleague of Insoo's from Milwaukee who was also training at MRI, said that they hit it off instantly (Lipchik, 2014). Either way, they were married on 25 June 1977 in Milwaukee.

I would like to take a moment to reflect on how lucky we have been to have had two such different and distinctive pioneers. In the normal run of things, one person has a great idea and then attracts disciples who try (in vain) to be like their guru; often the disciples are less skilful and more rigid than their predecessor. Steve and Insoo, while clearly being soul mates as well as colleagues, had such different styles; Steve the grump, a man of very few words, clip–board clasped to his chest, staring at the ceiling and apparently having an inner battle about which word he might venture next, alongside Insoo, bright, enthusiastic, charming, lively, amazed at her clients and openly appreciating so much about them.

In a very practical way this gave all of us who studied with them, worked alongside them and explored their ideas the chance to be ourselves in some way rather than try to be them. (I have seen a few apparently trying to be Insoo or Steve, with limited success.) Together they seemed to inspire each other, and extend their work in new ways both practically and conceptually. I would venture that neither of them could have done it alone.

Developing brief therapy

An 'MRI of the Midwest'

de Shazer and Berg moved back to Milwaukee and took up residence in a characterful house in the Wauwatosa area of the city. They came with the idea of setting up an 'MRI of the Midwest', a brief family therapy think-tank somewhat akin to the Palo Alto operation. de Shazer said later (Norman, McKergow & Clarke, 1997)

> ... our original question was 'What do therapists do that's worth doing?' The question was modified later to 'What do clients and therapists do that's worth doing?' That's the question we've been trying to answer since we started. That's the first major question. The second part of it is Wally Gingerich's question and that is 'How does the therapist know what to ignore?' And we're still working on those questions. There will never be a final answer.

They started by convening a group of colleagues to work together at their house during the evenings (de Shazer and Berg had day-jobs at Milwaukee Family Services). In those days before therapist licensing in Wisconsin, it was only possible to see clients in a state-certified mental health clinic, so they put out a call to friends, relatives and friends of friends to bring along their problems. Eve Lipchik (2014) recalls the observing team sitting on the stairs while practitioner and clients talked in the living room. As was standard family therapy practice, the therapist would take a break to discuss the case before delivering an end-of-session message to the clients. The whole team would then watch a video tape of the session and discuss it. Lipchik says that she had become disillusioned with the psychodynamic play therapy in which she was trained but was sometimes uncomfortable with the strategic interventions being delivered in these evening sessions.

Steve de Shazer continued to publish in peer-reviewed journals, writing about brief therapy with couples and families and the use of hypnotherapy techniques. The hypnotherapy paper (de Shazer, 1978) contains an exploration of the 'crystal ball' technique based on Erickson's pseudo-orientation in time (Haley, 1967) which has the client seeing and experiencing different futures including one where their problem was solved. de Shazer reports that he has used this idea with clients reporting sexual dysfunction; one impact was that clients no longer identified themselves as suffering from this disorder. At this point de Shazer reports using trance inductions to assist in this creative visualising. He later told me that he no longer used hypnotherapy because it seemed that he was working too hard, and that his client was not working hard enough! de Shazer returns to the crystal ball technique in his 1985 book *Keys* (de Shazer, 1985). This is not the famous miracle question which appeared in the mid–late 1980s, but it is an important precursor, a developed skill set which could be carried over into helping clients describe a miraculous future with their problem vanished.

The Brief Family Therapy Center

Sitting on the stairs was clearly not the most comfortable way to research therapy. In 1978 Steve and his colleague Jim Derks gave up their jobs with Family Services and invited members of the evening group to join a new licensed practice – the Brief Family Therapy Center (BFTC). Premises were rented at West Capitol Drive and fitted out as two therapy rooms connected by an observation room. Insoo stayed on at Family Services until the early 1980s in order to pay the bills. Eve Lipchik (2014) recalls that the decision to join wasn't easy – not only was a contribution of $1000 to the set-up requested, but there was no guarantee of any income.

The initial team comprised de Shazer and Berg, Jim Derks, Eve Lipchik, her fellow trainee Marilyn LaCourt and Elam Nunally (a professor of family studies at University of Wisconsin Milwaukee). In 2011, the surviving members of this team set down a detailed recollection of developments at this time (Lipchik, Derks, LaCourt & Nunnally, 2011). Later interviews with the participants by Kiser and Piercy (2001) emphasise that this was an unusual set-up; a new perspective, no funding, with both financial and professional risk for those involved who were committed to finding a better way.

Steve and Insoo also invited some graduate placement students to get involved, including Alex Molnar who became an important thinking partner for de Shazer. Someone who was very keen to join but didn't was Don Norum, also of Family Services. Norum wrote what is in hindsight a key paper in our field, 'The Family Has The Solution', in 1979 but was unable to get it published at the time. It finally appeared in the *Journal of Systemic Therapies* two decades later (Norum, 2000).

Around the start of the 1980s, Steve started the *Underground Railroad*, a newsletter which connected them with other practitioners with similar interests, including Bill O'Hanlon, Bradford Keeney and Brian Cade. It also attracted students and trainees who went on to play key roles, including Yvonne Dolan, Michele Wiener-Davis, John Walter and Jane Peller. The group worked to develop their ideas about effective therapy, based extensively on Erickson's methods, in a way which seems to me to owe more to the science of Francis Bacon than Karl Popper.

Rather than starting with a theoretical hypothesis and seeking to falsify or confirm it (in the Popper stance), the group did therapy as well as they could, observed it, discussed it, saw what seemed to be emerging, and tried out ideas based on that. Their work was based around observation rather than theory. This position was to turn out rather important in the decades to come, as it also influenced the nature of the practice which emerged.

One lasting development from this period was giving compliments at the end of the session. In his paper 'Brief Family Therapy: A Metaphorical Task' (de Shazer, 1980), Steve writes about how to help families accept tasks – to make the process 'as painless as possible'. One way is to make the task address the client's situation in a metaphorical way. The other is to offer compliments before the task – something the therapist and team are impressed with – which creates a 'yes-set' as the clients agree and nod to the compliments and then continue this acceptance as the task is proposed. de Shazer's first book, *Patterns of Brief Family Therapy*, was published in 1982, including ideas about building co-operation with clients, Buddhist and Taoist thought along with multi-perspective 'binocular change'. de Shazer later said it was out of date when it was published, as things were developing so fast (Norman, McKergow & Clarke, 1997).

Towards solutions

The BFTC group pressed on with their mix of development, research and practice. The group followed the Milan school of brief therapy, another off-shoot from MRI led by Mara Selvini-Pallazoli (Selvini-Pallazoli, Boscolo, Cecchin & Prata, 1978) in experimenting with invariant tasks – tasks given to a client family as a matter of course rather than through analysis of their particular context. One version of this, particularly with vague clients, was to ask them to bring a list next time of things they wanted to change. Eve Lipchik (2014) recalls that someone suggested asking a particular client what they *didn't* want to change; in her view this was a turning point from problem focused to solution focused. This task became, of course, the 'Formula First Session Task' described by de Shazer (1984, 1985).

Another shift in process was from resistance to co-operation. de Shazer had written about these as two different paradigms in 1982 (de Shazer, 1982a, 1982b), drawing a clear distinction between the Contest model of therapy and the Co-operation model. In the Contest model, the therapist wins when the clients co-operate; if they don't co-operate, they are 'resistant'. This resistance is said to be located within the family system as something they do rather than a product of the client-therapist interaction. de Shazer is clear that Erickson and the MRI had refined this notion but were still using the Contest metaphor.

In the Co-operation model, this notion of resistance is replaced by a more interactive and responsive concept.

> Each family, individual, or couple shows a unique way of attempting to cooperate, and the therapist's job becomes first to describe to himself that particular manner that the family shows, and then to cooperate with the family's way, and thus to promote change.
>
> (de Shazer, 1982a)

The Contest model, and with it resistance, was declared dead in the famous 'Death Of Resistance' (de Shazer, 1984), a work in progress since 1979. This statement was hugely controversial at the time; it was rejected 17 times and revised six times before ultimate publication.

de Shazer had begun working on the topic when a family described as 'highly resistant' by the referring clinicians were found to co-operate readily with the BFTC team (de Shazer, 1989). He quotes research from the period showing the average number of sessions declining from seven in 1979 to 4.5 in 1988, over 1000 cases, with an increased success rate of 80% from 72%. 'Resistance' ended up apparently buried in de Shazer and Berg's garden beneath a tombstone in the manner of murder mysteries, visible if one 'looks hard', reading 'Here lies Resistance/He was a good and useful fellow in his youth/R.I.P 1978'. The date of publication of this paper, 3 May, is now marked as SF World Day. de Shazer later published a similar but less well-known valediction to the concept of power in therapy (de Shazer, 1988a).

Another indication of Steve de Shazer's wide-ranging interests was the BRIEFER expert system project. BFTC research associate Wally Gingerich proposed constructing a computer program with decision trees to follow the progression of a therapy session. Hannah Goodman, a Master's degree student from UWM seeking an artificial intelligence project for her dissertation, was brought in and the project continued for several years (Gingerich & de Shazer, 1991). Although the idea of computer-driven therapy processes did not last at BFTC, the rigorous thinking required by the project may well have contributed to the formation of Solution Focused Brief Therapy as a new and distinct mode of practice with an overall form and distinctive tools; de Shazer made use of flow-charts in his crucial book *Clues* (1988b).

Around 1984 the BFTC team was changing. Jim Derks and Marilyn LaCourt left for jobs which paid health insurance, which BFTC was unable to offer. Others joined, often ex-students like Ron Kral and Kate Kowalski. People from around the world were starting to ask for training. James Wilk joined as therapist-in-residence from 1984–85 (Nunally, de Shazer, Lipchik & Berg, 1986) and went on to develop ideas about 'clinical epistemology' in his book *Shifting Contexts* with Bill O'Hanlon (O'Hanlon & Wilk, 1987). This book is not about SFBT but takes a fairly heavyweight view of some of the ideas circulating around this period, including the difference between abstraction and concrete detail in language. I found my way into SF via a chance meeting with Wilk in London when he was talking about working with 'minimal intervention' and have much to thank him for. It is a shame he has published so little since.

Another character who will play a greater role in the story also arrived at about this time. In 1984 Gale Miller, a sociology researcher from UWM, was contacted by Wally Gingerich to come and connect with BFTC as an in-house researcher, to study how the group was working together. Miller spent time at BFTC in 1984 and again from 1989. He says (McKergow, 2009) that the work changed markedly in this period; in 1984 the team were building on their eco-systemic work, while five years later a new form of practice had emerged. This was, of course, an early version of SFBT.

The advent of Solution Focused Brief Therapy

The BFTC team were in full flow in the mid-1980s. *Keys to Solution in Brief Therapy* (de Shazer, 1985) gave a kind of progress report including a lot about helping clients move from a complaint (which could be anything) to a 'problem' (which was workable), another look at the crystal ball technique, and the importance of co-operation. The 'keys' of the title are metaphorical skeleton keys, devices (or approaches) like the formula first session task which can fit many situations. We can also find early references to 'exceptions to the rule' (how clients construct complaints as 'always' happening, when there are other overlooked events occurring too) and Ockham's Razor (the priority of simplifying the clinical situation 'so that effective interventions can be designed' (p. 58).

However, this is not yet SFBT. The first sighting of a new form of therapy appears in the 'Brief Therapy: Focused Solution Development' (de Shazer et al., 1986). This paper is a direct counterpart (and tribute) to the MRI team's 1974 paper 'Brief Therapy: Focused Problem Resolution' (Weakland, Fisch, Watzlawick & Bodin, 1974); its form and main headings are the same, and it leads off with a comparison to the MRI's method. Brief therapy, the authors say, is not a matter of time limitation but of taking 'as few sessions as possible'. Only a small change is required, and therefore only a small goal is required also.

There is detail about 'constructing a complaint' (not just any old difficulty, but something that either persists or is at least seen as unchangeable), about seeking exceptions and establishing small goals as a way to know that treatment can conclude. The session may move on to discussing alternative futures without the complaint. There is a consultation break, and end-of-session message and a task. The authors take time to note that building expectations of change is important (yet another link to the MRI's paper, which talks about the work of Robert Rosenthal on the impact of the practitioner's attitudes (Rosenthal,

1966). The paper is a bold statement from a team which has become confident in its work and thinking. It concludes:

> In short, our view holds that clients already know what to do to solve the complaints they bring to therapy; they just do not know that they know. Our job, as brief therapists, is to help them construct for themselves a new use for knowledge they already have.
>
> (de Shazer et al., 1986, p. 220)

This stance is reinforced the following year with a new element in the SFBT vocabulary – pre-session change. Wiener-Davis, de Shazer and Gingerich (1987) report the 'accidental' discovery that changes in the problem situation often occur even before the first therapy session, and moreover that clients can often recall and describe these changes if prompted. Rather than discounting such reports as a 'flight into health', the authors frame this in Bateson's terms of 'a difference that makes a difference'. They describe a small-scale internal study of 30 clients. Of these, 20 could recall changes in the days leading up to the session which were both related to the reasons for coming to therapy AND were changes they wanted to continue to happen. In the remaining cases, it was common for clients to recall pre-treatment changes later in the session.

This paper seems to me to be a pivotal moment (perhaps among many such moments in this story). In this short five-page article, the BFTC team take on and reject psychoanalytic received wisdom, discover something fundamental through trial and error, and explicitly connect the results to Bateson and Erickson. They open a door which, they observe in the conclusions, could be useful to any kind of therapist, not only brief ones.

By this time, the BFTC team note that they are working to the same set of principles as the MRI, but with the priority order changed:

1   If it ain't broke, don't fix it.
2   Once you know what works, do more of it.
3   Stop doing what doesn't work and do something different.

The idea of stopping doing what doesn't work is now a fall-back position rather than the main strategy. It's still there but becomes increasingly unused in time as a main approach (though one could argue that doing more of what works often means doing less of what doesn't work).

At this point new publications are emerging from BFTC at speed; de Shazer produced 16 peer-reviewed articles and book chapters between 1986 and 1988, along with a major new book. *Clues: Investigating Solutions in Brief Therapy* (de Shazer, 1988b) is rightly seen as the touchstone of the SFBT we have come to know, learn and practise over the years. The book has precise flow-charts (page 86), likely inspired by work on the BRIEFER expert system, which makes the approach clear, at least in this initial form. It is useful at this point to compare the MRI brief therapy approach, the BFTC brief family therapy approach of the early 1980s and this 1988 SFBT approach in Table 3.1. This table will appear in future chapters suitably updated, to show the waxing and waning of key aspects of practice over time. It is not intended to be comprehensive.

Customers, miracles and scales

An important new element is the arrival of the customer/complainer/visitor distinction, connected to the need to construct a workable complaint (not just any old difficulty) with someone who wants to do something about it (a customer). Complainers had a complaint but felt no desire or ability to do anything, while visitors had no complaint (and were presumably present at the behest of someone else). These distinctions helped particularly in devising the end-of-session message. Trying to proceed in the normal way with someone who wasn't a customer tended to lead to trouble, so the first stage was to take time to ensure the stage was set for a worthwhile conversation. Over time

Table 3.1 Key elements from MRI brief therapy, BFTC eco-systemic therapy (c. 1982) and early SFBT (c. 1988) compared

MRI Brief Therapy	BFTC brief family therapy (c 1982)	Solution Focused Brief Therapy (c 1988)
Interactional view	Eco-systemic view including therapist and clients – 'death of resistance'	Customer/complainer/visitor relationships: Construct 'complaint'
Team behind the mirror as an aid to the therapist as they are working	Wider view of role of team with consulting break	Team helps construct end-of-session message
Attempted solution is holding status quo in place	Problem-free talk to start	Problem-free talk to start
Need to help the client 'do something different'	Examine patterns around the problem to identify potential spots for intervention	Gather specific concrete detailed information about exceptions – if found, explore what works
Gather specific concrete detailed information about problem and attempted solutions	Gather specific concrete detailed information about patterns around the problem	Set goals (small). If no exceptions, talk about hypothetical solutions and better futures
Break	Break	Break
Intervention designed to break pattern	Compliments	Compliments
Message as 'sales job' (their words) to stop doing the common-sense thing and do something different	Intervention: perhaps formula first-session task	Intervention: do more of what works (or easiest of what might work)

some people tended to forget that these were transient relationship descriptions rather than personal labels ('he's a complainer, she's a visitor') and that people moved around these positions. In the end the BFTC team gave up teaching them, but the idea of a customer survives today in a slightly different form, as we shall see in Chapter 5.

Two of what will come to be seen at SFBT's signature methods also start to appear about this time. Both the miracle question and scaling seem to have arisen through clients mentioning them and the therapist taking up the idea (seeking to follow their clients' language). The miracle question is mentioned briefly at the start of *Clues*, but appears nowhere else in the book, which makes me think it was arriving around the time the text was finalised. The miracle question will come to be seen as so fundamental to SFBT that de Shazer and Berg's final posthumous book will be entitled *More Than Miracles*, so closely has this particular way of working become entwined with the approach in the eyes of outsiders.

Steve wrote (de Shazer, 2004) that he had been using scales (introduced by clients) since 1970 but they had become more frequent and important over the years. This is certainly the case – as far as I can see, they don't explicitly appear in the literature until Lipchik (1988) and are fully explored in the landmark paper *Making Numbers Talk* (Berg & de Shazer, 1993). Of course, these ideas were seeds falling onto highly prepared ground where the BFTC team were already interested in talking about better problem-free futures and small differences. We will examine these methods in detail in later chapters.

Key points

- Steve de Shazer and Insoo Kim Berg both came into brief therapy from other fields.
- They set up the Brief Family Therapy Center (BFTC) in Milwaukee as an 'MRI of the Midwest', a therapeutic think-tank, in 1978.
- Working by trial and error, discussion and reflection, they built on the MRI's interactional view, developing the importance of change talk, co-operation and compliments to make brief therapy even briefer.
- Solution Focused Brief Therapy (SFBT) emerged as a distinct practice around 1988, based on building on exceptions to problems and setting small goals.
- Well-known methods such as the miracle question and scaling appeared subsequently, as the approach was refined and spread around the world.

References

Berg, I. K., & de Shazer, S. (1993). Making numbers talk: Language in therapy. In S. Friedman (Ed.), *The New Language of Change: Constructive Collaboration in Psychotherapy* (pp. 5–24). New York, NY: Guilford Press.

Cade, B. (2007a). A history of the brief solution-focused approach. In T. S. Nelson & F. N. Thomas (Eds.), *Handbook of Solution-Focused Brief Therapy: Clinical Applications* (pp. 25–63). Binghamton, NY: Haworth Press.

Cade, B. (2007b). *Insoo Kim Berg Obituary*. Retrieved from www.counselingsoft.jp/workshop3.html

de Shazer, S. (1974). On getting unstuck: Some change-initiating tactics for getting the family moving. *Family Therapy*, *1*(1), 19–26.

de Shazer, S. (1975). Brief therapy: Two's company. *Family Process*, *14*, 79–93.

de Shazer, S. (1978). Brief hypnotherapy of two sexual dysfunctions: The crystal ball technique. *American Journal of Clinical Hypnosis*, *20*(3), 203–208.

de Shazer, S. (1980). Brief family therapy: A metaphorical task. *Journal of Marital and Family Therapy*, *6*(4), 471–476.

de Shazer, S. (1982a). *Patterns of Brief Family Therapy*. New York, NY: Guilford Press.

de Shazer, S. (1982b). Some conceptual distinctions are more useful than others. *Family Process*, *21*, 72–84.

de Shazer, S. (1984). The death of resistance. *Family Process*, *23*, 11–17.

de Shazer, S. (1985). *Keys to Solution in Brief Therapy*. New York, NY: W. W. Norton.

de Shazer, S. (1988a). A requiem for power. *Contemporary Family Therapy*, *10*(2), 69–76.

de Shazer, S. (1988b). *Clues: Investigating Solutions in Brief Therapy*. New York, NY: W. W. Norton.

de Shazer, S. (1989). Resistance revisited. *Contemporary Family Therapy*, *11*(4), 227–233.

de Shazer, S. (2004). *Brief Therapy in Historical Perspective*. SFBT UWM online course, week 1 materials. Author's collection.

de Shazer, S., Berg, I. K., Lipchik, E., Nunally, E., Molnar, A., Gingerich, W., & Wiener-Davis, M. (1986). Brief therapy: Focused solution development. *Family Process*, *25*, 207–221.

Dolan, Y. (2005). *Steve de Shazer Obituary*. Retrieved from www.counselingsoft.jp/workshop3.html

Gingerich, W. J., & de Shazer, S. (1991). The BRIEFER project: Using expert systems as theory construction tools. *Family Process*, *30*, 241–250.

Haley, J. (1963). *Strategies of Psychotherapy*. New York, NY: Grune and Stratton.

Haley, J. (1967). *Advanced Techniques of Hypnosis and Therapy: Selected Paper of Milton H Erickson*. New York, NY: Grune and Stratton.

Kiser, D. J., & Piercy, F. P. (2001). Creativity and family therapy theory development: Lessons from the founders of solution-focused therapy. *Journal of Family Psychotherapy*, *12*(3), 1–30.

Lipchik, E. (1988). Purposeful sequences for beginning the solution-focused interview. In E. Lipchik (Ed.), *Interviewing* (pp. 105–117). Rockville, MD: Aspen.

Lipchik, E. (2014). The development of my personal solution-focused working model: From 1978 and continuing. *International Journal of Solution-Focused Practices*, *2*(2), 63–73. doi:10.14335/ijsfp.v2i2.23. Retrieved from www.solutions-centre.org/pdf/25-64-1-PB.pdf

Lipchik, E., Derks, J., LaCourt, M., & Nunally, E. (2011). The evolution of solution-focused brief therapy. In C. Franklin, T. S. Trepper, W. J. Gingerich, & E. E. McCollum (Eds.), *Solution-Focused Brief Therapy: A Handbook of Evidence-Based Practice* (pp. 3–19). Oxford: Oxford University Press.

McKergow, M. (2009). Interview with Gale Miller: The man behind the mirror behind the mirror at BFTC. *InterAction*, *1*(1), 78–87.

McKergow, M. (2015). Steve de Shazer: A different kind of cleverness (… and Paul Gonslaves). In M. Vogt, F. Wolf, P. Sundman, & H. N. Dreesen (Eds.), *Encounters with Steve de Shazer and Insoo Kim Berg: Inside Stories of Solution-Focused Brief Therapy* (pp. 114–117). London: Solutions Books.

Miller, G., & de Shazer, S. (1998). Have you heard the latest rumor about …? Solution-focused therapy as a rumor. *Family Process, 37*(3), 363–377. https://doi.org/10.1111/j.1545-5300.1998.00363.x

Norman, H., McKergow, M., & Clarke, J. A. (1997). Paradox is a muddle: An interview with Steve de Shazer. *Rapport, 34,* 41–49. Retrieved from http://sfwork.com/paradox-is-a-muddle 8 May 2020.

Norum, D. (2000). The family has the solution. *Journal of Systemic Therapies, 19*(1), 3–16.

Nunally, E., de Shazer, S., Lipchik, E., & Berg, I. K. (1986). A study of change: Therapeutic theory in process. In D. E. Efron (Ed.), *Journeys: Expansion of the Strategic-Systemic Therapies.* New York, NY: Brunner/Mazel.

O'Hanlon, W., & Wilk, J. (1987). *Shifting Contexts: The Generation of Effective Psychotherapy.* New York, NY: Guilford Press.

Rosenthal, R. (1966). *Experimenter Effects in Behavioral Research.* New York: Appleton–Century-Crofts.

Selvini-Pallazoli, M., Boscolo, L., Cecchin, G., & Prata, G. (1978). *Paradox and Counterparadox: A New Model in the Therapy of the Family in Schizophrenic Transaction.* Lanham, MD: Jason Aronson Inc.

Vogt, M., Wolf, F., Sundman, P., & Dreesen, H. N. (Eds.). (2015). *Encounters with Steve de Shazer and Insoo Kim Berg: Inside Stories of Solution-Focused Brief Therapy.* London: Solutions Books.

Weakland, J. H., & Fisch, R. (1992). Brief therapy: MRI style. In S. H. Budman, M. F. Hoyt, & S. Freidman (Eds.), *The First Session in Brief Therapy* (pp. 306–323). New York, NY: Guilford Press.

Weakland, J. H., Fisch, R., Watzlawick, P., & Bodin, A. (1974). Brief therapy: Focused problem resolution. *Family Process, 13*(2), 141–168.

Wiener-Davis, M., de Shazer, S., & Gingerich, W. J. (1987). Building on pretreatment change to construct the therapeutic solution: An exploratory study. *Journal of Marital and Family Therapy, 13*(4), 359–363.

Yalom, V., & Rubin, B. (2003). *Insoo Kim Berg on Brief Solution-Focused Therapy.* Retrieved from www.psychotherapy.net/interview/insoo-kim-berg

Chapter 4

The evolution of SFBT
Spreading the word and defining the practice

This chapter describes the development and spread of Solution Focused Brief Therapy (SFBT) around the world, engaging more people who brought their own ideas and innovations. The ideas also found homes in other fields including education, social work, coaching and management as well as wide-ranging applications across health care.

The global impact of the work originating in this small group in a Midwestern city better known for beer and motorcycles has been extraordinary. The way that it has happened is in large part due to the generosity and open-mindedness of Steve de Shazer, Insoo Kim Berg and the Brief Family Therapy Center (BFTC) team. Practice has continued to develop. This chapter looks at the journey towards an 'official' definition of SFBT, a concept which de Shazer might have struggled with, and why the background story of SFBT makes this a challenging and even controversial development.

SFBT goes global

As early as 1982, Steve de Shazer and Insoo Kim Berg were being invited abroad to teach about their work with visits to Norway and the United Kingdom. (Elam Nunnally also trained in Finland from the early 1980s.) Their travels pick up the pace in the mid-1980s, by which point they were clearly widely seen as having something new and interesting to say. And this really was new, and in some ways strange and unfamiliar.

In 1987, they were invited to Malmö, Sweden by Harry Korman and Martin Soderquist, who were working on treating people with drug problems using family therapy methods. Steve insisted that Insoo accompany him. Harry Korman (2020) recalls the first workshop; Steve showed a tape of his work with a cocaine addict who wanted to resist the urge to take drugs. It transpired in a matter of minutes of Solution-Focused questioning that she had in fact resisted the urge for three days prior to the session. Harry, practising strategic systemic therapy at the time, recalls thinking 'What the **** is going on? We would never have discovered that!'

Another early convert was British psychiatrist Dr Alasdair Macdonald. He recalls:

> I had established a strategic family therapy training team in Dumfries, Scotland. I read a paper by Steve concerning the BRIEFER algorithm. I was fascinated and shared it with the team, who liked it also. Brian Cade came to teach in Cumbria and some of us attended his workshop there. We decided to try SF for six months to see how it compared with our strategic therapy. We felt that SF was more respectful to the client, easier to do and produced results in fewer sessions, so we stayed with the model.
>
> Several of us went to workshops by Steve at BRIEF in London. From 1990 we started to offer workshops in Scotland and the North of England. After a while we attracted workers from Northern Ireland also. When I moved to Cumbria in 1995 I introduced SF to the local low secure unit. It worked so well that we had contracts to take on difficult cases from other regions, because we were the only team who always had empty beds.
>
> (Macdonald, 2020)

This combination of a simpler yet more effective way of working continued to gather champions and enthusiasts around the world. By the late 1980s, others were coming to Milwaukee to train and learn, and were also beginning to write about SFBT. Early books appeared by Michele Wiener-Davis and Bill O'Hanlon (*In Search of Solutions*, 1989) and the Brief Therapy Practice in London (*From Problem to Solution*, George, Iveson & Ratner, 1990). Connections were also forming with groups in Finland, Sweden, Belgium, Austria, Germany, Spain and elsewhere, as well as in Asia. This transition from SFBT being the work of the BFTC group to being co-owned, supported and developed was very important in the spread of the work – it is hard to see how the diversity of SF practice could have been achieved otherwise. And, as we will see, this diversity also makes it harder to be precise about what the work entails and therefore how to go about it.

More from Milwaukee

Steve de Shazer and Insoo Kim Berg continued teaching, writing, training, seeing clients and spreading the news about SFBT for the rest of their lives. Steve wrote two further books which attempted to contextualise the practice of SFBT, and indeed all talking therapy, alongside traditions of post-modernism and post-structuralism. *Putting Difference To Work* (de Shazer, 1991) draws on Wittgenstein and Derrida, among others, to focus not just on family-therapy-as-a-system but on language-as-a-system. The paper 'Doing Therapy: A Post-Structural Revision' (de Shazer & Berg, 1992) is probably the most concise statement of this focus on language and is well worth close study. *Words Were Originally Magic* (1994), the title quoting Freud, goes further – at the same time discursive (drawing on Wittgenstein again and also critiquing Lacan, Bateson (for muddled-ness) and Bandler & Grinder). de Shazer also examines therapy transcripts from his own practice alongside Weakland and family therapists Nathan Ackerman and James Gustafson.

A lot of the message is about 'staying at the surface', about focusing on what people say rather than any (imagined) subtexts, underlying structures, therapists' concerns and so on. *Words* in particular is full of case examples and dialogues, and also features a lovely moment where de Shazer mentions his therapist persona de Shazer-the-stupid (a thought that will resonate with anyone who saw Steve being puzzled by a client's statement and, apparently baffled, asking them for clarification). Alongside this he also mentions Weakland-the-dense (a similar style) and Insoo-the-incredulous (a very different but equally recognisable image; 'Wow'). The book is a tour-de-force and should, one might think, stand as de Shazer's crowning achievement.

Yet it doesn't. There is, in my view, a contradiction between the increasing drive for simplicity, staying on the surface, listening to the client without prejudice (as far as possible) on the one hand, and the intellectual gymnastics required to defend that position against a small number of interested combatants. After all, did one really require a critique of Chomsky or a working understanding of Wittgenstein's notion of language games in order to work with clients? No – only to argue with people who didn't 'get it'. The clients weren't interested – they wanted to improve their lives. The 'opposition' were not really engaging – they had their own traditions to celebrate and apply. Perhaps Steve was summing up all his huge intellectual ability and tussles over the years into a big statement to finally make it all clear. Except that to get clarity, it was almost a pre-requisite to have spent 20 years being Steve de Shazer.

Onwards and outwards

More books were starting to appear at this time. Ben Furman and Tapani Ahola's *Solution Talk: Hosting Therapeutic Conversations* (Furman & Ahola, 1992) appeared from Finland. Insoo Kim Berg published her first book the same year, *Working With The Problem Drinker* (Berg & Miller, 1992) (later retitled *The Miracle Method*), alongside Scott Miller, Director of Training at BFTC at that time. Miller has gone on to his own distinguished career in encouraging effective therapy, in particular using feedback from clients as a regular and continuing practice using Session and Outcome Rating Scales (for example Duncan, Miller & Sparks, 2011). The SRS and ORS have now been incorporated into SF practice in some circles (for example Burns, 2016).

The early 1990s marked a great explosion of interest in SFBT. I recall Dvorah Simon's brief therapy newsletter *News Of A Difference* (sent around on paper in those pre-Internet days). The first issue I saw in 1993 seemed to have about equal numbers of advertisements from practitioners offering MRI model brief therapy and SFBT. Before long, the majority were using SF.

One of the telling features of SF practice has long been how quickly and easily it transcended the mirrors of the family therapy room and started informing practice in many fields. Initially and unsurprisingly this started with different therapeutic settings – working with older people (Iveson, 1990), sexual abuse (Dolan, 1991), couples (Michelle Wiener-Davis' book *Divorce Busting* (Wiener-Davis, 1993) may be the first example of a book aimed at helping those in distress to apply SF ideas for themselves), working with women and children (Lethem, 1994). The use of the approach in child welfare and family settings was particularly notable, with Insoo Kim Berg's book *Family-Based Services* (Berg, 1994) leading the way; the influential *Signs Of Safety* approach was soon to follow (Turnell & Edwards, 1999). (This paragraph is only mentioning a few books from the early 1990s – there have been many more since then.)

Schools were another early setting for SF practice to be put into action. Michael Durrant's *Creative Strategies for School Problems* (Durrant, 1995) and John Rhodes and Yasmin Ajmal's *Solution Focused Thinking in Schools* (Rhodes & Ajmal, 1995) appeared, with Linda Metcalf's *Parenting Toward Solutions* (Metcalf, 1996) following a year later. A further sign of the adoption of SF ideas across the helping professions was the appearance of the first SF textbook. *Interviewing For Solutions* (De Jong & Berg, 1998) was, and still is for many, the go-to text; it has been through three revisions and is still a popular reference.

SFBT gets organised

In the early years SFBT was not organised in a formal way at all. It was more like a guerrilla movement, with a loosely connected informal network of enthusiasts each doing their own practice, linked by their connections with Steve de Shazer and Insoo Kim Berg. The co-founders spent a lot of time on the road visiting sympathetic groups, training, working and building interest. However, there was no formal organisation. This was not an oversight, but a deliberate plan.

The European Brief Therapy Association (EBTA) was formed in 1994 with support from de Shazer and Berg to support brief therapy of all kinds (although it has always been primarily a place for SF practitioners), following a meeting in Louisiana to honour the work of John Weakland the previous year. The founding members were Manfred Vogt and Wolfgang Eberling (NIK Bremen), Anders Claesson (FKC Stockholm), and Luc Isebaert and Marie-Christine Cabié (Korzybski Institute, Bruges and Paris) (Isebaert & Klingenstierna, 2012).

The first ETBA conference was organised by Luc Isebaert in Bruges, Belgium in 1994 with around 50 participants including a dozen or so MRI model brief therapists. The original form of the conference was novel and tells us a good deal about what de Shazer valued in these gatherings. No individuals could participate, only teams (or their representatives). There was no keynote address, only 60- or 90-minute workshops. Moreover, the workshops had no presenter, only conversations, and nobody could speak for more than ten minutes at a time.

We can see immediately how these rules point towards the valuing of sharing and mutual learning over authority and hierarchy. This spirit of generosity and low power-gradient has largely stayed with the SF community around the world, and it's one of the things we should be truly grateful for. Even at the time, though, some practical difficulties emerged. In particular, the exclusion of individuals was hard to enforce, and it proved hard to keep people to the ten-minute limit (Isebaert & Klingenstierna, 2012). Initially there were two conferences each year; by the following year in Bremen there were 250 people attending. EBTA was the de facto world SF body until 2002, when it was joined by the Solution Focused Brief Therapy Association (SFBTA) in North America.

Another novel feature of EBTA was that it was not a membership organisation in the usual way. As the EBTA history by Isebaert and Klingenstierna (2012) records it, the membership was defined as 'all those who had attended the last conference'. This definition held for 20 years; although impractical in many aspects, it had a simplicity. You're a member of a group if you're there; you aren't if you're not. Other more mainstream models were discussed and rejected, partly out of deference to de Shazer, who championed that the board should be composed like the editorial board of a scientific journal, appointed to represent their community. One obvious problem with this ephemeral membership was that it is incompatible with normal democratic organisation.

This format survived until around 2014, when a more conventional membership and elected board structure were introduced. The original form of EBTA certainly generated learning and exchange – I attended my first EBTA conference in 1997, and these were marvellous meetings where anyone interested could get up close with the leading lights of the field. What it also did, quite deliberately in my view, was prevent anyone or any group taking control of the field. The co-founders had eschewed this position and were quietly ensuring that nobody else could take it up either. There was not, and indeed could not be, one single 'proper' definition of what defined SF practice.

This may be surprising to the outsider but is entirely in keeping with Berg and de Shazer's notion of a flexible practice, the importance of focusing on the client rather than the precise method, and the driving priority of effective and brief treatment. It would make no sense at all to do SF therapy 'properly' and discover that the client had not seen any useful change, when some tweak or tactic might have proved more beneficial. Steve de Shazer always said that there was no orthodoxy, and indeed later published an influential paper about SFBT as a rumour (Miller & de Shazer, 1998). It keeps the focus on the practitioner and the work rather than on the method.

Steve and Insoo leave the stage

As the SFBT movement grew, Steve and Insoo spent more and more time 'on the road' teaching, speaking and working. Insoo developed her own writing, mostly about applications of SFBT in different settings and client groups. She engaged audiences around the world with her 'incredulous' and warm style. Steve also went on the road; his terse style and apparently abrupt attitude was less engaging with audiences (particularly those who were coming new to the approach) and so he was often to be found seeing clients, demonstrating his work and discussing it with trainees and experienced practitioners alike.

de Shazer and Berg often worked separately; on the occasions when they were together, they would enjoy long walks. They both seemed to find more interest in Europe than North America, where people were perhaps more interested in Steve's theoretical groundings. In the late 1990s, the BFTC shifted premises to a training building with office space as Steve and Insoo weren't in Milwaukee enough to have clients (McKergow, 2009). In the end they moved the office into the basement of their house. Both continued to work hard and travel extensively, although Steve was hampered by a chronic blood disorder. The final book to bear de Shazer and Berg's names is *More Than Miracles* (de Shazer et al., 2007), a project pulled together across their final years which sets out as clearly as possible the state of SFBT in the mid-2000s. It's an excellent and important book which strives for (and achieves) practical clarity and is another important milestone in the development of our practice.

Steve de Shazer became seriously ill in 2003 but recovered and resumed work. He visited London for a two-day workshop in September 2005 in good form, worked at BRIEF with several clients and an appreciative group and then left for his next engagement in Vienna. He was taken ill on the plane, was hospitalised and died there on Sunday, 11 September 2005 with Insoo by his side. His last recorded words (to Ferdinand Wolf, a long-time colleague and the Vienna seminar organiser who had wished him a good night), were to say 'This might not be a good night, but I hope it will be a not too bad night'. Two hours later he fell into a coma from which he did not wake (Wolf, 2015). In context, this is a very characteristic turn of phrase – Steve would often moderate instructions to workshop participants to have fun by adding 'but not too much!'.

Insoo kept up her work after Steve's death. Her own end came very suddenly while she was visiting her local gym in Milwaukee on 19 January 2007, went to the steam room to recover after a work-out and was found dead by the staff, as if asleep. It seems fitting that both of these innovators died 'with their boots on'. Neither showed any signs of wanting to retire. Their influence lives on in so many remarkable ways, and little else in this book would have happened without their presence and influence.

Defining SF work

The open stance favoured by de Shazer may have helped to keep things flexible, but problems were starting to arise in the field of research. A strict definition was seen as undesirable. However, other practices closely connected to social constructionism such as Appreciate Inquiry were building an audience without seeing a contradiction in having five generally agreed principles and four stages of work (see for example Cooperrider & Whitney, 2001). Papers were starting to appear which claimed to be about SFBT but seemed, to those familiar with the approach, to have varying (and sometimes little) connection with the work as understood within the SF community.

In 1997, at a special research meeting in Bruges, EBTA 'members' including Steve and Insoo drew up a list of elements which they felt were of defining importance to SF practice. If published research used these, then it could be considered as part of the SF canon. de Shazer and Berg published a short note about it (de Shazer & Berg, 1997) which is revealing of their stance towards defining their practice. They say that their approach has been a kind of 'naturalistic inquiry' into what therapists and clients do together that is useful, and list four features of a therapy conversation which 'might well serve as indicators that SFBT is happening'. These features are:

1   At some point in the first interview, the therapist will ask the 'Miracle Question'.
2   At least once during the first interview, and at subsequent ones, the client will be asked to rate something on a scale of 0–10 or 1–10.
3   At some point in the interview, the therapist will take a break.
4   After this intermission, the therapist will give the client some compliments which will sometimes (frequently) be followed by a suggestion or homework task (frequently called an 'experiment').

(de Shazer & Berg, 1997, p. 123)

de Shazer and Berg are at pains to point out that while this is a set of clues that 'SFBT is happening', it is not a recipe for how to do good therapy – there are many possible ways to do that. However, if all of these are not present, then SFBT is not being practised. They go on to say that too much focus on research and aggregating data may risk 'ignoring the client's goals, the client's evaluation of the therapy, and the client's own life, all of which are so important to SFBT' (p. 124).

This list is interesting in several ways. de Shazer and Berg have selected moments in the therapy session which can be initiated by the practitioner – the miracle question, scaling and so on. They say nothing in this list about what might happen next (presumably because it depends on the client's response, which is not within the practitioner's control). They include the break, part of their practice since the very start and inherited from family therapy and MRI brief therapy with the observing team. The giving of both compliments and (frequently) a suggested homework task is also vital.

As SFBT continues to evolve, we will see that some of these elements begin to recede. We will also see how the client's goal, evaluation and life can be incorporated into a new version of 'indicators that SFBT is happening' by seeing the development and growth of SFBT seen as conversation-building rather than question-asking. (This is not a binary either/or position but rather a shift in emphasis with increasing focus on what happens in between the 'set-piece' big moments like the Miracle Question, scaling questions and so on.)

Developing connections with national and topic groups

As the use of SFBT ideas in many areas continued to grow, it was perhaps inevitable that at some stage there would have to be some kind of formal organisation. This unsurprisingly started to happen first at a national level; the laws, rules and codes for therapy practice are set by countries in accordance with whatever norms they have adopted based on past therapies. Engaging with these systems is a powerful way (sometimes the only way) to move SFBT into mainstream acceptance.

The first country to form a national SF association was Finland. Ratkes – The Association for the Promotion of Solution and Resource Oriented Methods – was founded in 1995. The name is an abbreviation of the Finnish word *ratkaisukeskeinen*, an expression for something being solved. Ben Furman and Tapani Ahola (having been involved in leading brief therapy trainings with the Mannerheim League for Child Welfare) and Peter Sundman led the way. Peter, originally trained by MRI, and several others visited BFTC in Milwaukee in the late 1980s and a close connection with Steve and Insoo followed through annual workshops by them and by Elam Nunnally, who was married to a Finn and had trained people since the early days of BFTC.

Part of the challenge with official systems is that their requirements sometimes don't match the outlook of SFBT. The question then becomes whether compromises are possible and desirable. Part of this challenge with becoming integrated with the Finnish psychotherapy system was the requirement, based on assumptions of psychodynamic practice, that the practitioners be in therapy themselves for an extended period during their training. Then during the negotiations the family therapy group, including the SF workers, managed to renegotiate 'self-therapy' to 'self-exploration'. This was more workable, and Ben Furman managed to reduce the amount of time required still further. In 1998 SF therapy become officially recognised in Finland. It has since gone on, as in many countries, to be used in other fields too. Ben Furman's four-year run on prime-time TV helping people with their problems in an SF way also helped build local awareness of the approach.

Similar processes were starting to happen elsewhere. As the official systems are very different, there were also different experiences. In Germany, the law stipulated until recently that psychotherapy must be practised by a psychologist or medical doctor, which meant other forms of treatment being seen by some as lower-grade. In the United Kingdom, the UK Association for Solution Focused Practice (UKASFP) was formed in 2003, initially as a networking body. The regulation of therapy and counselling in the UK is more flexible than in Germany, and in the early years most people wishing to practise SFBT were already qualified under some other banner (family therapy, systemic therapy) and thus didn't need another qualification or recognition.

As time has gone on more and more people want to practise simply as SF therapists/counsellors, and so systems of recognition have been developing. The Solution Focused Brief Therapy Association (SFBTA) of north America was founded in 2002, and national associations are to be found in Sweden, Austria, Switzerland, Latvia, India, South Korea, Australasia and elsewhere.

2002 also saw the start of what became the SOLWorld community, dedicated to sharing and building SF practice in organisations, at a conference in Bristol hosted by the Bristol Solutions Group. Conceived in a similar-but-different non-organisational form to EBTA with no members, no board, no bank account and no money, the group has so far enabled over 40 international events including retreats, summer schools and conferences all aimed at coaches, managers, facilitators and those working in Organisation Development. Books also started appearing in this field including *The Solutions Focus* (Jackson & McKergow, 2002), *Brief Coaching for Lasting Solutions* (Berg & Szabo, 2005), *The Solution Tango* (Cauffman & Dierolf, 2006) and *Solution-Focused Management* (Lueger & Korn, 2006). The SOLWorld community included a strong Japanese group led by Yasuteru Aoki, who for many years organised a series of conferences in Japan.

Simplifying but not summarising

Along with increasing organisation in the SF world came a move to consolidate what was known so far – to look credible, to build on what was already there, and perhaps to attempt to make more impact on the broader worlds of psychotherapy, counselling and the wider helping professions. Steve de Shazer's original books in the early 1990s, while wide-ranging and innovative, had not set down in clear and easily understood terms what even *his* practice was, let alone something that others could follow. More general frameworks were appearing in the writings of others in the 1990s. The Brief Therapy Practice in London were quick off the mark (George, Iveson & Ratner, 1990) with a very understandable account. The Foreword to the book by Steve de Shazer reveals his potential concerns about attempts to convey this highly contextual and therefore not easily summarised practice:

> Frankly, I was afraid that [the authors] had developed a 'readers digest' version or a 'cook book' or (my worst nightmare) a statement, a manifesto about the right way to do brief therapy. Perhaps surprisingly, I did not worry about whether they had 'understood' my work and the work of my colleagues. After all, even a misunderstanding might turn out to be clinically useful. ... I was amazed to find evidence in Chapter One that they had gotten the idea. And, [in the rest of the book] I saw that not only had

they got the idea but they were able to use it with their clients in a useful way. ... They listened to the client, found out what she wanted and worked with her toward getting it. That is, of course, the core of solution focused brief therapy.

(de Shazer, in George, Iveson & Ratner, 1990)

This passage seems to me to sum up the difficulties in arriving at a neat 'official' version of SFBT, at least in the eyes of Steve de Shazer. SFBT is an approach which takes a great deal from the specifics of each client and case; what the practitioner might do is driven to a large extent by what the client says. The most important thing is that it works with clients, so anything which prioritises method over outcome is unsatisfactory. 'I did it properly but it didn't work' is a poor substitute for 'I cheated a bit and the client found a way forward'. This kind of flexibility is not to be found in models but more in the practitioners working with the models. In the passage earlier, de Shazer is not mainly concerned about whether the Londoners have understood *his* work, but whether *their* work is effective. That's the main thing. That they were doing it in a way which seems coherent with his own ideas is more of a bonus to him than anything else.

de Shazer's view seems to be that ideally everyone, with the benefit of time, would take years to sit with clients, research the brief therapy tradition, make lots of empirical experiments and examinations, and then reach an effective practice which is always under review. After all, that was how he did it. In taking the brief therapy stance of being more interested in the individual client than their diagnosis, de Shazer was resisting the urge to categorise clients (and treat them using a medical model of examine-diagnose-prescribe) and is instead using his conversational skill to work with them as individuals. He also seems to be resisting taking a similar approach to his own practice – summarising it into a series of steps, a 'cook book', which might exclude interesting useful possibilities.

An 'official' version of SFBT?

The lifetime-exploration approach espoused by Steve de Shazer, while philosophically robust and driven by principle, is neither efficient nor even available to the vast majority of practitioners who wanted to learn about SFBT rather than devise it for themselves. De Jong and Berg's *Interviewing For Solutions* (1998) offered something more accessible, which was consolidated by others. In the UK, Bill O'Connell (1998) produced accessible texts which helped him to launch a Master's degree programme in SFBT. Research was beginning to accumulate, collected by EBTA research co-ordinator Alasdair Macdonald (2007, 2011); much of it was favourable to SFBT. As national SF organisations engaged with their own requirements for licensing and recognition, it was inevitable that some kind of widely used framework would appear.

In 2007, Björn Johansson and Eva Persson began to host meetings of what became known as the Karlstad Group, addressing this question by looking for links, connections and parallels with other fields. I was a regular participant along with Peter Sundman, Gale Miller, Ferdinand Wolf, Wolfgang Gaiswinkler and Marianne Roessler and others. This work evolved over time into an EBTA study group on the theory of SF practice led by Peter Sundman which has produced very substantial work over several years (Sundman, 2017). Once again, the main purpose of this definition was to assist in defining the practice for the purposes of research rather than seeking to limit what an individual practitioner might do with a client.

There were also drivers towards accreditation of practitioners. This form of professionalising had been rejected by de Shazer and Berg at a time when most SF practitioners had come to this way of working have qualified in some other form of practice. In the early years of the 21st century, however an increasing number of people were coming into the field who wanted to specialise in SF work from the start. There were different views as to how to achieve this. The International Alliance of Solution-Focused Teaching Institutes (IASTI) was formed in 2008, with a conventional model of approved trainings leading to various levels of certification.

Others felt that this kind of hour-counting process did not really fit with the SF priority to do as little as necessary; some people seemed to become fluent in the practice in a short time while others appeared to do years of study and still not 'get it'. The Association for Quality Development of SF Consulting and Training (SFCT) established a system of reviewing pieces of work from 2009, where candidates presented their work for feedback and discussion with experienced practitioners. The idea was that this was more like a driving test than a training programme: if good work could be shown, that was enough. Solution Focus in Organisations – SFiO has the same model. A similar ethos was applied by the United Kingdom Association of Solution Focused Practice (UKASFP) where practitioners submit a single session which shows key pieces of SF work in action.

In 2011, an authoritative collection of the hundreds of research studies undertaken was curated by Cynthia Franklin and published through Oxford University Press (Franklin, Trepper, McCollum & Gingerich, 2011). This is a landmark collection by any standards – the 25 chapters detail research and experience in applying SFBT in many settings from domestic violence through children, schizophrenia, alcohol treatment, management (a chapter contributed by me, McKergow, 2011), life coaching, schools, child protection and more.

The second chapter of this book (Trepper et al., 2011) is entitled 'Solution Focused Brief Therapy Treatment Manual'. It is deliberately constructed in the same way as treatment manuals for other accepted forms of therapy, and is intended to present SFBT as a respectable, useful, well-founded mode of practice, particularly in a north American context where the National Institute of Mental Health requires such manuals to ensure replicability of future research.

This manual helpfully outlines key interventions in both general and specific terms. The general include:

- Positive, collegial, solution–focused stance
- Looking for previous solutions (in order to utilise them, not stop them as in the MRI model)
- Looking for exceptions
- Using questions rather than directives or interpretations
- Using present and future oriented questions rather than past oriented questions
- Compliments
- Gentle nudging to do more of what works.

We can compare the specific interventions included in the manual against the previous two iterations of SFBT practice from the table in the previous chapter (Table 4.1):

Table 4.1 Key elements from BFTC eco-systemic therapy (c. 1982), early SFBT (c. 1988) and the SFBTA treatment manual (2011) compared

BFTC brief family therapy (c 1982)	Solution Focused Brief Therapy (c 1988)	SFBT treatment manual (2011)
Eco-systemic view including therapist and clients – 'death of resistance'	Customer/complainer/ visitor relationships: Construct 'complaint'	Collegial and collaborative relationship
Wider view of role of team with consulting break	Team helps construct end-of-session message	Team (if there is one) helps construct end-of-session message
Problem-free talk	Problem-free talk	Pre-session change, construct solution-focused goals (small, presence of a solution)
Examine patterns around the problem to identify potential spots for intervention	Gather specific concrete detailed information about exceptions – if found, explore what works	Miracle Question
Gather specific concrete detailed information about patterns around the problem	If no exceptions, talk about hypothetical solutions and better futures. Set goals (small).	Scaling Questions, Constructing Exceptions, Coping Questions (if needed)
Break	Break	Break
Compliments	Compliments	Compliments
Intervention: perhaps formula first-session task	Intervention: do more of what works (or easiest of what might work)	Experiments and Homework Assignments

Looking at this progression, some things are clear. We are no longer interested in patterns around the problem at all. Focus on the future (as developed by small goals and the Miracle Question) is now further up the agenda. The constructing of exceptions has moved down the order, but is still present – even though an 'exception' requires a problem definition to be meaningful ('an exception to what?'). The break, compliments and some kind of task, experiment or homework have evolved but are still right there at the end of the session. We will return to this table again towards the end of the next chapter, with the next generation in view.

Key points

- SFBT spread rapidly from its Milwaukee roots, in something resembling a 'guerrilla movement' more than a formal organisation.
- The practice was further developed by other groups and spread into other fields, across the helping professions and into schools, coaching, organisation management and many other fields.
- Steve de Shazer and Insoo Kim Berg were reluctant to take on formal leadership roles, and instead promoted mechanisms of exchange, mutual learning and shared responsibility among the SFBT community.
- A more settled version of the practice gained currency from the mid-1990s, with more focus on the future and the Miracle Question, and on using scales.
- There have been various approaches to accrediting SF practitioners over the years, none of them completely accepted across the field.
- Authoritative statements culminating in a 'treatment manual' finally materialised after the deaths of the founders. The evolution of the practice, however, continued.

References

Berg, I. K. (1994). *Family Based Services: A Solution-Focused Approach*. New York, NY: W. W. Norton.

Berg, I. K., & Miller, S. (1992). *Working with the Problem Drinker: A Solution-Focused Approach*. New York, NY: W. W. Norton.

Berg, I. K., & Szabo, P. (2005). *Brief Coaching for Lasting Solutions*. New York, NY: W. W. Norton.

Burns, K. (2016). *Focus on Solutions: A Health Professional's Guide* (2nd rev. ed.). London: Solutions Books.

Cauffman, L., & Dierolf, K. (2006). *The Solution Tango: Seven Simple Steps to Solutions in Management*. London: Marshall Cavendish.

Cooperrider, D. L., & Whitney, D. (2001). A positive revolution in change. In D. L. Cooperrider, P. Sorenson, D. Whitney, & T. Yeager (Eds.), *Appreciative Inquiry: An Emerging Direction for Organization Development* (pp. 9–29). Champaign, IL: Stipes.

De Jong, P., & Berg, I. K. (1998). *Interviewing for Solutions*. Pacific Grove, CA: Brooks/Cole.

de Shazer, S. (1991). *Putting Difference to Work*. New York, NY: W. W. Norton.

de Shazer, S. (1994). *Words Were Originally Magic*. New York, NY: W. W. Norton.

de Shazer, S., & Berg, I. K. (1992). Doing therapy: A post-structural revision. *Journal of Marital and Family Therapy*, *18*(1), 71–81.

de Shazer, S., & Berg, I. K. (1997). What works? Remarks on research aspects of Solution-focused brief therapy. *Journal of Family Therapy*, *19*, 121–124.

de Shazer, S., Dolan, Y., Korman, H., McCollum, E., Trepper, T., & Berg, I. K. (2007). *More Than Miracles: The State of the Art of Solution-Focused Brief Therapy*. Philadelphia, PA: Haworth Press.

Dolan, Y. (1991). *Resolving Sexual Abuse: Solution-Focused Therapy and Ericksonian Hypnosis for Adult Survivors*. New York, NY: W. W. Norton.

Duncan, B. L., Miller, S. D., & Sparks, J. A. (2011). *The Heroic Client: A Revolutionary Way to Improve Effectiveness Through Client-Directed, Outcome-Informed Therapy* (2nd ed.). Hoboken, NJ: John Wiley.

Durrant, M. (1995). *Creative Strategies for School Problems: Solutions for Psychologists and Teachers*. New York, NY: W. W. Norton.

Franklin, C., Trepper, T. S., McCollum, E. E., & Gingerich, W. J. (2011). *Solution-Focused Brief Therapy: A Handbook of Evidence-Based Practice*. Oxford: Oxford University Press.

Furman, B., & Ahola, T. (1992). *Solution Talk: Hosting Therapeutic Conversations*. New York, NY: W. W. Norton.

George, E., Iveson, C., & Ratner, H. (1990). *Problem to Solution: Brief Therapy with Individuals and Families*. London: BT Press.

Isebaert, L., & Klingenstierna, C. (2012). *A Brief History of EBTA*. Retrieved from http://blog.ebta.nu/about-us/history

Iveson, C. (1990). *Whose Life? Working with Older People*. London: BT Press.

Jackson, P. Z., & McKergow, M. (2002). *The Solutions Focus: The SIMPLE Way to Positive Change* (2nd ed.). London: Nicholas Brealey Publishing.

Korman, H. (2020). Private communication.

Lethem, J. (1994). *Moved to Tears, Moved to Action: Solution Focused Brief Therapy with Women and Children*. London: BT Press.

Lueger, G., & Korn, H. P. (2006). *Solution Focused Management*. Augsberg, Germany: Rainer Hampp Verlag.

Macdonald, A. (2007). *Solution-Focused Therapy: Theory, Research and Practice* (2nd ed., 2011). London: Sage Publications.

Macdonald, A. (2020). Private communication.

McKergow, M. (2009). Interview with Gale Miller: The man behind the mirror behind the mirror at BFTC. *InterAction*, *1*(1), 78–87.

McKergow, M. (2011). Solution-focused approaches in management. In C. Franklin, T. S. Trepper, W. J. Gingerich, & E. E. McCollum (Eds.), *Solution-Focused Brief Therapy: A Handbook of Evidence-Based Practice* (pp. 327–341). Oxford: Oxford University Press.

Metcalf, L. (1996). *Parenting towards Solutions: Positive Techniques to Help Parents Use the Skills They Already Have to Raise Responsible, Loving Kids*. Upper Saddle River, NJ: Prentice Hall.

Miller, G., & de Shazer, S. (1998). Have you heard the latest rumor about ...? Solution-focused therapy as a rumor. *Family Process*, *37*, 363–377.

O'Connell, B. (1998). *Solution Focused Therapy* (2nd ed., 2005 & 3rd ed., 2012). London: Sage Publications.

O'Hanlon, W., & Wiener-Davis, M. (1989). *In Search of Solutions: A New Direction in Psychotherapy*. New York, NY: W. W. Norton.

Rhodes, J., & Ajmal, Y. (1995). *Solution Focused Thinking in Schools: Behaviour, Reading and Organisation*. London: BT Press.

Sundman, P. (2017). *Introduction to EBTA Practice Definition*. Retrieved from http://blog.ebta.nu/the-solution-focused-modell

Trepper, T. S., McCollum, E. E., De Jong, P., Korman, H., Gingerich, W. J., & Franklin, C. (2011). Solution-focused brief therapy treatment manual. In C. Franklin, T. S. Trepper, W. J. Gingerich, & E. E. McCollum (Eds.), *Solution-Focused Brief Therapy: A Handbook of Evidence-Based Practice* (pp. 20–38). Oxford: Oxford University Press.

Turnell, A., & Edwards, S. (1999). *Signs of Safety: A Solution and Safety Oriented Approach to Child Protection*. New York, NY: W. W. Norton.

Wiener-Davis, M. (1993). *Divorce Busting: A Revolutionary and Rapid Program for Staying Together*. Upper Saddle River, NJ: Prentice Hall.

Wolf, F. (2015). Three episodes with Steve de Shazer: Personal and professional. In M. Vogt, F. Wolf, P. Sundman, & H. N. Dreesen (Eds.), *Encounters with Steve de Shazer and Insoo Kim Berg: Inside Stories of Solution-Focused Brief Therapy* (pp. 183–186). London: Solutions Books.

Building descriptions, stretching worlds

Chapter 5

Evolving the next generation of SFBT

This chapter examines the evolution of Solution Focused Brief Therapy (SFBT) into the 21st century. This is a story of gradual change, shifts in emphasis and building on what went before. It results, in my view, in the emergence of something that presents some fundamental differences from the SFBT of the 1980s and 1990s. This book is about showing the connections and showing how what we know now can open the door for yet more development in the future.

I wrote about this shift in practice in a paper entitled 'SFBT 2.0' (McKergow, 2016) where, with the aim of clarity, I set about juxtaposing the new developments with the original versions of SF (called SF 1.0 for the purposes of the paper). While many people appreciated my efforts to concisely set out the ideas in a clear form, some did not appreciate the terminology of a software upgrade and felt that I was trying to consign the older versions to the dustbin of history. This was not my aim.

With the greater scope afforded by this book, I hope I can succeed in showing the evolution and development of the practice over half a century and stressing that this is a gradual rather than discontinuous process. These later developments were presaged by the evolution in the work of de Shazer and Berg and other key SF practitioners. There is a moment now to take stock of where we are and where we are heading. More clarity about what we do and a better story around how it works, while potentially treading on a few toes, seems to be an advantage for the coming decades.

Conversation as intervention

We might say that for many years SF practitioners have hedged their bets about the contributions of the therapeutic conversation itself, as opposed to the tasks and homework, in helping to bring about change for the client. This is neatly summed up in the second revised edition of *Problem To Solution* (George, Iveson & Ratner, 1999, p 22). Reflecting on their decade of experience with SF (at that point), the authors recount a teenage client who asked whether the interview had been about collecting information so they could tell him what to do, or just a process of questions and answers. They don't explicitly answer the point but say how Steve der Shazer's own practice had blended the two until task and process seemed almost indistinguishable. Even at that point, at the end of the 20th century, they wonder where this is leading:

> As the task becomes more important, the therapist's thoughts, views and actions become more dominant. This does not make for poor therapy but will eventually lead to a level of difference that will not be confineable within a single model.
>
> (George, Iveson & Ratner, 1999, p. 22)

Their work, and that of increasing numbers of others, has moved on over the next two decades. In seeking to make tasks less and less important, they have opened the doors for a rethink of SF practice. Some people don't see it as a rethink – a few have been doing this for years, others want to honour the work of de Shazer and Berg by sticking with what they wrote about, while yet others seem to value a harmonious practitioner community over open and sometimes difficult conversations about differences in practice. The rethink is the topic of this book – the next generation of SF practice.

Focused description development

An important aspect of this rethink is clarity in what the practitioner is seeking to do. In next generation SF work, this is characterised as helping the client build detailed descriptions of scenes from their lives in the future, present and past which connect with their best hopes or project.

As with previous developments in the field over the past half century, this evolving approach to brief therapy was set out in a paper with a clue in the title. After *Brief Therapy: Focused Problem Resolution* (Weakland, Fisch, Watzlawick & Bodin, 1974) and *Brief Therapy: Focused Solution Development* (de Shazer et al., 1986), Chris Iveson and I presented *Brief Therapy: Focused Description Development* (Iveson & McKergow, 2016). This step allows a re-configuration of SF practice, allowing many of the existing elements to be seen in a new way. Other elements, including tasks, recede in importance. This reconfiguration offers a number of potential advantages:

- More clarity on what the practitioner is listening for from the client, and how they might respond
- More clarity on what the practitioner is aiming to do – they can now listen largely free from the worry about having to produce an intervention or 'understand' the client and their situation
- More clarity on what the practitioner is doing (as opposed to what the practitioner might be expected to be doing but isn't)
- More clarity on why all this might be a good thing to do; it allows some progress in the vexed area of 'SF theory'.

As we will see, this focused and detailed description development is based on building conversations about what the client would notice (in the future), notices (in the present) and did notice (in the past). This includes a whole range of experience of the client themselves and their surroundings including other people. It is not simply about what the client can do but also about what in their context is suggesting to them that it might be time to act. This blurring of perception and action fits in with the enactive and embodied perspective, as we will see in the next chapter.

Leaving the problem behind

SFBT practitioners have always been interested in how to make progress without diagnosing or investigating people's problems; indeed, this could be seen as the field's single most important defining feature. However, the 'problem' has proven stubborn in its presence as the field has developed. If 'exceptions' are important, then the immediate cry is 'exceptions to what?'. The problem lurks in the background, still necessary although it is much less central. In *Putting Difference to Work* (de Shazer, 1991) Steve tried but could not quite manage to remove the notion of problem altogether. Instead the word is always written ~~problem~~, in the *sous-rature* style of Heidegger and Derrida, to denote its irrelevance to the 'solution'.

The next development, recognising that it isn't necessary to even know the client's problem, came from a number of sources including the work of John Walter and Jane Peller (Walter & Peller, 1992) and Harry Korman and Martin Soderquist (Korman & Soderquist, 1994). In London, Chris Iveson and his BRIEF colleagues began to ask 'What are your best hopes from coming here?' which invites the client to think about an outcome, instead of asking 'What brings you here?' which elicits a problem account (George, Iveson & Ratner, 1999). With this question the client is freed from the need to describe a problem (though many clients still choose to do so).

Hypothetical futures in SF practice – from last resort to first port of call

Steve de Shazer's (1988) book *Clues: Investigating Solutions in Brief Therapy* prioritises searching for exceptions over 'building hypothetical solutions'. However, we can also see a focus beginning to develop on getting concrete and detailed descriptions of such solutions. de Shazer notes that:

> Tasks can be readily designed when the client's description of a hypothetical solution includes enough behavioral details (i.e. concrete and specific goals) that can be given as tasks much as if they were exceptions.
>
> (p. 96)

Here we see a blurring of the distinction between the past (exceptions) and the future (hypothetical solutions). de Shazer goes on to note that where more than one potential aspect of the future suggests itself as a task, the client is asked to do the easiest, particularly something small and easy to do experimentally.

We also get first published version of the miracle question:

> Suppose that one night, while you were asleep, there was a miracle and this problem was solved. How would you know? What would be different? How will your husband know without your saying a word to him about it?
>
> (p. 5)

This is seen as a way to help in setting goals with the client which are more specific and concrete than 'feeling better' or other global and non-specific wishes. This, writes de Shazer, can be useful in assessing the salience of exceptions, and also of re-assessing the complaint discussed earlier with the client, bringing it more into line with the answers to the miracle question.

By the time of Steve de Shazer's next book *Putting Difference to Work* in 1991, the miracle question seemed to be more consolidated as part of BFTC's repertoire:

> What will you notice different the next morning that will tell you there has been a miracle? What will your spouse notice?
>
> (p. 113)

de Shazer notes that the second part of this question is a little more difficult than simply imagining you have replaced your chair. Once the question becomes interactional, it is like being asked to imagine someone else's imagining what kind of new chair you purchased. He also notes for the first time how the framework of the miracle allows clients to bypass their structural, causal assumptions. They do not have to imagine the process, only the results. This allows them to bring more of their previous non-problem experiences into the conversation, which is no longer about simply eliminating the complaint.

Why a miracle?

The origins of the miracle question are described in the first edition of *Interviewing For Solutions* (De Jong & Berg, 1998). Insoo was interviewing a woman who 'seemed burdened by the weight of the world' – she had many difficulties including out of control children, a husband drinking heavily and about to lose his job, and it seemed that she could not cope with another day. Insoo asked, as was standard practice at BFTC at the time, about what would need to happen for their time together to be seen as useful. The client heaved a long deep sigh and said that there were so many problems that maybe only a miracle would help. Insoo, alert as ever to her client's language, picked up the word and asked,

> OK, suppose a miracle happened, and the problem that brought you here is solved. What would be different about your life?

(p. 77)

To Insoo's amazement, the woman who had seemed to overwhelmed and unable to go on began describing a vision of a different life, both for her children, her husband and, crucially, herself too. 'I will have more energy, smile more, be calmer with the children ...' and so on. A miracle perhaps but also very workable goals and aims for the client.

This particular element has come to represent SFBT in the eyes of outsiders. It is so unique and memorable that it's often the first thing other practitioners notice. Indeed, de Shazer and Berg's posthumous book was entitled *More Than Miracles* (de Shazer et al., 2007), to emphasise that there are other elements to the work. What makes it such a useful device?

Future focus

The miracle question is very definitely about the future. Not only that, but it is also about a *better* or *preferred* future. This alone makes an unusual line of inquiry, at least in the prevailing therapeutic context where the investigation of problematic pasts was considered de rigueur and the search for unseen causes of mental disturbance, which apparently had to be talked through in order for any progress to be made, was the order of the day. To start to look into the future breaks a number of assumptions, particularly that the client is at the mercy of their disorder which must be stopped or cured before any meaningful progress can be made.

Looking into the future begins instead to draw attention to the client's agency in their own life, their ability to influence their own situation. Interestingly, at around the same time as the miracle question was being developed, a number of other approaches including neuro-linguistic programming (NLP) and visualisation were also drawing on this future focus. NLP tended to focus on very specific goal-setting in the future (see for example Knight, 2010), while in a gentler vein Dina Glouberman's book *Life Choices and Life Changes Through Imagework* (1989) was instrumental for many, including me, at the time. However, the miracle question is a special form of future focus which is more than simply turning in the direction of the future.

What is the miracle question *for*?

That the miracle question leads into some useful conversation seems to be confirmed by its continuing importance in the field. It's a good thing to be doing – but why? There have been various purposes given in the past, which started as quite firm rationales and have become fuzzier. In the shift described in this book, they can become clearer again, if somewhat different.

Preparation or action?

The original miracle question from 1988 was designed as an aid to clarify the goals of the client, in situations where there were no clear exceptions to their problem or complaint. More recently this rationale is still given as the prime reason, albeit that this is now a potentially useful route for all clients. Indeed, Macdonald (2011) quotes research from Ferdinand Wolf and colleagues in Vienna that showed that clients giving *any* response to the miracle question was linked with increased chances of a positive outcome to the therapy (p. 22). By 2007, de Shazer and collaborators are giving four possible reasons for asking the miracle question (pp. 40–41):

1   It is one way to create goals for therapy – and there are many other ways to do this, so the miracle question might be a little elaborate.
2   It can be an emotional and 'virtual' experience – in some (but not all) sessions the clients behave as if they are experiencing what happens the day after the miracle.
3   Prepares for exceptions – the details constructed in the miracle conversation can help prime the client to notice small pieces of those details in the past.
4   Part of creating a progressive story – clients often arrive at therapy with a 'digressive' story of things going from bad to worse. The miracle conversation can lead into connections with the client's experience which are starting points for a story of how life might be (and perhaps is even already) getting better.

Reasons 1 and 3 can be clearly seen as part of the classic SFBT picture; the miracle conversation is part of preparing for the real work of change which happens in connecting with experiences in the clients' past which can be expanded and built upon. Reasons 2 and 4, however, are signs of a different route where the miracle conversation is not preparation but is rather the real work at hand. This conversation itself – the imagining of a better future in detailed and interactional terms – is what builds potential and actual change for the client, right there in the session.

I realised this myself gradually over many years of running training courses for solution-focused coaches, facilitators and others. Seeking short and focused training exercises, I developed activities to practise asking the miracle question and then expanding on the answers, over as little as ten minutes. Rather than forcing 'role-plays' on people, I suggested that they pick something about their own lives that they'd like to improve, and discovered that many people emerged from even this brief conversation – without any scales, exceptions, compliments or anything else – with new ideas and possibilities.

Aha! or drip-drip-ooh

I also discovered that these ideas did not usually arrive as flashes of inspiration, 'aha' moments or bolts from the blue. Rather they seemed to gradually form so that while I felt differently and had more ideas at the end of the conversation, I wasn't quite sure how and when these changes had occurred. It was rather like the formation of a stalactite through the dripping of limestone-rich water: after the conversation something new had definitely formed, but nobody had arrived to stick it in place, it had just appeared apparently from nowhere during the conversation.

From exceptions to instances

The importance of 'exceptions to the problem' was an early piece of the SFBT jigsaw as it came together in the Brief Family Therapy Center (BFTC) in Milwaukee under Steve de Shazer and Insoo Kim Berg. The idea of 'exceptions to the rule' of when problems occurred appeared in de Shazer's book *Keys To Solution in Brief Therapy* (de Shazer, 1985) and in some ways marks a defining moment in the development of our field. The Mental Research Institute (MRI) take on brief therapy, on which de Shazer, Berg and their colleagues were building, had seen a necessity for interrupting the problem pattern to allow new (and hopefully more useful) behaviour to emerge. By noticing that clients could already recount exceptions without needing to break the pattern, the BFTC team opened the door to leaping over this problem-focused step and moving directly to discussions about 'better'.

At first these exceptions were central to the work, as events from the past which could be potentially repeated or reused in some way to bring to bear on the current problematic situation. In *Clues*, de Shazer (1988) distinguished between deliberate exceptions, created knowingly by the client, and spontaneous exceptions which seemed to happen without the client's effort or action. The former were seen as particularly useful as they could be examined in the therapy session to explore exactly how the client created them, and could therefore deliberately take steps to build more examples in the future. The latter needed more consideration, and so therapist and client explored precisely the differences between these spontaneous exceptions and the normal problem, with the client often being charged with the task of predicting when these moments might occur in the coming days.

Past exceptions have drifted away from this prime position over the years in favour of looking first at the future. In order for exceptions to make sense, one always needs to ask 'exceptions to what?' which brings the problem back into view. Different practitioners tackled this in different ways. The BRIEF group in London started speaking not of exceptions to the problem but rather of 'times when the miracle has happened' (George, Iveson & Ratner, 1999). They then moved to the rather more elegant terminology of 'instances' (Iveson, George & Ratner, 2011). Jackson and McKergow (2002) introduced the slightly curious term 'counters' (things that count or matter) to include such times; they also included traces of other useful elements from the past including evidence of strengths, useful co-operation and any other grounds for optimism.

An instance is a more focused concept than an exception. The latter is 'any time the problem doesn't happen when it might', whereas the former is 'something that connects with what we are hoping for'. Of course, there is an overlap between these, but while an exception needs a problem, an instance needs a future description or at least a hope to define it. It is a more elegant concept. An instance is a neat way to discover not merely events and behaviours that could well be useful but also other interesting differences such as strengths-in-use, resourceful awareness and skill, co-operation with others and contextual awareness ('how did you *know* to do that?').

Building descriptions

The view of SFBT as description-building grew through the 2000s. A crisp statement of the full possibilities appears in Guy Shennan and Chris Iveson's chapter *From Solution to Description* (Shennan & Iveson, 2011), which somewhat ironically appears in the same volume as the 'treatment manual' described in the previous chapter (Trepper et al., 2011). The authors point to initial studies which show that this form of description-building therapy leads to even further reductions in duration, on average around a session less for each client. They also say clearly that these small initial studies need expanding, which I hope will be one result of this present book.

In this view, there are three key elements to the practice. In order to build descriptions, we need to know at some level what these descriptions are to be about. A problem statement is not useful for this (other than as a stepping stone), so we need to know what the client is seeking; 'Where do you want to go?', as opposed to 'Where have you been?'. These three elements are based on the assumption that every client, including those mandated to attend, have a good reason – a desired outcome – for being there.

1   What are your best hopes from our work together? (The 'contract' or what Jackson and McKergow (2002)) call the 'platform' and Korman refers to as the 'Common Project' (Korman, 2004)

2   How will you know that these hopes are being realised? (The client's preferred future)

3   What are you already doing that might contribute to your hopes being realised? (The history of the preferred future in the past and present)

There are many versions of these questions but what they share is a focus on description and only description. The broad description of an outcome, a more detailed description (perhaps beginning with a miracle question) and a description of past and present instances of the hoped-for future happening (often summarised in a scale).

Adding detail

One consequence of shifting our attention to description building is an increased awareness of exactly how clients can be encouraged to build on their descriptions and add detail, without being led by the therapist in terms of content. The second part of this book will explore the practicalities in detail, but here are some key description-expanding questions which are commonly deployed alongside the SFBT 'big questions' such as miracle and scaling. These include:

- What difference would that make?
- What difference would that make to person [Y]?
- What would be the first tiny signs that [thing M] was happening?
- Who else would notice [thing M] was happening? What would they notice?
- What would person [Y] do when they noticed you doing [thing M]?
- What would you do in response to that?
- What else?
- What happens/happened next?

All these questions build on something the client has already said and are encouragements to the client to continue. They do not offer suggestions that reflect the therapist's interests and ideas. The extent to which SFBT practitioners are particularly focused in this process has been seen in research deriving from microanalysis of therapeutic dialogues, of which more in the next chapter.

These small description-building questions can also be used in different combinations with great effect. They are clearly visible in recent SF work. Peter De Jong, a very experienced and longstanding SF practitioner, microanalyst and collaborator with Insoo Kim Berg for many years, joined me (McKergow, 2019) to compare two sessions from different eras; a session carried out by Insoo Kim Berg (*Over The Hump*, available on video from BFTC and chosen by him) and a Chris Iveson session (*Mary and the cuddle*, reported in Iveson and McKergow, 2016 and chosen by me). We both viewed them separately to see what we saw, drew distinctions and made notes, and then compared our observations. Of course, there were plenty of similarities – both sessions are clearly SFBT and not something else. However, there were also some clear distinctions.

In what is a complicated session because there are a lot of children in the room, Insoo didn't get a 'project' agreed with the clients but rather assumed it.

She may have been justified in doing that because of the situation, but there it is. Insoo then asked the miracle question, got some 'headline' answers but didn't expand much on them. She tended to get a response (to the miracle question, or a scale) and then repeat it, whereas Chris tended to dive into more detail from whatever starting point. He used the question 'what difference would that make?' six times (in comparison with Insoo's no times) and variations on 'what might you notice?' over 20 times (again, Insoo no times).

Peter De Jong concluded at the time that these sessions show 'very clear variations which could be very profitable to explore'. He also said that we were 'reaffirming the spirit of SF' by looking directly at the work in action. We will see some examples later in the book of how a practitioner can help their client start from one small remark (perhaps 'I'd feel better') and build it out into a detailed and multi-perspective series of description in the client's life.

Three-part interactional sequences

The United Kingdom Association for Solution-Focused Practice (UKASFP) has developed an accreditation process firmly rooted in this description-building concept. They have introduced the idea of three-part interactional sequences as being a key element in building these descriptions, which should ideally be shown to become accredited as a practitioner. These sequences contain at least three steps of change:

When there is a sign of change or progress (which might be a behaviour, a thought or a feeling), the practitioner helps the client to build the sequence by asking about:

- what others would notice or have noticed (depending on whether it's a future or past sign);
- what those others would do or have done differently as a result; and
- the impact of this on the client – how would/did they respond to that?

Whether the practitioner is seeking accreditation or not, these is an excellent model to follow. It includes the detail-building questions mentioned earlier in a recursive way, bringing the two-way interactions between the client and others into focus. There are strong echoes here (for me anyway) of the interactional view pioneered by the Mental Research Institute, Palo Alto, which we reviewed in Chapter 2 and were a key starting point for Steve de Shazer.

A series of descriptions – narrative qualities

An under-explored element of SF practice, particularly as it has evolved, is that clients do not experience the creation of these descriptions (in the session) in the same chronological order as they would in everyday life; descriptions of the future often precede descriptions of the past and present. However, in practice this is not problematic at all. Just as there are movies which play with the order of events, having flashbacks and flash-forwards, I have very rarely come across clients who have any difficulty in putting the scenes together and making sense of them. This ability to create connections, relationships, consequences and logic from a series of linked events seems to be a fundamental part of our ability as human beings. Even if other species have forms of language, the human variety is vastly richer and allows us to conjure complex tales and connections.

This idea of language and story-telling (and therefore also story-understanding) as a human fundamental was introduced by communications theorist Walter Fisher (1987), who proposed that our species (*homo sapiens*, 'wise man') might be better referred to as *homo narrans* ('storytelling man'). It was extended by British science writers Jack Cohen and Ian Stewart (Pratchett, Stewart & Cohen, 2002), who thought that 'homo' is a rather extravagant claim and that *pan narrans*, the 'storytelling ape', would be more accurate.

One key element to note is that it is the client who should 'join the dots' between the various descriptions. It can be very tempting for us, hearing the client's words in action, to see some apparently key connection, action, or obvious conclusion. Don't. Our way of helping the client is to help them assemble their ideas, not do the work for them. Steve de Shazer often implored us to 'not work harder than our clients', and this is a prime place to heed that directive. They will come to conclusions that fit for them.

Moving away from family therapy norms and customs

We saw in chapters 2 and 3 how the MRI developments in family therapy and brief therapy, and subsequent developments in Milwaukee, were built on a model of having a team of therapists observing through a one-way mirror, gathering views, consulting with the leading therapist and in particular aiding the construction of an end-of-session message to the client.

As early as 1990, Ben Furman and Tapani Ahola pointed out (Furman & Ahola, 1990) that the secrecy inherent in the one-way mirror set-up did not match the new approaches based on co-operation rather than a contest between client and practitioners. They advocated removing the mirror and having team discussions in front of the client, in the form of reflecting teams (Anderson, 1987). This form of practice was later extended by Harry Norman, John Henden and the Bristol Solutions Group (Norman, Hjerth & Pidsley, 2005).

There are good reasons, practical and theoretical, for reconsidering this practice. If we continue to explore the role of the therapist as being the elicitor of detailed descriptions rather than the designer of interventions, then some key things follow:

1   There is no need for a team anymore. The conversation is for the client to hear, and the single therapist is part of that. The idea of others watching,

hidden from view, seems not only costly but also perhaps rather odd in an era when openness and transparency are highly valued.

2   There is therefore no need for a break, as there is no intervention to design and nobody with whom to consult. Of course, there may be good reasons for the practitioner to take a deep breath and think about what has been said, but the idea of leaving the room to do this seems out of place.

3   There is not the same need for compliments in a sustained barrage, as the prelude to selling some kind of intervention. That is not to say that compliments are forbidden – more that the purpose of them changes into potential reframing of difficulties and normalising of challenges and can be used at any time during the session.

4   And of course there is no intervention. Some who are committed to exploring the limits of this new view would even say that any conversation about possible actions and next steps is unnecessary – the client will do something if they see fit, and if they don't see fit then there is no point asking about it. There may be a summary by the practitioner at the close of the session.

Working in an organisational context, I might still ask the client about their thinking on possible next small steps – the idea being that it's very normal to agree actions in these contexts, to the extent that some people assume that if they haven't agreed an action then they positively don't have to do anything, which is not the impression I seek at all. The focus is usually on helping them focus on *small, concrete* and *accessible* actions, much more likely to get done than large and distant actions and so more likely to make a difference.

Whatever, this is now at most a light touch final question to the clients rather than a complex intervention with coin tossing, pretending, squirt gun fights in the garage, formula first session tasks or acting differently on alternate days of the week, and all the other aspects that featured in the strategic family therapy playbook.

Ending the session – no tasks or actions, more appreciative summarising

We have just seen that the end of the session has lost many of the trappings which used to be taken as read in the early days. There is no ritual of break, compliments, tasks. However, we have to bring things to a close in some way. Appreciative summarising by the practitioner can usefully be done here – it shows you've been listening and offers the client the chance to hear some of the things they've been saying again, perhaps in a different order. One way to help the client to look at smaller (and hence more do-able) details is to engage in a description of tiny signs that one point higher on the scale has been reached.

Another is to have the client scale their confidence of progress, or that progress can be maintained.

One other aspect of ending sessions is to offer power more clearly to the client, in terms of what happens next. So we might expect to see less of 'please make an appointment for next Tuesday', and more of 'I hope that's been useful for you ... would you like to come back to continue our work together?'. Steve de Shazer always said that therapy should take as many sessions as it takes and not one more, so we should be looking to help the client decide if and when they wish to return. And if they think that's enough, then it's a cause for gentle celebration.

The next generation of SF practice

To summarise, these 21st-century developments add to, rather than replace, the SFBT emerging from the Milwaukee team. This new focus on descriptions allows us to add a new column to the table of evolution (Table 5.1):

Table 5.1 Key elements from early SFBT (c. 1988), the SFBTA treatment manual (2011) and next generation SF practice compared

Solution Focused Brief Therapy (c 1988)	SFBT treatment manual (2011)	Next generation SF practice
Customer/complainer/ visitor relationships: Construct 'complaint'	Collegial and collaborative relationship	Best hopes ('everyone is a customer for something')
Team helps construct end-of-session message	Team (if there is one) helps construct end-of-session message	Probably no team and no break
Problem-free talk	Pre-session change, construct solution-focused goals (small, presence of a solution)	Preferred future detailed descriptions (starting with Miracle question or similar)
Gather specific concrete detailed information about exceptions – if found, explore what works	Miracle Question	Scaling leading to detailed descriptions of 'instances' supporting preferred future
If no exceptions, talk about hypothetical solutions and better futures. Set goals (small).	Scaling Questions, Constructing Exceptions, Coping Questions (if needed)	Perhaps descriptions of (N + 1) on the scale
Break	Break	Usually no break
Compliments	Compliments	Appreciative Summarising
Intervention: do more of what works (or easiest of what might work)	Experiments and Homework Assignments	Invitation to return if client wishes to do so – either now or later

The role of the practitioner is clarified in this evolution; a builder of descriptions rather than looking for behavioural interventions to deploy. The conversation is the intervention, and the tiny details in the descriptions all open up the possibility of action. Precisely how this form of practice can help people, even those with seriously debilitating mental health problems, is the topic of the next chapter.

Key points

- SFBT has continued to evolve in the 21st century.
- The conversation can now be seen as the main intervention, not the means to information for constructing an intervention.
- SF conversations can be viewed as building descriptions of future, present and past which align with the realisation of the client's best hopes, based on signs of progress.
- This involves many 'small' questions deployed skilfully alongside the 'bigger' questions such as the miracle question and scaling questions.
- As the conversation is now the main intervention, there is less (or even no) need for a break, compliments at the end of the session or a task.

References

Anderson, T. (1987). The reflecting team: Dialogue and meta-dialogue in clinical work. *Family Process, 26*(4), 415–428.

De Jong, P., & Berg, I. K. (1998). *Interviewing for Solutions*. Pacific Grove, CA: Brooks/Cole.

de Shazer, S. (1985). *Keys to Solution in Brief Therapy*. New York, NY: W. W. Norton.

de Shazer, S. (1988). *Clues: Investigating Solutions in Brief Therapy*. New York, NY: W. W. Norton.

de Shazer, S. (1991). *Putting Difference to Work*. New York, NY: W. W. Norton.

de Shazer, S., Berg, I. K., Lipchik, E., Nunally, E., Molnar, A., Gingerich, W., & Wiener-Davis, M. (1986). Brief therapy: Focused solution development. *Family Process, 25*, 207–221.

de Shazer, S., Dolan, Y., Korman, H., McCollum, E., Trepper, T., & Berg, I. K. (2007). *More Than Miracles: The State of the Art of Solution-Focused Brief Therapy*. Philadelphia, PA: Haworth Press.

Fisher, W. R. (1987). *Human Communication as Narration: Toward a Philosophy of Reason, Value, and Action*. Columbia: University of South Carolina Press.

Furman, B., & Ahola, T. (1990, May/June). Glasnost therapy: Removing the barriers between clients and therapists. *Family Therapy Networker*, 61–63.

George, E., Iveson, C., & Ratner, H. (1999). *Problem to Solution: Brief Therapy with Individuals and Families* (rev. & exp. 2nd ed.). London: BT Press.

Glouberman, D. (1989). *Life Choices and Life Changes through Imagework*. London: Mandala/Unwin Paperbacks.

Iveson, C., George, E., & Ratner, H. (2011). *Brief Coaching: A Solution Focused Approach*. London: Routledge.

Iveson, C., & McKergow, M. (2016). Brief therapy: Focused description development. *Journal of Solution Focused Brief Therapy*, 2(1), 1–17.

Jackson, P. Z., & McKergow, M. (2002). *The Solutions Focus: The SIMPLE Way to Positive Change* (1st ed.). London: Nicholas Brealey Publishing.

Knight, S. (2010). *NLP at Work: The Essence of Excellence* (3rd ed.). London: Nicholas Brealey Publishing.

Korman, H. (2004). *The Common Project*. Retrieved from www.sikt.nu/wp-content/uploads/2015/06/Creating-a-common-project.pdf

Korman, H., & Soderquist, M. (1994). *Talk about a Miracle*. Retrieved from www.sikt.nu/wp-content/uploads/2015/06/Talk-Miracle.pdf

Macdonald, A. (2011). *Solution-Focused Therapy: Theory, Research and Practice* (2nd ed.). London: Sage Publications.

McKergow, M. (2016). SFBT 2.0: The next generation of solution focused brief therapy has already arrived. *Journal of Solution Focused Brief Therapy*, 2(2), 1–17.

McKergow, M. (2019). Response to Harry Korman's reflections on SFBT 2.0 paper. *Journal of Solution Focused Brief Therapy*, 3(1), 74–78.

Norman, H., Hjerth, M., & Pidsley, T. (2005). Solution focused reflecting Teams in action. In M. McKergow & J. Clarke (Eds.), *Positive Approaches to Change: Applications of Solutions Focus and Appreciative Enquiry at Work*. Cheltenham, UK: Solutions Books.

Pratchett, T., Stewart, I., & Cohen, J. (2002). *Science of Discworld 2: The Globe*. London: Ebury Press.

Shennan, G., & Iveson, C. (2011). From solution to description: Practice and research in tandem. In C. Franklin, T. S. Trepper, E. E. McCollum, & W. J. Gingerich (Eds.), *Solution-Focused Brief Therapy: A Handbook of Evidence-Based Practice* (pp. 281–298). Oxford: Oxford University Press.

Trepper, T. S., McCollum, E. E., De Jong, P., Korman, H., Gingerich, W. J., & Franklin, C. (2011). Solution-focused brief therapy Treatment manual. In C. Franklin, T. S. Trepper, W. J. Gingerich, & E. E. McCollum (Eds.), *Solution-Focused Brief Therapy: A Handbook of Evidence-Based Practice* (pp. 20–38). Oxford: Oxford University Press.

Walter, J. L., & Peller, J. E. (1992). *Becoming Solution-Focused in Brief Therapy*. New York: Bruner-Maazel Inc.

Weakland, J., Fisch, R., Watzlawick, P., & Bodin, A. (1974). Brief therapy: Focused problem resolution. *Family Process*, 13(2), 141–168.

Chapter 6

'Stretching the world' of the client

Some widely held views among SF practitioners deserve scrutiny, including the not-knowing stance, an attitude held dear by many practitioners to the extent of denying any expertise at all. From this, arises the idea that explanations smack of theorising and should be avoided: clients are the experts.

Steve de Shazer wrote in *Putting Difference to Work* (de Shazer, 1991):

> But the question 'How does it work?' always seems to arise. My position has been that one cannot know how it works, one can only know that it does work. Answers to the question 'how does it work?' always involve speculation. ... To speculate, to conjecture, is a matter of storytelling; it is fiction.
>
> (de Shazer, 1991, p. xv11)

de Shazer goes on to say that he has, even so, found that people seem to like it when he introduces parallels which help them see what happens, without obscuring it. He goes on to a fascinating account drawing on Wittgenstein, Derrida, Mikhail Bakhtin and many others in an intellectual tour de force.

Thirty years on, I think that it is time to look at this again. This line of post-structural storytelling has not proven compelling or even particularly useful outside a small part of the SFBT community. It carries little weight in the wider circles within which we work: healthcare, therapy, education, management. If a hard-pressed health service is looking for an efficient way to carry out therapy, looks at SFBT and asks, 'how does it work?', they are scarcely likely to be reassured by references to Derrida and Baudrillard.

The not-knowing stance

As we saw in Chapter 2 about the interactional view, the SFBT approach is based on a far-from-conventional view of mental illness and helping people with problems. This is a challenge when it comes to sharing and spreading the approach. When we visit a medical doctor, we have a complaint or symptoms. The doctor listens to these, examines us, perhaps asks for tests, and then tells us what is wrong with us. The treatment we are given (or perhaps offered, following the evolution of informed consent for patients) follows. As we will see, there is a widely held view (not held by me and the SF world) that mental illness is fundamentally no different.

SFBT, on the other hand, does not depend on the 'problem' at all. There is no diagnosis. There is a way of engaging the client in conversation to help them build towards a better life. So what is the practitioner doing, if not trying to diagnose and problem-solve on behalf of the patient? One answer is to be found in the idea of a not-knowing or non-expert stance. Sometimes called a 'beginner mind' (a concept from Zen, Suzuki, 1970), it is a vital counter to our normal everyday desire to help people by understanding them, empathising with them, joining in with them, sharing our experience and so on.

Listening to clients with a beginner mind is (to try) to be open, to hear them without judgement or desiring to 'help' by jumping in. This open-ness to the client's experience and lack of judgement about them is key in SF and other practices. The Collaborative Therapy school of Harlene Anderson and Harry Goolishian, which also has roots in the MRI brief therapy tradition, makes a particularly strong practice in this area (see for example Malinen, 2004). In more general terms, this position has become associated with the postmodern movement in therapy (including narrative, collaborative, solution focused and social constructionist).

There is a great practical advantage to the not-knowing position. As a practitioner, I feel I can sit down with anybody and make a start, building towards something better, without needing to understand and research their problems, diagnosis, life history or whatever. In circumstances where some kind of intake survey or history needs to happen for other administrative reasons, practitioners often separate it from the therapy by doing it in another room and even with another person, to emphasise the clean start to the practice. Asking about people's hopes and what they want to happen and listening closely to the answers is a worthy skill in almost any situation – particularly where people are stuck and don't know what to do (or do what know to do, but somehow aren't doing it).

'Carl Rogers with a twist'

This not-knowing stance appears in the work of Milton Erickson half a century ago, where Erickson advocated not trying to enforce his views on his clients but rather 'attempting to invoke the client's individuality in seeking the best modality of therapeutic response' (Erickson & Rossi, 1979, p 25). It is also very associated, in a pure form, with the person-centred approaches pioneered by Carl Rogers from the mid-20th century (Rogers, 1951).

Rogers advocated a non-directive approach, offering genuineness, respect and empathy with unconditional positive regard, thereby providing space for clients to explore their own experience and move towards self-growth by simply reflecting back their statements and offering space for them to go on. This remains a popular approach in the 21st century, not least because of its humanistic and open attitude to the multitude of human experience. Bill O'Hanlon said that SFBT could be characterised as 'Carl Rogers with a twist' (O'Hanlon & Beadle, 1994) – the twist being that rather than simply reflecting back what clients said, the reflection could be subtly adjusted to nudge attention in the direction of improvement. For example 'I'm depressed' could be reflected as 'You've been depressed'.

Insights from Ludwig Wittgenstein?

In his last decade Steve de Shazer became increasingly interested in the philosophy of Ludwig Wittgenstein and his views on language (as a fluid interactional practice to get things done) and mind (as a social ability to interact). Wittgenstein attempts to de-muddle philosophy, language and life, mainly by looking at how language works and how it can bewitch and mislead us. Anyone wishing to explore this should start with Ray Monk's excellent biography *The Duty of Genius* (Monk, 1990), which presents the work alongside Wittgenstein's life in an accessible way. His later work (Wittgenstein, 1953) presents arguments which show that the 'inner' world of experience is not separate from the 'outer', that reliance on explanations is a misleading superstition, that language and meaning are continually flexing in practice, that perfect understanding is impossible, and that we should therefore stay on the surface and look at specifics rather than generalities. (This is the briefest of summaries of decades of difficult work, and Wittgenstein himself would be appalled that I had attempted such an act of wilful ignorance!)

Steve de Shazer explored these Wittgenstein connections with gusto, often in partnership with German logician and constellations therapist Professor Matthias Varga von Kibéd. There are tapes and recordings of their conversations (for example de Shazer & Varga von Kibéd, 2003). *More Than Miracles* (de Shazer et al., 2007) contains probably the best of how this relates to SFBT practice. It is well worth reading. de Shazer was always at pains to say the Wittgenstein did not provide any 'missing theory' of SFBT, but that there were interesting parallels. And indeed there are.

And … there is also some incongruity. Dense arguments from Wittgenstein are used to show why the 'usual' kinds of therapy conversations, about feelings, underlying causes, diagnoses, hidden emotions, overwhelming inner urges, parental trauma etc, are at best muddled and riddled with confusion, at least compared to the kind of 'simple' everyday language favoured by SFBT practitioners.

However, the train of thought started by Wittgenstein has continued to run over the years and is now re-appearing, with much additional detail and clarity, in the field of enactive cognition. This is a more open view of how 'mental' and behavioural phenomena are united, and how what might look like a behavioural conversation is engaging the client at the most fundamental levels of life. We shall come to this later in this chapter.

An explanation of SF practice?

I want to offer a different kind of explanation for how SFBT works. This does not throw out the connections and parallels with Wittgenstein so prized by de Shazer, but it builds on it in a practical way using developments in enactive cognition which have appeared over the past decade. I think it offers an intuitive and useful way to look at what we do, in a way which helps point to how that might make a difference to our clients. After all, it seems strange to an outsider that we propose to treat 'mental illness' with a practice which apparently says nothing about 'mental' or indeed 'illness'.

In encouraging a not-knowing position for the practitioner, SFBT practice has always stayed away from offering explanations to the client about how come they are where they are. This is, of course, in stark contrast to many other traditions which see the building of 'insight' in the client as a pre-requisite to progress. I would like to make clear here that this is not the kind of explanation I am proposing. We help the client to describe various scenes from a better life without any explanation, nor any need for explanation (assisted by the inexplicable miracle).

I am much more interested in explanations *about* our practice; having a comprehensible (and hopefully plausible and attractive) answer to fellow professionals and hard-pressed commissioners of our services about what we do and how it might help. There is a tradition of SFBT folk delighting in not-knowing about this too. They take a lead from Steve de Shazer earlier, insisting that it is enough that it *does* work. It seems to me that this is incurious in the extreme; it makes them look (to others not in the not-know) like hillbillies who insist that drinking the juice from a willow-tree to help skin problems and fever worked for their grandfather, works for them and will work for you too. This is a scientific dead-end; understanding *how* things work makes them accessible to others and helps to build and develop them. Following this more progressive route, someone else analysed the juice of the said willow tree and found it to contain salicylic acid, now a World Health Organisation 'Essential Drug' (WHO, 2020) for skin conditions and a basis for aspirin.

An exploration into 'how SFBT works' will need to take account of the close focus on and acceptance of the client, their experience and their language. It will need to address the concern of SFBT practitioners that having a 'theory' will distract them from listening to the client. I will show why listening to the client is important, as part of the theory. It will also shed light on the way that 'the more they talk about it, the more real it is'. This is not a new idea; it has been around for decades as a generally held (if not universally acknowledged) truth. Steve de Shazer said it out loud as an observation in a

1994 workshop which we can all still hear (de Shazer & Berg, 1994). But how exactly does this work?

The answer will need to be understandable quickly and instinctively to the world at large. Cognitive Behavioural Therapy (CBT) is currently widely used and respected, and it has just such a story: that extreme or unhelpful thoughts produce undesirable (for the client) behaviour. Correcting the thinking is therefore the first step to changing that behaviour (BABCP, 2020). This is very plausible, given the general understandings of the relationship between thought and action. It's also wrong, as Wittgenstein would point out; from where does the brain get input? It looks like thinking controls action, in the same way that it looks like the sun goes around the earth. Getting away from the assumption that 'inner' phenomena such as thoughts, feelings and attitudes generate 'outer' behaviour, speech, gesture etc. is one of the key benefits of looking at the world in a Wittgensteinian way.

Privileging the brain

From a cognitivist perspective, the world is somehow created by the brain, which is seen as a kind of controlling computer of the body within which it is contained. The brain forms and stores representations, which then form the basis for action. This view has become so everyday as to largely escape questioning and forms the basis of CBT, among many other things. In parallel, the field of counselling has become filled with talk of internal feelings, emotions, drives, urges or motivations, all of which are apparently seen as somehow driving or controlling external behaviour, as any reader of popular magazines knows.

This has led to a kind of neuro-fetishist view, where brain and mind can almost be interchanged and anything significant must somehow be traced back to the brain. The past couple of decades have seen the rise of 'brain science' where pictures of parts of the brain 'lighting up' are used as proof that something is happening. I heard one leading scientist refer to this trend as 'the new phrenology', the Victorian practice of assessing a person's character from the bumps on their skull. If the brain is in control, then the brain must be the centre of attention. The mind is in the brain, so therefore 'mental' illness (and health) are to be sought there too.

The enactive paradigm

Developments over the past 20 years have brought a new contender into focus – the enactive paradigm. Rather than the body being used by the brain, enactivists see the person using their brain to think, act, remember and so on. Philosopher Rom Harré (2002) introduced the task/tool metaphor to show how this works. Harré pointed out that we say a person digs a ditch (say) using a spade. The spade does not dig the ditch, the person uses it to dig the ditch. We can therefore choose to study spades, or to study digging – but if the latter is our goal, we will need a person to be doing it. Studying the spade is not enough.

By analogy, replacing the spade with the brain, a person uses their brain to think. The brain does not think, the person thinks using their brain. So we can choose to study brains, or to study thinking – but if the latter is our goal then we will need a person to be doing it. In this neat way Harré helps to put the brain in its proper place – as a key tool for a thinking person. Brain science is a perfectly proper subject. But if we want to study thinking (and by extension other 'mental' phenomena) then we will need a person to be the focus of attention, not a brain.

Where is 'the world'?

To see things anew, we can start by taking a look at what we mean by the 'world' of the client. This is the kind of question which gets picked over by philosophers and largely ignored by everyone else. It's worth exploring here briefly – if we are going to examine 'stretching the world' we should make sure we understand what we're talking about.

In everyday parlance, the world is all around us. It might be the planet Earth, it might be everything we can see, it is what we inhabit. And how do we know about it? That's where the contention starts. For most people that's not problematic – we perceive it by seeing, hearing, touching, smelling and tasting it – both for ourselves and through reports from others. This view of the world was dominant until the mid-20th century, when interest in minds, brains and crucially computers began to converge in what was termed cognitive science.

So where is the world, if not in the brain or the head? Enactivists (for example Thompson, 2007; Stewart, Gapenne & Di Paolo, 2010) think that rather than looking 'inside', we are better to take an embodied view. Rather than trying to separate mind and body, they prefer to bring them together, call the result a person and then look at how that person interacts with the world, including other people. That person's experience is of central interest; a first person phenomenology (Merleau-Ponty, 1945), not a mere by-product of cognitive processes. Enactivism, and SF work, takes the client's experience very seriously indeed. (And of course, if the person has a brain injury or illness, that will affect their interactions, just as a broken spade will impede digging.)

Happily, there is already an older tradition which takes this view, which is coming back to the fore; the world as possibility for interaction, the 'Umwelt'.

Umwelt – world as possibilities for interaction

Jakob von Uexküll was a German biologist working in the early decades of the 20th century. He became interested in how organisms interacted, or knew to interact, with their environments. He proposed the idea of an Umwelt (von Uexküll, 1920); a species-specific subjective self-in-world reference frame, constituted by 'carriers of significance' – signs of opportunities for interaction which were important to the creature. Von Uexküll gives the example of a tick (a small insect existing by sucking animal blood) – sensitive to light (an aid in climbing to the top of blades of grass), the 'odour' of butyric acid (emitted by hairy mammals like dogs) and warmth (to tell them whether they are on a suitable creature or not). These are signs of what makes the world of the tick – other matters such as the time of year or the state of the stock market are simply not of concern (to the tick).

This kind of argument was extended by American psychologist J. J. Gibson, who proposed that humans (and other species) see the world as *affordances* – opportunities for interaction. Gibson (1977) proposed that perception is not a neutral sense-gathering activity but rather a key part of action, and so we perceive a wooden café chair not as an interestingly twisted construction of steamed shaped wood coated with varnish but rather as a place to sit. (We may of course reflect on the chair too, taking a new look at it rather in the same way that Marcel Duchamp forced fresh perspectives on a ceramic urinal by placing it in an art gallery and calling it 'Fountain'.) Note that this is species-specific; a small bird flying into my office might see a guitar on a stand as a place to perch, whereas I see it as an opportunity to make music rather than as a seat. That this perspective goes beyond merely human behaviour is very satisfying to me – I see it as linking back to Gregory Bateson's interest in the widest possible application of communicational principles.

The Umwelt of a tick is very small and focused. As humans, we possess at least two key tools not available to the tick which expand our range of affordances – memory and language. Whereas the tick responds to warm fur in its immediate vicinity right now, we can remember many things which are not immediately present – I know to go to the kitchen when I am hungry and want an apple. I don't dispute that many animals have memory at some level too, which helps them make their living. With the question of language however, humans are way ahead of any other species. We can bring things like crocodiles into our presence with language, we can learn and pass on information with language, we can co-ordinate and co-operate with language.

With language and memory, affordances and Umwelt move from being broadly species-specific to being individual (with cultural and social elements too). Each of us will perceive what might be thought to be the same scene differently. Imagine walking through a forest with a botanist, an artist and a survivalist. The botanist notices different plants, talks about how they grow and multiply and where they are normally found. The artist is noticing the light, the colours, the shapes, and can produce work which somehow brings these things into a new representation. The survivalist knows what can be eaten, what is poison and how to make useful artefacts like cords and hammocks from what's lying around. It's the 'same' forest – and yet these are three different Umwelts.

A world as a 'field of affordances'

Looking at worlds as Umwelts and affordances has returned to the agenda with the rising interest in the paradigm of enactive cognition (see for example Varela, Thompson & Rosch 1991; Chemero 2009; Hutto & Myin 2013). In contrast to the prevailing cognitive paradigm of brain-as-computer, enactive cognition sees the brain as a linking organ playing a part in a much wider process of action/perception, processes that are intimately linked. Anthony Chemero's work has been important in the past decade in making clear that affordances develop in relatively fast (learning, within the lifespan of an organism) and slower evolutionary timescales. For example, double-thumb smartphone typing was unknown before the 21st century, but now many people use it to communicate. Gibson's idea of the critical role of affordances in perception has been further extended by Sanneke de Haan and others (2013) with their idea of 'landscapes' and 'fields' of affordances.

An affordance appears in the interaction between an organism and its environment. So it doesn't make sense to speak of an affordance as simply 'out there' in the environment, or 'in here' in the organism – we need both. A chair may offer a sitting opportunity to a human – but it also offers sleeping to cats, eating to moths, chewing to dogs, and so on. de Haan and her co-authors (2013) present this idea of the 'landscape of affordances' as 'all possibilities for action open to a specific form of life' (p. 7), which depends on the abilities available to this form of life – the entire field of possibilities open (say) to human beings, or dogs, or ticks. They then narrow this down further by proposing a 'field of affordances', the relevant possibilities for action that an individual is responsive to in a concrete situation.

This field of affordances corresponds to the 'world' of the individual – the opportunities for interaction which are noticeable and usable. Of course, this is an excerpt from the landscape of affordances, the set of all possible interactions for humans. For example, my office has a large chunky door frame which I use to enter and exit. My friend David, a climbing enthusiast, uses it to practise pull-ups to strengthen his fingers – indeed, his world is full of handholds, lines of ascent, ledges and opportunities for gymnastic exertion, which is probably why he is much skinnier than I am. (And yes, he also uses the door frame to enter and exit.)

One can easily grasp how worlds of (say) someone who is depressed might be rather small with not many possibilities and little chance to change them, or how an OCD sufferer's world might be dominated by washing their hands or checking the gas.

Mental health – where to look?

In my view the work of Sanneke de Haan and her colleagues opens up huge possibilities for all kinds of clinical work, which are only just beginning to make an impact on practice. de Haan herself has begun to extend her work into the realms of psychiatry (de Haan, 2020). Here I am building the other way, from practice towards conceptual.

How to describe mental illness has been a matter of debate for many decades. Some would like to insist that there is 'really' only brain illness, making the mistake of confusing the brain and the mind/mental. Of course, brain diseases and conditions are real, have difficult consequences for the sufferer and need treating. Alzheimer's disease, Parkinson's disease and epilepsy are examples. The brain illnesses are not usually categorised as 'mental'. (This is not to say that SFBT ideas cannot be used with Alzheimer sufferers to help them live better lives – they can.)

However, conditions like depression are not brain diseases; according to the British NHS there are no reliable physical tests for it (NHS, 2020). The US National Institute of Mental Health (NIMH) has stated that 'Brain scans alone cannot be used to diagnose a mental disorder, such as autism, anxiety, depression, schizophrenia, or bipolar disorder'(NIMH, 2020, p. 2). It has even been said that 'Depression can damage parts of the brain' (Schmaal et al., 2016), which seems to see the brain as an innocent victim of depression rather than the active cause.

Psychiatry is the medical field of addressing mental disorders. It has modelled itself on other medical fields in seeking to treat these illnesses in a diagnostic way, essentially categorising them and using research to establish the best ways of treatment, in the same way as a physical illness. The results, however, have been less than illuminating. The Diagnostic and Statistical Manual (APA, 2013) has grown bigger and bigger over its five major revisions since 1952, with ever-growing extent (130 pages growing to 991) and numbers of disorders (up from 108 to 354) (Khoury, Langer & Pagnini, 2014). There is, sadly, less and less clarity over what to do about them. Accusations have been made that these diagnoses are being used to medicalise the normal ups and downs of life in the interesting of pharmaceutical companies (see for example Frances, 2013).

A more promising approach in recent decades has been the biopsychosocial model of mental health originally proposed by George Engel (1977). This pluralist model looks to include elements from biological, psychological and social realms, and it is a step away from the strict objectivity of science. It starts to include more concern for the person as an individual in their specific context, including psychological concepts such as self-esteem and temperament alongside social elements, family relationships and circumstances. However, it's not the answer; although the broadening of focus is welcome, it seems to simply say that 'everything' could be relevant and so doesn't help much in actually figuring out what to do.

An enactive perspective – 'the world' of the client is out-of-tune

There is a long-standing, if somewhat overlooked, tradition of looking at mental illness not as something inside the patient/client, but as some kind of disturbance on the client's way-of-being in the world, based originally on phenomenology and recently extended by enactivists. German psychiatrist Thomas Fuchs offers an interesting way into a general discussion about enactivism and mental illness. In his paper (Fuchs (2013) examining depression not as an inner and individual complaint, but as a detunement/disturbance (*Verstimmung* in German, which translates as an unpleasant out-of-tune-ness) of 'the resonant body that mediates our participation in a shared affective' (which is very much stated in embodied and enactive terms). Fuchs harks back to phenomenologist psychiatrist Jan Hendrick van den Berg's pithy aphorism (van den Berg, 1972):

> The patient is ill; this means, his world is ill.

Fuchs elaborates on this position:

> In this sense, the illness is not in the patient, but the patient is in the illness, as it were; for mental illness is not a state in the head, but an altered way of being in the world.
>
> (Fuchs, 2013, p. 222)

Taking the statement 'the world of the patient is ill', it is easy and tempting to fall back into a cognitivist picture that the world of the patient is inside the head of the patient. From an enactive perspective, the world of the patient is 'out here', in the interactions of the patient with their world. de Haan (2020) has comprehensively developed this idea towards psychiatry with four inter-linking domains: physiological, experiential, sociocultural and existential. An enactivist perspective addresses all four domains. She defines mental illness as a disorder of sense-making, how the individual experiences the world, and states the importance of personal phenomenological experience as a way to approach this. I propose that SFBT is a good fit for how to do this.

The 'world of the patient' is the patient's field of affordances. Remember that this is an excerpt from the total landscape of affordances open to the patient's form of life. This is dynamic on many levels – including short-term learning and long-term evolutionary. So, if we take mental illnesses as conditions of a person (as opposed to a brain disease), we could tentatively define this form of mental illness as:

•   A persistent Verstimmung (disturbance/detuning) of a field of affordances.

These terms are carefully chosen:

Persistent: not very temporary – we all have temporary disturbances in our worlds and deal with them by everyday actions. We feel a bit miserable and decide to go out for a walk and see some friends, for example. These are everyday ups and downs and are dealt with routinely most of the time. Only if the 'ordinary' ways of dealing with something prove ineffective can we start thinking in terms of illness. Readers may recall that the necessity of persistence was first put forward by John Weakland and colleagues at the Mental Research Institute, Palo Alto, in the 1970s, as we saw in Chapter 2 (Watzlawick, Weakland & Fisch, 1974; Weakland, Fisch, Watzlawick & Bodin, 1974). It is still sound.

Verstimmung: This is a German word which has a number of meanings difficult to entirely sum up in English. These include disturbance, detuning, and leaving a bad mood. This is not a breakage – there is a sense in which the disturbance can be corrected. This is not, of course, referring to a bad mood which 'accompanies' the illness, the *Verstimmung* is key to the whole picture.

Field: This refers to the field of affordances relevant to this person in this context. This inevitably brings a first person perspective into action – different people will naturally have different fields of affordance, and in particular the therapist/practitioner will not be able to take on the client's field of affordance.

Of affordances: This is, again, neither in the person nor in the environment but in the relationship between the person and their environment, as shown in possibilities for action and engagement.

SFBT as 'stretching the world'

Psychotherapy has been characterised (and caricatured) as 'two people talking, trying to figure out what one of them wants'. All talking therapies have in common at least the talking element (though the topics of the conversation vary dramatically between approaches). We can also note the findings of Wampold (2001) that all talking therapies are about as effective as each other in pure outcome terms.

What has never been done, as far as I know, is to look at talking therapy explicitly in the way it stretches and changes the client's field of affordances. On this basis, therapies which seek to address mental distress by a focus on long-passed causalities such as childhood trauma and familial relations might be expected to take a long time to work (having little in the way of immediate consequence), whereas therapies focusing more on details of a better future, some of which is already at hand, might be expected to bring more rapid progress.

If we are to look at talking therapy as helping to stretch the client's field of affordances in useful ways that connect to progress, we might expect to look for:

• The therapist taking the client as an active participant in the joint process
• The therapist taking the first person perspective/descriptions very seriously
• The therapist not attempting to discover what has caused the problem but rather establishing a conversational narrative around progress in the past, present and future

- The conversation being focused on small details of a 'better world' – signs that things were and are improving.

One might expect that such a stretching of the field of affordances might have an emergent quality about it – sometimes neat, sometime messy, sometimes clear, sometimes confusing. To stretch a field of affordances is not the same as to provide key steps for action to the client. Might such a therapy be effective? Well, we have been talking about it at length in this book: the next generation of SFBT.

How SFBT stretches the world

What is going on when we engage the client in describing tiny signs of progress, of the miracle happening, that things were going better, that they are now closer to ten on the scale? We are helping them generate new, or at least newly relevant and important, affordances: 'stretching their world'. The client describes 'better'

- In their own language
- In the future, past and/or present
- In everyday terms
- In detail
- In particular, in terms of 'noticing' and 'signs'.

The language of 'tiny signs' and 'noticing' could hardly be more suited to such a task. Every time a new detail emerges in the conversation in terms of a sign or action, that becomes a potential affordance. Not all the potential affordances will be important – that only becomes apparent later on when the client experiences their stretched world first hand after the session.

Case example: putting things up in my room

The client is a 16-year-old school student, referred by the school who were concerned about the student's fragility in exams, especially as there are important tests just around the corner. The school also informed the practitioner that they had previously self-harmed. The client's best hopes (which we will see forming in Chapter 9) are broadly to feel better, have a growing self-confidence, be able to go into exams properly and stay in them and be able to speak up in lessons more.

   This is a short but verbatim extract from a miracle future conversation, about going into lessons with these hopes realised. I have added a commentary. Note the way in which new possibilities for interaction appear in the conversation, created by the client in the conversation. These new possibilities stretch their world. This is a future gallery conversation; the same kind of things can and do happen in building descriptions about the past and present.

Transcript	Commentary
P: Who would be the teacher who would be most surprised to see that? To see you walk into the lesson and have that eye contact?	
C: Erm ... probably my current Maths teacher.	Finding a specific context, rather than speaking in general.
P: Ok, what's their name?	
C: Mr S.	
P: Ok ...And how would you know that Mr S was surprised by that?	
C: Cause we'd actually have a conversation rather than just like a quick 'morning' and then me shuffle off into my seat.	A detailed concrete specific description is starting to be built here ...
P: Yeah ... So you'd have a conversation ... Who do you think would start the conversation?	Practitioner wants to dig further into the detail.
C: Probably him ...	
P: Ok.	
C: Cause he says 'morning' to everyone as they walk in ...	
P: Yeah.	P not rushing on, waiting for more ...
C: And like if you ... like actually engage, he'll be 'oh how was your weekend?' That little chit chat before the lesson ... whereas if you just walk in and say 'morning' and then go off then you don't.	Very good to get this detail from the client – the description is coming to life
P: Ok, so he'll start a conversation with you, because you're engaging and having that eye contact yeah ... and he might ask you about your weekend ...	Practitioner reminds client that we are talking about having eye contact ...
C: Yeah just random stuff.	
P: And how are you going to respond to that? Given your growing self-confidence, belief in yourself ...	Now building descriptions of the interaction between client and teacher as a series of responses.

Transcript	Commentary
C: Positively.	
P: Yup ... yeah ... And then what effect might that have on Mr S? The fact that you've engaged, looked at him as you've walked in, and you've responded, you know, really positively to his question ...	Back to the teacher ...
C: Erm ... Good that I'm ... responding.	Client is still thinking about it ...
P: Yeah.	
C: The fact that ... yeah ...	
P: And how might, err ... I wonder, cause that's a short piece of time isn't it, it's just that as you're walking in ... How might that influence the rest of the lesson? Walking in with confidence, eye contact, conversation together ...	Practitioner linking this brief moment into a bigger picture of the lesson.
C: More confident for the rest of the lesson ...	
P: Yeah ... And how would Mr S know that you were more confident? How would that show?	Making the rather abstract word 'confident' into more detailed specific language.
C: To put my hand up ... Or like if he asks me randomly, cause sometimes it's like 'oh you answer' and stuff ...	'Put my hand up'.
P: Yeah ...	
C: Like I wouldn't, like ... not know what to say or stammer.	
P: Ok. And how would you ... Instead of stammering, how would you come across?	
C: Just like be able to say my thoughts, like flowing better ...	'Say my thoughts, flowing better'.
P: Yeah.	
C: And like louder so I'm not really quiet.	'And louder'.

It is quite clear that there are now more significant possibilities in the moment of walking into the class with Mr S, and different ways of doing it, that the client has created for themselves. The world is stretched – there are more possibilities, more affordances, newly relevant affordances. None of this was impossible before, but it has now taken on a new role and potential significance for the client. The moment of meeting the teacher is now sited within the bigger context of hopes for a better life.

Why 'stretching' the world rather than 'changing' or 'rebuilding'?

The idea of 'stretching' seems to me to fit this situation particularly well, for a number of reasons.

- A stretch requires effort from the client. When the first response to (say) a miracle question is 'Ummmm', that is a good sign that the client is going to have do some work! New thinking often takes time and effort. If the client simply reels answers 'off pat', that's a sign that they are not perhaps in new territory as yet, and the practitioner should dig into some more fine detail.
- A stretch may show tendency to return somewhat towards original size. We can't know how much of newly stretched world will persist, and it may relax back somewhat after the session. We have to wait and see.
- Changes will continue after the session too. The client will leave the consulting room with their world already stretched and will live into their new worlds. The impact of that only appears over time.
- 'What's better' questions at follow-up sessions can be seen as asking about how the newly stretched world is fitting for the client, how they are experiencing it, what else they need to do. This kind of conversation also fits well into the world-stretching paradigm.

Conclusions

We started this chapter looking at the reasons why SFBT practitioners have been nervous or reluctant to engage in discussions about 'theory', as any concern with that might prevent them focusing fully on their clients and their language. We have ended up with a theory which *depends* on close focus on the client and their language, making sense of it in both a practical sense (it informs what we do) and a conceptual sense (it helps to understand quite how doing that might help the client). These detailed conversations are not about anything that looks 'mental' by the normal understanding of the word, but the enactive view helps to draw a broader outline around that concept.

Key points

- SFBT practitioners have resisted theories and explanations of our work for sound and principled reasons, including wishing to focus undistracted on the client and keep a beginner mind about what might be going on for them.
- This may be principled in some ways, but it interferes with outsiders and fellow professionals understanding and engaging with what we do. A useful narrative can serve our field here.
- The field of theory and explanations about mental illness is widely contested, from brain science to medicine to biopsychosocial narratives.
- An enactivist perspective allows us to reconceive 'mental' from an inner story into an interactional one, with the world of the client (their Umwelt) being their affordances, their possibilities for interaction.
- One potential definition of 'mental illness' could be 'a persistent Verstimmung (unpleasant out-of-tune-ness) of affordances.
- SFBT can be thought of as 'stretching the world' of the client by grounding tiny interactional detail in the therapeutic conversation.

References

American Psychiatric Association. (2013). *Diagnostic and Statistical Manual of Mental Disorders* (5th ed.). https://doi.org/10.1176/appi.books.9780890425596

British Association for Behavioural and Cognitive Psychotherapies (BABCP). (2020). *What Is CBT?* Retrieved from www.babcp.com/files/Public/what-is-cbt-web.pdf

Chemero, A. (2009). *Radical Embodied Cognitive Science.* Cambridge, MA: MIT Press.

de Haan, S. (2020). *Enactive Psychiatry.* Cambridge: Cambridge University Press.

de Haan, S., Rietveld, E., Stokhof, M., & Denys, D. (2013). The phenomenology of deep brain stimulation-induced changes in OCD: An enactive affordance-based model. *Frontiers in Human Neuroscience, 7,* 653. Retrieved from www.frontiersin.org/articles/10.3389/fnhum.2013.00653/full

de Shazer, S. (1991). *Putting Difference to Work.* New York, NY: W. W. Norton.

de Shazer, S., & Berg, I. K. (1994). *From Problem to Solution, Part 1* (Audio). Retrieved from https://youtu.be/7a71M1b7YOU. 16 July 2020, 22 minutes into the recording.

de Shazer, S., Dolan, Y., Korman, H., McCollum, E., Trepper, T., & Berg, I. K. (2007). *More Than Miracles: The State of the Art of Solution-Focused Brief Therapy.* Philadelphia, PA: Haworth Press.

de Shazer, S., & Varga von Kibéd, M. (2003). *Conversations about Wittgenstein.* Recording from the Plenary at the 2003 SFBTA conference. Santa Fe, NM: SFBTA.

Engel, G. (1977). The need for a new medical model: A challenge for biomedical science. *Science, 196,* 126–129.

Erickson, M. H., & Rossi, E. (1979). *Hypnotherapy: An Exploratory Casebook.* New York, NY: Irvington Publishers.

Frances, A. (2013). *Saving Normal: An Insider's Revolt against Out-of-Control Psychiatric Diagnosis, DSM-5, Big Pharma, and the Medicalization of Ordinary Life.* New York, NY: William Morrow.

Fuchs, T. (2013). Depression, intercorporeality, and interaffectivity. *Journal of Consciousness Studies, 20*(7–8), 219–238.

Gibson, J. J. (1977). The theory of affordances. In R. Shaw & J. Brnasford (Eds.), *Perceiving, Acting, and Knowing*. Mahwah, NJ: Lawrence Erlbaum Associates Publishers.

Harré, R. (2002). *Cognitive Science: A Philosophical Introduction*. London: Sage Publications.

Hutto, D. D., & Myin, E. (2013). *Radicalizing Enactivism: Basic Minds without Content*. Boston, MA: MIT Press.

Khoury, B., Langer, E. J., & Pagnini, F. (2014). The DSM: Mindful science or mindless power? A critical review. *Frontiers in Psychology, 5*, 602. doi:10.3389/fpsyg.2014.00602

Malinen, T. (2004). The wisdom of not-knowing: A conversation with Harlene Anderson. *Journal of Systemic Therapies, 23*(2), 68–77.

Merleau-Ponty, M. (1945). *Phénoménologie de la perception (Phenomenology of Perception)*. Paris, France: Editions Gallimard.

Monk, R. (1990). *Ludwig Wittgenstein: The Duty of Genius*. New York, NY: Free Press.

NHS. (2020). *Clinical Depression*. Retrieved from www.nhs.uk/conditions/clinical-depression/diagnosis/

NIMH. (2020). *Neuroimaging and Mental Illness*. Retrieved from www.naminys.org/images/uploads/pdfs/Neuroimaging%20(FAQ).pdf

O'Hanlon, W. H., & Beadle, S. (1994). *A Field Guide to Possibility-Land*. Omaha, NE: Possibility Press.

Rogers, C. (1951). *Client-Centered Therapy: Its Current Practice, Implications and Theory*. London: Constable.

Schmaal, L., Veltman, D., van Erp, T., et al. (2016). Subcortical brain alterations in major depressive disorder: Findings from the ENIGMA major depressive disorder working group. *Molecular Psychiatry, 21*, 806–812. https://doi.org/10.1038/mp.2015.69

Stewart, J., Gapenne, O., & Di Paolo, E. A. (Eds.). (2010). *Enaction: Toward a New Paradigm for Cognitive Science*. Cambridge, MA: MIT Press.

Suzuki, S. (1970). *Zen Mind, Beginner's Mind*. New York: Weatherhill.

Thompson, E. (2007). *Mind and Life: Biology, Phenomenology and the Sciences of Mind*. Cambridge, MA: Harvard University Press.

van den Berg, H. (1972). *A Different Existence: Principles of Phenomenological Psychopathology*. Pittburgh, PA: Duquesne University Press.

Varela, F., Thompson, E., & Rosch, E. (1991). *The Embodied Mind: Cognitive Science and Human Experience*. Cambridge, MA: MIT Press.

von Uexküll, J. (1920). *Theoretische Biologie*. Berlin: Paetel.

Wampold, B. E. (2001). *The Great Psychotherapy Debate: Models, Methods, and Findings*. Mahwah, NJ: Lawrence Erlbaum Associates Publishers.

Watzlawick, P., Weakland, J. H., & Fisch, R. (1974). *Change: Problem Formation and Problem Resolution*. New York, NY: W. W. Norton.

Weakland, J. H., Fisch, R., Watzlawick, P., & Bodin, A. M. (1974). Brief therapy: Focused problem resolution. *Family Process, 13*(2), 141–168.

Wittgenstein, L. (1953). *Philosophical Investigations* (Trans. G.E.M. Anscombe). New York, NY: Macmilllan.

World Health Organisation (WHO). (2020). *WHO Model Lists of Essential Medicines*. Retrieved from www.who.int/medicines/publications/essentialmedicines/en/

Chapter 7

The role of the practitioner

What exactly is the role of the practitioner in Solution Focused (SF) work? There have been considerable shifts in what practitioners do over the past 30 years. In the beginning, as we saw in Chapters 2 and 3, the therapist was there to engage the client in conversation to help in the construction of a task which would help them move on. This meant doing a lot of noticing of events mentioned by the client which seemed to be relevant, either because they were 'exceptions' to the usual problematic patterns, or they showed something useful about the client's strengths, know-how, skills and so on.

Of course, it is possible and even likely that these conversations also influenced the client directly, without the task. As we saw in Chapter 5, the influence of the conversation, as opposed to the task, has become a key development in the 21st century. In Chapter 6, I proposed that the conversation is now about expanding the possibilities open to the client – stretching their world. This chapter will explore the role of the practitioner: how does this world stretching happen? The answer will be 'both more, and less, then one might suppose'.

The practitioner as world-stretcher

A key part of recent developments is an increase in the level of detail sought by the practitioner in terms of the client's descriptions – not just that something would happen, but exactly what, what would be the first signs that others noticed, what difference would that make, what would happen next, and so on. In pursing this co-creation of tiny details with the client, the practitioner is not preparing an intervention; they are in the process of making an intervention.

The gradual accumulation of detail, grounded in the conversation (as we will see in the microanalysis section later in this chapter) brings new possibilities for action into the client's awareness, as affordances. Note that these new possibilities were not exactly unavailable to the client before – they are not outwith the bounds of possibility (the landscape of affordances). However, the conversation brings them directly into the client's reach as something relevant to a better life. I recall a client once saying that they would squeeze their orange juice differently on the day after the miracle. They already had fresh orange juice – but it now seemed to play a somewhat different part in the make-up of their day and their life.

Notice too that everything in an SFBT conversation happens from someone's perspective – the client, those around them, and occasionally even the practitioner's view (as in a summary or compliment). The grammar is about specifically named people doing particular things, with and for each other. It is not a generalised description, it is not carried out in the molecular impersonal language of science and medicine (Harré, 2002), it is about what these particular people notice about themselves and about each other. This may be one reason why SFBT has not carried far into the scientific and medical fields – the terms of engagement are so different. Science (including psychology) is more interested in finding general truths and reliable knowledge across populations. SF is always about *this* situation with *these* particular people.

One thing to bear in mind is that while the therapy conversation is going on, neither party knows quite where it is going and what will emerge. Similarly, when the client walks out of the conversation at the end, we never know what will ensue. The world of the client is already stretched – but what that will mean for the client as they tackle their lives from a new standpoint is never sure. We have to wait and see. When the client comes back for another session (assuming that they wish to do so) the practitioner will start by asking 'what's better?' – inviting the client to recount ways in which they have noticed new and better happenings.

One fascinating possibility is that this process of world-stretching is more akin to physiotherapy – the exercising and building of limbs and muscles – than conventional psychotherapy. In psychotherapy, the 'therapeutic alliance' is usually considered vital, where the particular practitioner and client build up a relationship. Under normal circumstances this is probably to do with the client trusting the therapist enough to reveal intimate details of their unhappy past. In SFBT, where the focus is around the fine detail of a better future, present and past, there is perhaps less (or even no) need for such a relationship. As the questions are for the client to hear (rather than the therapist) then it may be that a different (similarly trained and oriented) practitioner could continue. There are anecdotal reports (including from BFTC) of this happening on occasions where the usual therapist was indisposed and a replacement took over, with little apparent concern from the client. I am not suggesting that this should happen, but the possibility is inherent in this view of the client being the key audience for the co-created conversation.

Building descriptions

Without an end-of-session task the therapist would not need to be collecting information for its construction. And it's not the therapist listening to understand the situation, so they can go away, converse with others and produce a task. This kind of listening – to understand and prepare a response – is so natural and every day to us that it's hard to conceive of another way to do it. Listening in order to say something sensible, relevant and helpful is second nature. But here we are not going to say anything! It's a different form of engagement.

The practitioner is listening to help the client expand on their descriptions of relevant times or scenes in the past, present and future. This is a different and very focused kind of listening with detailed attention to the actual words used by the client rather than the general sense of what they say. The practitioner can then pick up part of what the client has said and offer it back for expansion and elaboration.

This detailed listening and engagement has been there in SF practice from the outset. However, recent developments are helping the therapist focus even more single-mindedly and closely on the language of the client. The practitioner must, of course, keep some kind of track of wider issues – if the safety of the client or anyone else is at risk then other actions need to be taken. But if we take the prime role of the therapist as listening for description development, of noticing, then the practice can take a new turn both in practical and conceptual terms. This chapter will investigate the practical consequences of such a turn.

Explanation or description

> We must do away with all explanation, and description alone must take its place.
> Wittgenstein (1953), *Philosophical Investigations*, 109

Arguments from Wittgenstein can be used to attempt to show the muddles inherent (from his perspective) in different kinds of therapy conversation. But they can also be used in a more helpful way to show what we might do instead: build descriptions. Wittgenstein, and de Shazer, were wary of explanations, both about the client's life and indeed about our practice.

As far as working with the client is concerned, we are not seeking explanations of how they came to a troubled state. Such details lie in the world of the problem. Take a client who says they are depressed; there are potential explanations at many levels from chemicals in the brain, physiology of the nervous system, life history, workplace conflict, familial relations, childhood trauma, economic deprivation, political oppression and even diet and exercise. Most fields choose one of these areas to focus on. With SFBT we can step over this choice, and instead help the client focus on the world of solution, filled with descriptions of their everyday better life in the future, present and past from which the client draws their own conclusions. We don't try to 'join the dots' and make sense for them.

This is one reason why the miracle question is so effective as a starting point. It presupposes that a miracle, a sudden and inexplicable event, has occurred in the night while the client is asleep. The client only discovers afterwards that the miracle has happened by describing scenes from the day after the miracle.

They missed the (imaginary) moment when the transformation occurred, and so cannot know quite how it happened. So the qualities of a miracle – sudden, inexplicable and useful, an event without a cause – are an excellent way to help the client separate the experience of life after the miracle (a description) with quite how they got there (an explanation).

Keeping the preferred future separate from 'how to get there' has long been part of good SFBT practice. Indeed, this is a key difference from the usual pattern to be found in business and self-help books of goal – plan – action – success. In the latest SFBT there is no goal, no plan and no (or not much) action. What there is instead is the client, assisted by the practitioner, building descriptions around a theme of the client's best hopes. The practitioner asks questions which help the client to start a description (perhaps a miracle or scaling question) and then works with them by asking much smaller questions to expand it. Building this description allows us to more easily avoid the muddles pointed out by Wittgenstein not by understanding them (hard work) but by simply doing something coherent.

The client then, as the session progresses, experiences a kind of shift of awareness so that at the end of the conversation they know what to do next. The small details in future, past and present widen the landscape of their worlds, their possibilities for action. This contrasts with hoping for an 'aha' moment, a flash of realisation which opens the door to immediate resolution. I used to think (25 years ago) that this was the aim. I have occasionally seen it happen (and indeed it is to be welcomed on those rare occasions, as is any helpful learning or realisation from the client). However, I have come to realise that our work is more often about a gradual dawning, a realisation at the end of a conversation that something is different. It's more like drip–drip–drip than whizz–bang, climbing a mountain (which is hard work) and finally turning around and getting an amazing view which wasn't there at the start.

So far we have been thinking about the practitioner asking questions, and the client answering them. Recent developments from conversational microanalysis, however, have shown that both participants are even more involved than we might suppose.

Developments from microanalysis

From the very outset SFBT has developed by examination of actual practice. From Steve de Shazer, Insoo Kim Berg and their teams sitting on the stairs in Milwaukee to observe sessions and discuss them, through extensive use of transcriptions and tapes in teaching, to these latest development in description building, a great deal of development has been driven by pragmatic and focused reflection.

This is perhaps taken to one logical conclusion in the form of microanalysis. We first met Janet Bavelas in Chapter 2 of this book, all the way back in 1967 as a co-author of *Pragmatics of Human Communication* (Watzlawick, Bavelas & Jackson, 1967). After a distinguished career in researching communication and dialogue, Dr Bavelas returned her attention to the field of therapeutic communications in the early 2000s and has since led ground-breaking studies of actual dialogues. She has been heard to quietly observe that 'communication theory seems to have studied everything ... apart from actual communication' and has brought an incredibly detailed focus to studying SFBT sessions and comparing them with other disciplines.

This is a rich, detailed and absorbing field. Space is limited here, and I hope to draw out some salient points. Fortunately, Bavelas' papers are archived on her website and can be freely explored (Bavelas, 2020).

Questions and formulations

In an early study comparing SFBT sessions with client-centred therapy sessions, Bavelas & Tomori (2007) looked at two key aspects. At a basic level, the therapist's dialogue participation can be seen as either questions or 'formulations' (statements). Questions are clearly designed to generate answers, while formulations could be reflections (of what the client has just said), summaries, statements of the therapist's understanding, and so on. Both are ways of taking the conversation forward. Categories for 'both' and 'neither' questions and formulations were also used – more of this later.

The SFBT sessions showed roughly equal numbers of questions and formulations by the practitioner. The client-centred sessions, on the other hand, consisted almost completely of formulations, with just two questions across the two sessions. That SFBT shows up, in practice, with a relatively high proportion of questions is not surprising, but the level of difference is stark.

Positive and negative

In the same study the sessions were also analysed to see how many of the therapists' utterances were positive (connecting with the client's hopes and successes), negative (connecting to the client's problems) or neither. In the SFBT sessions positive outnumbered negative by about six to one. The client-centred sessions saw a dramatic difference, with negative utterances outnumbering positives by around four to one. The authors say they are in no doubt about the client centred practitioners desire to be sympathetic to their clients and wonder whether this result may be unintended. They also note that the overall impact of a series of problem-focused and negative statements on the client is likely to be predictable.

In a later study Smock Jordan, Froerer & Bavelas (2013) compared microanalysis results from three SFBT sessions with three using cognitive behavioural therapy (CBT). They again found that the SFBT practitioners used more positive utterances than negative, often by a considerable margin, while the CBT sessions showed more of a roughly equal balance. Moreover, in both cases the client was likely to respond in the same vein, positive or negative. The authors note that the practitioners tended to perpetuate and build on these answers, so establishing different 'routes' in the conversation.

Building formulations

Over several years around the start of the 2010s, Janet Bavelas worked closed with experienced SFBT practitioners Harry Korman and Peter De Jong to investigate even more closely how SFBT seemed to work in practical second-by-second detail. She noted (Bavelas, 2011) that formulations can be 'open' or 'closed'. Open formulations, although not questions, are intended to promote a response from the interlocutor, which can be signalled by a pause for the response, a raised questioning intonation. A closed formulation, on the other hand, is not intended to promote a response and may be followed by the practitioner continuing to speak, changing the subject or some other signal. This is more than simply the words spoken. So, in a simple example:

C: I've found that going for a walk helps me calm down …
P: Going for a walk … (Raised intonation, pause, tell more more, open formulation)

Or

P: Going for a walk. (Falling intonation, no pause, sounds like changing the subject, closed formulation)

Preserving client language

Another aspect of formulations is the extent to which the client's language is preserved by the therapist. Korman, Bavelas & De Jong (2013) examined sessions from SFBT, CBT and motivational interviewing (MI) in this regard. They measured the extent to which the client's language was preserved in the therapist's formulations either exactly (verbatim), or deictically (referred to in summary by a demonstrative pronoun such as 'that' or 'it'), or in altered form (typically a synonym or paraphrase). They also noted where therapists added their own words.

These results showed that the two SFBT excerpts (from Berg & Korman) showed the highest percentages of retained client language, both in terms of the totals (93% and 86% respectively and language retained exactly (38% and 57%). Correspondingly, these two sessions showed smaller amount of new language added by the therapist; 7% by Berg and 14% by Korman. The other

CBT and MI sessions showed added language at 37%, 5% and 43%. These findings confirmed what had been a clear but somewhat implicit preference for preserving and using the client's language wherever possible.

Of course it is simply not possible to use everything a client says; there is also deciding what to omit. This is another skill for the SF practitioner, as we shall see in the following chapters.

Questions as interventions

The phrases co-creation and co-construction tend to get bandied about in all kinds of ways these days, from involving clients in their own treatment programmes in medicine to vague notions of social construction as being something amazing, difficult and hard to pin down. SFBT, on the other hand, has been relatively clear, at least in recent years, about the notion of co-creation of meaning in dialogues and interaction. One the one hand, we are taking a hard and concrete look at language and dialogue (which would surely meet with nods of approval from the MRI originators). On the other hand, this move leads to some slightly uncomfortable truths about the role and responsibility of the therapist.

McGee, Del Vento and Bavelas (2005) looked at the idea of an interactional model of questions as therapeutic interventions. Rather than asking questions for the purpose of information gathering (which would be consistent with a task-based model of therapy) the authors note how SFBT therapists ask questions to introduce new possibilities and co-construct new meanings. They say that in this view, therapists and clients are not simply sending information about the client back and forth to each other. Their dialogue is actively shaping a new version of the client's life. This is a key point in the evolution of SFBT; although this idea was not a new one, Bavelas and her colleagues had shown *how* this was happening in the process of questions and answers. They identified key elements of how questions can be shaped to lead in this direction:

- **Orientation** – the question constrains and orients the answerer towards a particular aspect of their experience
- **On-The-Spot Reviewing** – to answer the question, the answerer must do considerable on-the-spot review work, searching through their experience (or imagination based on experience) for the requested specifics
- **Embedded presuppositions** – questions can contain embedded presuppositions, which are usually accepted without comment by the answerer, yet are malleable and can be corrected by the therapist if they turn out not to be useful
- **Acceptance** – in answering the question, the answerer implicitly accepts the presuppositions as common ground, and 'owns' their answer, at which point the initiative returns to the questioner.

A short example helps illustrate these rather abstract points in action. The client has been talking about how in her miracle day she would be going to a job interview (rather than perhaps sitting around at home).

C: I'd make sure I was more presentable when I left the house to drop Anton off at school.
P: How are you looking more presentable, on this morning after the miracle?
C: My hair isn't sticking up all over the place … and I will have clothes on that didn't look like they had just been pulled off the floor.

The clients offers the words 'more presentable'. This is the orientation for this particular section of dialogue. The therapist picks up those words and asks about how she will be looking more presentable. There are two presuppositions here:

1   that she will know somehow how she will look more presentable, and
2   there has been a miracle!

Note that the second presupposition has been simply accepted without question – it was introduced as part of a miracle question some time before and is now part of the dialogue. To answer the first part, the client has to on-the-spot review her experience and come up with an answer. She does this without batting an eyelid (as is often the case). She has accepted the presupposition that she knows and now owns her answer. The therapist can now continue to build the description.

Notice how different things might be without the presupposition of self-awareness regarding 'more presentable':

C: So I'd make sure I was more presentable when I left the house to drop Anton off at school.
P: Do you know how you are looking more presentable, on this morning after the miracle?
C: Ummm … no.

The therapist has not presupposed that she knows the answer but has instead asked her explicitly whether she knows. This is a yes/no type question rather than an open 'how' question, and it gives the option of a 'no' response. Given that option, that's what she gives the therapist. We see how a tiny, detailed change in the question turns it into a whole different intervention. We will look at detailed dialogues later in this book, and this kind of choice will come up time and again.

Co-creation of meaning in practice

Later research shows that the practice of solution-building turns out to be even more complex and interwoven than simple question-and-answer processes. In another important contribution De Jong, Bavelas and Korman (2013) showed in even more detail exactly how the kind of details produced by clients were 'grounded' in the conversation, accepted by both parties. Building on the work of psycholinguist Herbert H. Clark (1996) and drawing on their own examples, the Bavelas team produced a firm view of how this acceptance happened and new meanings secured as the conversation proceeded. In later work (Bavelas, Gerwing & Healing, 2017; De Jong, Smock Jordan, Healing & Gerwing, 2020) they refer to this three-part process as 'calibration' and offer a more sophisticated framework around it.

In its simplest form, a grounding or calibration sequence consists of three steps involving both the person who is contributing information at that particular moment and the person being addressed:

1   The speaker presents some information.
2   The addressee displays that he or she understood it.
3   The speaker confirms the addressee's display of understanding.

Note that very often the speaker is the client, though of course the process can work either way. To give a simplistic example, suppose that a hotel concierge has been asked for the phone number of a restaurant by a guest:

CONCIERGE: It's 552 8262
GUEST: 552 8262
CONCIERGE: Yes, that's right.

Between them, the guest and concierge have grounded the fact that the phone number is 552 8262. Of course, there are ways that people abbreviate and smooth this process. The concierge might respond 'Uh-huh' and nod rather than say 'Yes, that's right'. The guest might just respond '8262' as they note the number down rather than repeat the whole thing. There are ways that the second and third step can be included into subsequent questions and formulations, such as '(nodding) ... And are they open tonight?'. It is unusual and discomforting if the third step does not take place in any way at all – the matter is still up in the air.

This is a complex area, but the main conclusion is simple and stark. It takes two to construct meaning. The therapist and client are both complicit in the conversation and the meanings that are constructed. This can come as a shock to some practitioners who pride themselves on their 'neutrality' and 'client focus'. Microanalysis shows that there are no neutral words, there is no way not to communicate and influence – an idea coined in the abstract by Gregory Bateson over half a century before and laid bare in the tiny details of conversational interaction.

Of course, in real life things get more complicated than this ploddingly simple example. Grounding sequences overlap and can be achieved by tiny

Table 7.1 Microanalysis detail showing grounding and lexical choice

	Transcript	Grounding sequence	Overlapping sequences
#1	Client: 'Well, right now I'm dealing with a drinking problem'.	1a: presents new information	
#2	de Shazer: 'Mm-huh'.	1b: displays understanding with a minimal response	
#3	Client: 'Yeah'. (very softly)	1c: confirms the display of understanding, also with a minimal response. **1: Grounded that right now the client is dealing with a drinking problem.**	
#4	(de Shazer paused while looking down and writing, then says 'OK, and, uh' and pauses again.)		(At de Shazer's second pause in #4, the client started to speak (#5) but broke off again as soon as de Shazer spoke again (#6)/ At #6 they were synchronised again.)
#5	Client: 'Sometimes I drink –'.		2a: presents new information
#6	de Shazer: 'You say "right now"' (with emphasis)	1b': second display of understanding of what the client said in #1, this time more explicitly	
#7	Client: 'Well, I've been dealing with it –'	1c': client confirms de Shazer's display of understanding (in #6) by beginning to give more information on what 'right now' meant **1': grounded that he is dealing with it "right now"**	2b: displays understanding
#8	de Shazer (overlapping): 'Mm-hm'.		2c: confirms de Shazer's display as accurate by continuing on this theme.
#9	Client (continuing): 'but right now I'm just feeling that it's the time of my life to really get into it, to do something about it'.	3a: presents new information	**2: grounded that he has 'been dealing with' (his drinking problem).**

(from Bavelas, De Jong, Smock Jordan & Korman, 2014, pp. 17–18) responses rather than full statements. To take a therapeutic example from Bavelas, De Jong, Smock Jordan and Korman (2014), here is Steve de Shazer starting a client interview (Table 7.1). He has asked 'What brings you in?'.

This all takes just 17 seconds, even given de Shazer's measured style of working. It makes clear and open some aspects that have been with us all along but not really noticed:

- there is more to the exchanges than simple exchanges of questions and answers
- that the grounding of information is a joint activity between client and practitioner
- that the practitioner is paying *very close* attention to the actual words used by the client
- that a lot of the grounding happens in minimal responses like 'Um-hm' as well as repeating and re-using words
- that the process of constructing meaning is a continuous one, involving all concerned in the conversation.

These elements of grounding using minimal responses and joint co-operative processes are not themselves unique to SFBT; indeed, if we take this view seriously, they are part of pretty much any conversation. However, if we take a perspective of SF work as description-building, then they are crucial in both grounding the client's words and encouraging them to expand.

Just to be clear, this co-creation is more than the simple 'backchannel' of communications where the receiver acknowledges what the sender is saying. The same kinds of activities occur – nodding, smiling, encouraging noises ('um-hm'), leaning forward with interest, writing things down, but they are seen by Bavelas and her colleagues not as part of a turn-taking routine but as a continuous process in which both parties are involved. This means that we are now even more interested in these small contributions, often coming from the practitioner, which help in the construction of meaning.

Of course, there can also be grounding of words introduced by the practitioner, again involving both parties. If this happens in SFBT these are often strengths, useful qualities, things that the client can be complimented on. In other forms of therapy the practitioner might introduce technical words from their model and get the client to help ground them. We will see how and when this happens in subsequent chapters where sections of actual sessions will be presented and annotated.

Choosing key words

Bavelas and her co-workers have found three strands in their analysis of SFBT dialogues. Along with (positive and presuppositional) questions and formulations, the practitioner is engaged in 'lexical choice' – choosing which (if any) of the client's words to include, and which of their own to add. In normal everyday conversations this is such an unconscious competence that we do it without thinking – meeting a friend for a coffee or chatting over dinner with friends. However, therapy conversations are not normal and everyday; they are purposeful skilled activities designed to help someone talk about their situation in novel ways.

Look again at the Steve de Shazer excerpt from earlier. The client opens up to de Shazer's initial question by saying:

CLIENT: Well, right now I'm dealing with a drinking problem.

Most people would pick up on the 'drinking problem' piece of this utterance, and perhaps come back with something like 'How long have you had this drinking problem?' or simply 'a drinking problem?' de Shazer, on the other hand, picks up on the other element of the response:

DE SHAZER: You say 'right now' (with emphasis).

As he says this, de Shazer also talks over the client's attempt, 'Sometimes I drink – ', to expand on the drinking problem. But note that de Shazer is not rejecting or denying the client's language about a drinking problem. Indeed, he has been part of grounding that very topic. And he is choosing other words to pursue the next piece of the conversation – 'right now'. These words are there, at the surface, in the conversation. de Shazer could have overlooked them, but he didn't. This is a skill, and it's a skill that needs to be learned.

Staying with the client's words

You will probably notice the importance of listening to, and using, the client's actual words. This requires close attention. This focus is helped by the fact that we are not trying to 'understand' or interpret the client in the conventional sense. Hear the words, pick key words, help them to expand. This is important for two reasons – practical and ethical.

The practical implications are neatly illustrated by Ferdinand Wolf in his chapter in *Encounters with Steve de Shazer and Insoo Kim Berg* (Wolf, 2015). Wolf saw Steve de Shazer ask a client what might be the benefits of their work together, and she replied 'I would prwldbdl'. de Shazer continued, 'And if you would prwldbdl for some time, what difference would that make for you?' An answer came, the conversation continued, various possibilities were examined, and finally de Shazer came into the consulting room (behind the mirror) and asked 'Can anyone tell me, what the hell does 'prwldbdl' mean?' Wolf observed that de Shazer was quite happy to use this 'word' as he didn't need to know what it meant, only to use it to progress the conversation. The client, who was quite happy with the session, seemed to know what it meant, and that was enough.

The ethical reason why this is so important – to me at least – comes from the work of German philosopher Jürgen Habermas. In his 1971 book *Knowledge and Human Interests* (Habermas, 1971), he writes about violence as 'systematically distorted communication'. When we change the client's language, we do violence to them. I have come to see the valuing of the client's language in SFBT as an ethical stance. If we are to change it directly by proposing a 'better' word, then we are taking control away from the client about how they express themselves. This is, for me, akin to kidnapping them and leaving them stranded in an unknown location, all the while insisting that it's for the best.

And of course, Steve de Shazer was well aware of this too. In his paper 'Radical Acceptance' (de Shazer, 1997) he writes:

> It turns out that clients are more reasonable than we expect and they can be counted on to modify their views once we have accepted them. Such modification is, however, unlikely if the therapist points out the unrealistic nature of the client's picture of the miracle or suggests that their rating is somehow 'wrong'. The client's answer needs to be accepted fully and literally – this is where the art of the approach comes into things.
>
> (de Shazer, 1997, p. 378)

This may be simple but, as de Shazer says in the paper, many people find it far from easy! The skill of both 'emptying your own head' (so as not to attempt to interpret what the client says from your own experience, and at the same time to 'stay out of the client's head' (so as not to attempt to hypothesise what is 'behind' the client's words) is a tough ask. It comes with practice to those who can take time to work with it.

The value of seeing description-building as a key process, and the insights from microanalysis discussed earlier, give a much fuller picture of how this acceptance is not an end but a start. The client's first words are fine – and yet there is always the possibility of more to say.

The role of the practitioner ...

Having taken this tour around some different views of what the practitioner is, and is not, doing in SFBT, we can make a summary. The role of the practitioner is to stretch the world of the client, by grounding tiny interactional detail in the therapeutic conversation:

- To acknowledge the client's problematic situation (without adding to it)
- To be very interested in how the client would notice progress
- To help the client establish their best hopes, the 'theme' of the work

- To help the client build descriptions of different scenes from their everyday life with these best hopes realised, in the future, present and past, from their own and others' perspectives
- To help the client make a start on these descriptions with 'large' questions like a miracle question, scaling questions etc. (first level)
- To help the client add concrete, observable, tiny detail to these descriptions using 'small' questions like 'what difference would that make?', 'what would be the first tiny sign that [person X] would notice?', etc. (second level)
- To participate with the client in the conversation, to keep going and explore further, by small co-ordinated acts including nodding, smiling, writing, leaning forward, saying things like 'um-hm', often as the client is talking, as well as asking questions and making statements (third level)
- To form questions, formulations and choose words from the client to help them focus on words which are connected to the client's hopes and useful experience, and therefore overlook other words which may be more connected to problems and stuckness.

This is quite a list. Fortunately, we will be examining how it all works in practice in subsequent chapters, where actual therapeutic conversations will be shown with a commentary to help see these points in action.

For the sake of clarity, here are some things which are not usually the role of an SF practitioner:

- 'Diagnose' the client's problems – even if they agree with you
- Tell the client specifically what they should do next
- Try to explain the client's unhappy situation
- To introduce big words and ideas which come from their own experience and knowledge rather than the practitioner
- Interpret the client's situation according to some prior model rather than simply letting the descriptions speak for themselves.

This chapter has been very much about *what* the practitioner does. It is firmly based on deploying expertise in listening, question framing, description building and summarising.

Key points

- The role of the practitioner has evolved over the years, from a task-builder through various intermediate stages to a description-builder and world-stretcher.
- This involves very careful listening indeed to the clients' exact words.
- Taking a 'not-knowing' or beginner's mind position – about the client, their experience and their hopes – is key.

- Building descriptions is a good practical way to avoid the muddles described by Ludwig Wittgenstein and stay out of the potential mess of explanation.
- Recent research in microanalysis of SFBT sessions has shown the importance of retaining positive elements client language in questions and formulations (statements).
- The co-construction of the therapy session is the result of both parties working together continuously with engaged gestures and encouragement rather than a neat question–and–answer process.
- Clear focus on client language, 'radical acceptance', is valuable from both practical and ethical standpoints.

References

Bavelas, J. B. (2011). Connecting the lab to the therapy room: Microanalysis, co-construction, and solution-focused therapy. In C. Franklin, T. Trepper, W. J. Gingerich, & E. McCollum (Eds.), *Solution-Focused Brief Therapy: From Practice to Evidence-Informed Practice* (pp. 144–162). Oxford: Oxford University Press.

Bavelas, J. B. (2020). *Webpage of Janet Beavin Bavelas*. Retrieved from http://web.uvic.ca/psyc/bavelas/

Bavelas, J. B., De Jong, P., Smock Jordan, S., & Korman, H. (2014). The theoretical and research basis of co-constructing meaning in dialogue. *Journal of Solution-Focused Brief Therapy*, 2(2), 1–24.

Bavelas, J. B., Gerwing, J., & Healing, S. (2017). Doing mutual understanding: Calibrating with micro-sequences in face-to-face dialogue. *Journal of Pragmatics*, 121, 91–112. Retrieved from http://web.uvic.ca/psyc/bavelas/2017%20Calibration.pdf

Bavelas, J. B., & Tomori, C. (2007). Using microanalysis of communication to compare solution-focused and client-centered therapies. *Journal of Family Psychotherapy*, 18(3), 25–43. doi:10.1300/J085v18n03-03

Clark. H. H. (1996). *Using Language*. Cambridge: Cambridge University Press.

De Jong, P., Bavelas, J. B., & Korman, H. (2013). An introduction to using microanalysis to observe co-construction in psychotherapy. *Journal of Systemic Therapies*, 32, 18–31.

De Jong, P., Smock Jordan, S., Healing, S., & Gerwing, J. (2020). Building miracles in dialogue: Observing co-construction through micro-analysis of calibration sequences. *Journal of Systemic Therapies*, 39(2), 85–109.

de Shazer, S. (1997). Radical acceptance: A commentary. *Families, Systems & Health*, 15(4), 375–378.

Habermas, J. (1971). *Knowledge and Human Interests* (Trans. Jeremy J. Shapiro). Boston: Beacon Press.

Harré, R. (2002). *Cognitive Science: A Philosophical Introduction*. London: Sage Publications.

Korman, H., Bavelas, J. B., & De Jong, P. (2013). Microanalysis of formulations in solution focused brief therapy, cognitive behavioural therapy and motivational interviewing. *Journal of Systemic Therapies*, 32(3), 31–45.

McGee, D. R., Del Vento, A., & Bavelas, J. B. (2005). An interactional model of questions as therapeutic interventions. *Journal of Marital and Family Therapy*, 31, 371–384.

Smock Jordan, S., Froerer, A., & Bavelas, J. B. (2013). Microanalysis of positive and negative content in solution-focused brief therapy and cognitive behavioral therapy expert sessions. *Journal of Systemic Therapies*, 32, 47–60.

Watzlawick, P., Bavelas, J. B., & Jackson, D. (1967). *Pragmatics of Human Communication: A Study of Interactional Patterns, Pathologies and Paradoxes*. New York, NY: W. W. Norton.

Wittgenstein, L. (1953). *Philosophical Investigations* (Trans. G. E. M. Anscombe). New York, NY: Macmilllan.

Wolf, F. (2015). Three episodes with Steve de Shazer: Personal and professional. In M. Vogt, F. Wolf, P. Sundman, & H. N. Dreesen (Eds.), *Encounters with Steve de Shazer and Insoo Kim Berg: Inside Stories of Solution-Focused Brief Therapy* (pp. 183–186). London: Solutions Books.

Next generation Solution Focused practice

Chapter 8

Introducing the Solution Focused art gallery

Solution Focused (SF) practice has always been a very flexible occupation. One of the challenges in teaching it and helping people understand it is that the second-by-second focus (of building a therapeutic conversation) can seem ill at ease with the architecture of a session (perhaps across an hour of work).

The focus on description development lets us include a high-level metaphor which can help. As the session goes along, the practitioner will help the client to construct a series of descriptions of their life both in the future (after the miracle, with things going better with regard to their hopes) or of episodes in the past and present which support that better future. In this way, the client will leave the session having experienced themselves in different moments in time. One way to look at this is like visiting an art gallery – seeing different pictures on the walls, which are linked by the theme of the exhibition.

From questions to 'rooms' and 'tools'

Questions have always been at the heart of Solution Focused Brief Therapy (SFBT). Indeed, the original videos produced by the Brief Family Therapy Center (BFTC) showing Steve de Shazer and Insoo Kim Berg at work are subtitled to help viewers keep up with what's happening in the session. The titles say, 'Miracle Question', 'Scaling Question' and so on. The focus is on the question. There are now even books collecting huge numbers of 'SF questions' (for example, Bannink, 2010), as if a question alone can be 'solution-focused'. (Any question can be asked in a myriad of different ways, and only some of them might be SF.)

Of course such questions are an important element of SF practice. However, the point of these questions is not simply to be asked – it is to start or build on a section of the interview/session. A miracle question and a single answer may make a little progress, but the real meat lies in what happens next – the expansion of the answers into descriptions in conversation. It therefore makes sense to focus on these chunks of conversation rather than the questions alone, as discrete elements.

So, a 'better future' conversation is a starting question (perhaps a miracle question) PLUS all the follow ups about first tiny signs that the miracle has happened, who else might notice, what would they notice, what happens next, what difference that makes, to whom, and so on. And then there are all the tiny responses, 'mm's, nods, gestures by the practitioner in grounding the conversation and encouraging the client. This has of course always been part of SF practice; our attention is now drawn even more to the 'small' questions and responses in between these big set-piece questions which tend to mark the start of a whole new section of the conversation.

The art gallery

Chris Iveson and others have introduced an 'art gallery' metaphor for a therapy conversation. Somewhat typically Chris is a little shy about his role in this; it was taken up by Elliott Connie (2015), I mentioned it (McKergow, 2016), as did Adam Froerer (2017) and Froerer, von Sziffra-Bergs, Kim and Connie (2018). The idea has subsequently been used by Peter Röhrig and Martina Scheinecker (2019) among others. This art gallery has a series of rooms with different things to look at and examine (Figure 8.1). These rooms might include:

- Ticket office – getting some best hopes from the client, a 'ticket' to proceed with the work
- Future Gallery – a set of pictures or descriptions of a better future for the client and those around them with these best hopes realised
- Instances Gallery – a set of pictures or images of instances in the past or present that connect with this preferred future (which may be constructed using a scale from 1–10)
- Gift Shop – the final room, which may feature a series of pictures or images of N + 1, smaller vignettes or signs along the way that progress is being made. Stopping here is optional!

These are not the only possible rooms. Adam Froerer talks of a Resources room (Froerer, 2017), where different elements of the client's life showing their resources are gathered. The point of this metaphor is that once inside the gallery (with a ticket or project), the rooms may be visited in any order, and different amounts of time spent in each room. Although there is definitely a direction of travel implied from entrance to exit, during the session the client and therapist may spend more time in one room than in others, may go back and revisit something, or perhaps discover something else they hadn't noticed before, and so on. This is not a route map but a guide to what will inevitably be an individual journey.

These 'rooms' help the practitioner keep track of where they are and what's going on in the conversation. It's generally good to stay in one room for a while, not dash frantically from one room to another. If, during a future conversation, an interesting and relevant 'instance' appears, the therapist may make a note of it and go to visit it later rather than diverting immediately to see it now and losing the thread of the preferred future conversation. Therapist and

A solution-focused art gallery

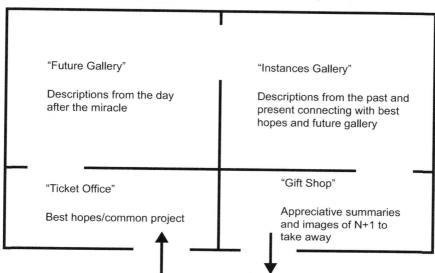

Figure 8.1 A solution-focused art gallery

client can move from room to room together, backtracking if necessary. The key distinction here is making the most of each room or phase (examining the detail of the different works which turn out to be on show) rather than leaping between rooms (a tendency I observe in many beginners to SFBT who seem to want to apply all the ideas at once).

This development was presaged by the work of Jackson and McKergow (2002/2007) on 'solutions tools'. These too were an attempt to find a larger unit of conversation than the question/answer, to help learner practitioners and coaches keep track. Jackson and McKergow attempted to give snappy names to these tools, such as Future Perfect (preferred future) and Counters (including instances and also relevant resources).

Jackson and McKergow's terms don't always translate well into other languages, but they have proved durable over the past two decades in helping practitioners to make the most of the conversation they are having (by sticking with it) rather than rushing off to other conversations when a tempting morsel is dangled by the client. There is also the advantage that the tools concept does not impose a 'correct order' for the tools to be utilised, giving flexibility to the practitioner within an easy-to-carry framework.

It can be useful for the practitioner to appreciatively summarise each scene and each room before moving on. This gives another chance for key words to be grounded, consolidating the new descriptions and for direct and indirect complimenting. We will now take a tour of all four of these main rooms.

Key points

- Attention has moved away from the 'set-piece questions' of SFBT (miracle, scaling and so on) and onto the way the conversation is developed following these questions.
- These sections of conversation can be likened to rooms in an art gallery, where the client's descriptions may be found and admired in any order.
- The main rooms in the SF art gallery include (but are not limited to)

  - The ticket office – getting some best hopes from the client, a 'ticket' to proceed with the work.
  - The future gallery – a set of pictures or descriptions of a better future for the client and those around them with these best hopes realised.
  - The instances gallery – a set of pictures or images of instances in the past or present that connect with this preferred future (which may be constructed using a scale from 1–10).
  - The gift shop – the final room, which may feature a series of pictures or images of N + 1, smaller vignettes or signs along the way that progress is being made.

- Smaller description-building questions can be used to build individual descriptions in each room.
- Appreciative summarising is a useful way to conclude a visit to one room before moving to the next.

References

Bannink, F. (2010). *1001 Solution-Focused Questions*. New York, NY: W. W. Norton.

Connie, E. (2015). *3 Things to Make Using SFBT Easier*. Retrieved from www.elliottconnie. com/3-things-to-make-using-sfbt-easier/

Froerer, A. (2017, March 31). *The Power of Solution Focused Language*. Presentation at the Solution Focused Safari Conference, Johannesburg, South Africa.

Froerer, A., von Sziffra Bergs, J., Kim, J. S., & Connie, E. (Eds.). (2018). *Solution-Focused Brief Therapy with Clients Managing Trauma*. Oxford: Oxford University Press.

Jackson, P. Z., & McKergow, M. (2002/2007). *The Solutions Focus: The SIMPLE Way to Positive Change* (1st ed.). London: Nicholas Brealey Publishing.

McKergow, M. (2016). SFBT 2.0: The next generation of Solution Focused Brief Therapy has already arrived. *Journal of Solution Focused Brief Therapy, 2*(2), 1–17.

Röhrig, P., & Scheinecker, M. (2019). *Lösungsfokussiertes Konflikt-Management in Organisationen*. Bonn, Germany: managerSeminare Verlags.

Chapter 9

The Ticket Office
Permission to start/enter

In our art gallery view of Solution Focused Brief Therapy (SFBT), we meet the client at the ticket office. We start by trying to get a 'ticket' – to see if we can find a project where the client wishes to change some aspect of their life. This is the first step in building a world stretching conversation, and it is a defining part of Solution Focused (SF) work; the client themselves plays a decisive part in deciding what the project is to be about. There may of course be other constraints, about which we can be open and honest. However, the client will ultimately decide what the work is to be about and choose how they wish to engage with it.

This is all a long way from expert diagnosis, where the practitioner will call the shots about what is wrong and what should be done. Of course the client may arrive with the words of other experts ringing in their ears, leading them to perhaps be expecting some kind of medical consultation. Getting things off on the right foot is perhaps the most important part of SFBT; once we have a project and an engaged client, the other elements of the work begin to flow naturally.

A word of confession; when I wrote *The Solutions Focus* with Paul Z Jackson decades ago (Jackson & McKergow, 2002), I thought this part of the work was relatively easy and so didn't give it much explicit attention. I was wrong. I have come to realise in the ensuing years that this is the crux of SF practice. If a project can be negotiated, everything else begins to fall into place. If the project is vaguely defined or over-simplified, then the subsequent work can start to get muddled. Getting a sound basis at the outset is perhaps the most important step in building towards solutions with our clients. And the project sometimes evolves along the way.

Defining a common project

When we meet our clients, we usually have no idea what they want. We may have an idea about how come they were referred to us, or some inkling about problematic circumstances. We have perhaps heard stories about them from colleagues, about how they are and how difficult others have found them. The first thing is to set all that aside. We are keen to meet the clients as people, not as problems or diagnoses. Starting with an open 'beginner mind', at least about the clients themselves, is key.

We may need to gather some basic information from the clients, their names and addresses, ages, circumstances, referrals, perhaps medical information. Some people like to do this in a separate room and even with a different person taking the details, to emphasise that this is not a part of the therapeutic conversation, which is going to be about a better life for the client.

Getting a ticket

We are hoping to work with the client to establish that they want something better in their lives, something which will make a useful difference to them (and perhaps to others), and that is important enough for them to start working towards today. You may recall that in some versions of SFBT there were experiments about seeing whether the client was in a customer, complainer or visitor relationship at the start. A customer broadly satisfied the criteria from earlier, a complainer saw that there was a problem but didn't see themselves in having a role in working on it, and a visitor saw no problem and no need for change at all (de Shazer, 1988).

These days we are much more inclined to assume that everyone is a customer for something. They may not know immediately exactly what they seek, and so it's our role as practitioners to sit with them and encourage them to think about it. This is sometimes quite straightforward; on other occasions it can take time and considerable skill.

The 'ticket' is going to tell us the theme for the work, the 'common project' (Korman, 2004). It's like the title of the exhibition in the SF art gallery, the theme that binds all the different descriptions together. It plays a key role in the way that the client 'joins the dots' and draws conclusions and inspiration from the conversations. The client will define this in the end, in their own words (rather than professional therapy or medical language). We don't want to teach the client how we as professionals may think about their situation, we want to expand their own language and thinking about it to open up new possibilities. We want the client to be trusting their own language and judgement as much as possible rather than making decisions about them and for them at the outset and then having to wean them back into the picture.

Not a goal

We saw in earlier chapters how the role of goals has changed over the years in SFBT. At the very start, the idea of goal-focused therapy was already a big step away from the traditional aim of building insight rather than 'mere' new behaviour. The brief therapy tradition takes the view that changes in the here and how can move the situation on, with no need to excavate the past. SFBT goals were typically small rather than large, behavioural and specific rather than abstract and internal (feelings, emotions etc) and appeared in the initial stages of treatment.

What is the purpose of a goal? Where I come from, in the organisational sphere, goals are used to drive action and determine success. We agree that we want to sell 1000 widgets by the end of the year or land a man on the moon by the end of the decade, and we get on with it. There is a clear success criterion, and we will know if we get there or not. A time element is crucial – without a deadline, it's just a dream (as a top-line US consultant once told me).

It seems to me that SF goals have never really worked in that way. They were not an end point for the client but a sign that treatment is moving the right way and can be ended. They are part of setting a direction, making things smaller and nearer (as do many of our methods). They are rarely used to determine success – that's up to the client at the time. They are more likely to be used as milestones along the path to something better.

Another and much clearer question is whether the common project is a goal. It is not. There may well be goals in the client's life, and they form part of the context for the work. We will later see a session transcript where the client, at school, has important exams coming up which cannot be dodged and at which they wish to succeed. The work will not be about passing the exams or not (a goal) but about equipping the client to work more effectively at school (and also move on from self-harming into the bargain). The goal forms part of the backdrop to the work rather than being the key factor.

What are your best hopes?

Having carried out any formalities, the session begins. There are all kinds of things we can ask the client at the outset, all of which will carry some form of expectation or presupposition. We can rule out a few candidates to start with:

*   **'What's the problem?'** – is clearly about what is thought (very possibly by someone else) to be wrong with the client and is not what we are interested in at all.
*   **'How can I help you?'** – clearly suggests that the practitioner will be doing the helping, whereas we are more keen to imply that the client will be doing much of the work.
*   **'What brings you in?'** is again likely to be construed as being about the problem.

We want an opening that immediately points the client towards the future rather than the past, and towards a better future at that. One question which does this well (at least in English) is

*   **'What are your best hopes for our work together?'**

Look at the presuppositions. We will be working together, which sets the ground for a co-operative relationship. What are your hopes? The Oxford dictionary definition of hope as a noun is:

a feeling of expectation and desire for a particular thing to happen

So for something to be a hope, is should be both desirable and somehow possible. This is quite subtle. A paradigmatic example is a client who has lost their arm in an accident. They may well 'wish' that their arm would return – but they cannot really 'hope' that it will (pending some dramatic development in medical and cyborg science).

A hope is a good place to start. A 'best hope' asks the client to think as big as they can, at the top end of the scale, for what might just conceivably be possible. One of the key elements of SF work is combining big thinking with tiny details and signs, and this is a place to encourage the client to think as big as they can. I acknowledge here that the translation of 'best hopes' into other languages including German, Spanish and Finnish is not straightforward – experimentation is needed.

Possible initial answers to 'best hopes?'

Sometimes, the client will respond with a neat statement of things they are hoping for. At that point, we can accept it and begin to expand on it by asking 'what difference would that make for you?' and so on. But sometimes that doesn't happen.

'...' (Thoughtful or puzzled silence)

Don't panic, and don't say anything for now! This is a somewhat unusual question, and so may well take some thinking about. Wait. Pay attention. Don't interrupt. Let the client work for themselves. Some practitioners seem to be nervous of silence and think they must have asked the question 'wrongly'. No, your client is just thinking. Wait. Please.

'I don't know ...'

This can sometimes follow a thoughtful silence and might get a similar response. Of course they don't know ... yet. It will take some thinking about. Keep them thinking. Nod slowly. Say something like 'yes, it's a tough question ...'. Don't change the subject, for a while at least.

'My problem is that ...'

Sometimes people will want to tell you about their problems and difficulties anyway. Perhaps they expect to be asked about it. Perhaps they have been rehearsing it on the way over to see you. Whatever, it happens sometimes. Once again, don't panic. If there is ever to be a time for problem talk in an SF session, it is now. Listen hard, accept what they say and look for a chance to get back to their best hopes. This is a good time to use the circles of acknowledgement and progress.

Circles of acknowledgement and progress

One simple model I like to use when teaching or reflecting on my own practice is the circles of acknowledgement and progress. Imagine two circles on the ground – the circle of acknowledgement and the circle of progress (Figure 9.1). You are standing with a foot in each circle.

As an SF practitioner, you are looking to balance acknowledgement questions/statements and progress questions/statements. You therefore stand with a foot in each circle. When things are going well, and the client is talking about 'better', then you can shift your weight onto the progress foot. You will be asking questions to expand on 'better'. However, you still keep the 'acknowledgement' foot in contact with the ground, as you will still be looking for chances to acknowledge the client's tough situation, their coping, their struggle. A lot of SF work looks like this – plenty of questions about 'better'.

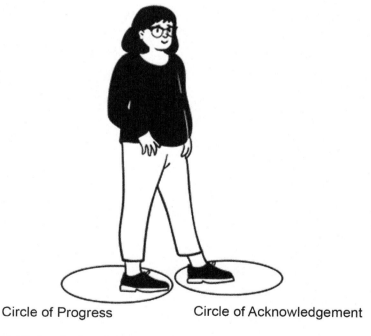

Circle of Progress   Circle of Acknowledgement

Figure 9.1 Circles of acknowledgement and progress

However, if the client is finding things tough or challenging, then you may want to put more weight on the 'acknowledgement' foot. Slow down. Accept that the client is finding it tough for now. You can do this, as de Shazer did in the short microanalysis example in Chapter 7, with as little as a 'mm–hm'. This is not being problem-focused, it's taking the client seriously. Sometimes if they don't think we've heard or recognised their struggle, they want to tell us again and be less inclined to come along with our progress questions.

The idea is that we never lose contact with either circle. There will always be chances to acknowledge, and always clues which may lead to progress. Even if we shift our weight from one foot to the other, both are always on the ground. If we only look for progress, we may risk trying to go faster than the client. If we only look to acknowledge, things may slow down or even stop.

In this opening phase of the conversation in the Ticket Office, we can look to acknowledge the problems and difficulties, and at the same time look for anything in the client's responses which may be somehow connected with a better future. For example:

CLIENT: It's been awful. ... I have been stuck in the house, afraid to go outside, not seeing anyone for weeks on end ... if only I could see my sister ...
PRACTITIONER: Ooh, that's tough. *(Acknowledging.)* So ... you'd like to see your sister? *(Progress based on what the client has said.)*

Expanding on best hopes

Once the client starts to talk about hopes for the future, we can start to build on them. Listen carefully for the client's key words – remember that we are looking to preserve as much of the client's language as possible in a spirit of respect, pragmatism and efficiency.

Often the client may start out with a hope that is not really their only concern but is part of a bigger picture. So for example:

• 'I want to get a job'
• 'I'd like to be in a relationship'
• 'I'd like to be back in school'.

These are all steps towards something else. They look like goals, but they are more like routes to something else. And there is a way we can move immediately towards exploring those bigger issues.

'What difference would that make?'

This question is one we will meet again and again in the next few chapters. It encourages the client to place their words into a broader context, to think about how they hope things might develop, to start to connect with the benefits of change. Note that 'what difference' is a neutral question, which allows both positive and negative answers. In practice though, if the client is thinking about a hope for the future, the differences will usually be positive. Don't worry if a negative one comes along though – it's all part of weighing things up.

'Who else would notice a difference? What difference would they notice?'

This is part of expanding the project to involve other people, at least in the picture of those who have an interest. Remember, in SF everything happens from someone's point of view. So it's important to identify who exactly might be noticing differences when hopes begin to be realised. Find out the names as well as the relationships (apart perhaps from Mum and Dad or however the client refers to them, if they are in the picture). So it's best friend Jackie, Rob at the gym, Rhona the hairdresser, Mr Grimsdale the boss, and so on. We will be using this tactic even more when we get into future descriptions in the next chapter.

'What else?'

For some people this is the definitive SF question. It's certainly one which can be used in many situations once the client has begun to list things which are somehow connected with an element or description of a better future, or instances with their past. Don't ask it when they are telling you about their problems though (as one novice student of mine did and was surprised at quite how many problems their client had!).

A name for the project

To make questions in the following sections of an SF session flow well, it's useful to be able to refer to the best hopes by some kind of code name. Sometimes the words of the client can give you this directly, which is a good option. Sometimes things get more complicated and longer, where there may be different aspects and people involved. In those cases, I like to ask the client to propose a good name for the project, an idea I got from Ben Furman and now use all the time.

This has a number of useful functions. It sums up the conversation so far, giving a sense of closing this part before we move on. It gives the client a chance to come up with their own name, to which they feel some attachment and investment. And the name can then be used as part of future questions in a neat and effective way. Whether or not you choose to explicitly find a name, you will be wanting a phrase, preferably from the client, to use to refer to the project, their hopes, the differences those hopes would make and everything else. The name is best in short and useable form, a word or a short phrase.

PRACTITIONER: So, what would be a good name for this project about your hopes for (x, y and z)?
CLIENT: (pause) How about 'Lively Health'?
PRACTITIONER: (writing it down) Lively Health ... excellent!

Having a name for the project makes more difference than it should, in my experience. It sums up what may have been quite an involved piece of conversation, it can stand for it in questions, it seems to help the client think about the work as something they have defined and have the leading role in. And it literally only takes a moment.

In his later years, Steve de Shazer used to often say to the client at this point that 'there are no guarantees but I promise to do my best and I hope you will too', while looking expectantly for a confirming nod or response. This has the effect of clarifying that this will be an active process for the client and firmly enlists them in the work.

Case example 1: Mary and the cuddle

The following chapters feature extracts from actual SF sessions. These are verbatim transcripts, and so include some natural stumbles, ems and ers and small noises/contributions. We saw in chapter 7 how even these little parts of a conversation have a role in grounding and calibrating what is being said between the participants. These conversations were, of course, improvised in the moment and so are not perfect. It is the imperfections that help to show the actual practice, as opposed to the in-principle simplification.

This first case example shows how brief this process can be. This case concerns Mary, a woman in her mid-40s who attended BRIEF in London, referred by her GP following depression and the GP's concern at the risk of suicide. We will meet her again in Chapter 10 in her Future Gallery. The practitioner is P, the client C.

Session Transcript	Commentary
(The session starts with a moment's conversation about the practice of SF and what it's about, which has been edited out.)	Mary, familiar with other forms of therapy, had asked about SF.
P: Okay, so what are your best hopes from it? If it turns out to work for you, what do you...?	'It' is the treatment process, which had been discussed in the abstract a moment before.
C: Well, just as I said to no longer be ... I feel like I am vacuumed and sucked into the past and that it has a massive control over who I am today. It affects every bit of my being.	Client's first answer is (as often happens) about what's wrong for her, not (yet) her best hopes ... and it's still a starting point.
P: Sure.	Practitioner is acknowledging client and listening for key words.
C: I can't ... you know, I just want ... I have always ... I have started to compare myself to like a butterfly. I feel I am trapped in that cycle and I am not able to just ... it might sound ridiculous but just be free and to fly. You know?	

Session Transcript	Commentary
P: And if you could, what difference do you think that would make?	The first of our 'building' questions ...
C: I think just ... you know, a very simple, pure, like you know, basis for me looking into this. It is just to find a way to be at peace with who I am.	
P: Okay.	'acceptance of where I have come from, but hope for where I am going'
C: You know? To kind of have a level of acceptance of where I have come from, but hope for where I am going and a bit more focus on that.	
P: And if you did have more kind of hope for where you are going and if the past no longer can kind of mess with your future, what difference do you hope that will start to make in your life?	And again ... note that the practitioner is keeping it small, 'what difference do you hope that will *start to make* in your life'.
C: I think I will be more emotionally balanced. That I will be probably more consistent in who I am and my being. You know? Because I feel I could have, maybe even in a day, I can change from being positive and hopeful to being depressed, negative, scared. So it just sucks me back in. every time I have it, I am gone. It looks like a magnet bringing me back.	
P: Okay.	OK, now we are getting towards a workable project.
C: I'm probably making no sense, aren't I?	
P: Hold on. so look, if tonight while you are asleep a miracle happened and it didn't get rid of the past, but it stopped the past messing with your future, but you were asleep when it happened so you didn't know, what is the first thing you notice when you wake up tomorrow that began to tell you this sense of peace and acceptance?	Practitioner has listened hard and boldly summarises what he has heard of the client's best hopes ('it didn't get rid of the past, but it stopped the past messing with your future') into a miracle question, moving on to the next stage of the work.

This takes no more than a moment or two. One might say that the practitioner could have confirmed the project with the client a little more firmly, but he has listened hard and taken the client's words very seriously. We will see how things develop in the next chapter.

Case example 2: putting things up in my room

The client is a 16-year-old school student, referred by the school, who were concerned about fragility in exams, especially as there are important tests just around the corner. The school also informed the practitioner that they have previously self-harmed. We met this client briefly in Chapter 7, during their exploration of entering a classroom after the miracle.

This is quite a long Ticket Office conversation. It illustrates the practitioner's patience and skill at keeping the conversation going and developing a solid ticket for the project.

Session transcript	Commentary
(A bit of preamble around filling in forms has been deleted from the start of the session)	
P: So, what would be your best hopes for, for these sessions? So we can have up to six in total ... erm ... What would you like to get from them? What would be your best hopes from them?	Starting right away by asking for best hopes.
C: Like ... To feel better about myself. P: Ok.	This is a very normal and workable answer. It's a bit vague but that's quite OK at this stage, we can build on it and explore it.
C: Is that right?	It seems the client may be a bit nervous ... the practitioner puts her at her ease.
P: Well, there's no wrong answers, absolutely not. ... They're all right. ... So to feel better about yourself, yeah ... and if you were able to achieve that, yeah, so if you were able to start feeling better about yourself, what difference do you think that would make?	Building on the initial answer with 'what difference would that make?'
C: I'd have more self-confidence ... P: uh-huh ...	(No doubt the practitioner is noting down some key words here – 'self-confidence') Practitioner encourages client to keep going ...
C: and I wouldn't feel like such a failure.	This is a 'negative' – they wouldn't feel like that. So practitioner works to discover what would be happening (much more interesting from an SF perspective) with 'instead'.
P: So greater self-confidence and wouldn't feel like such a failure; what would you be thinking and feeling instead? If you weren't thinking that you were a failure, what would replace that?	
C: That actually ... it is ... That I am doing ok, and it's not as bad as my mind makes me think it is.	

Session transcript	Commentary
P: So actually you are doing ok and it's not as bad as ...	Practitioner reflects these useful words to encourage client to keep going – 'Rogers with a twist ...'
C: My mind thinks it is ... I always think I'm failing when I'm not.	
P: So start to feel better which would lead to greater self-confidence, this kind of knowledge that actually I am doing ok, rather than your mind telling you that it is bad, that you are a failure ... ok ... What else do you think? What else would feeling better and having this self-confidence lead to?	Practitioner summarises what the client has said so far about what she wants, using the actual words, and asks 'what else?' to keep it going.
C: I wouldn't panic as much. I'd be able to go into exams properly.	Aha. Another angle from the client.
P: Ok ... So going into exams properly ... What does that ... err ... look like for you?	Practitioner seeking descriptive clarity here.
C: Stay in the exam and not have a panic attack and come out.	
P: Ok ...	
C: Cause I can't do that in the real ones.	(Client is referring to 'mock' exams, trial runs for the actual exams which come later)
P: So to be able to stay in the exams ... And what would you ... In terms of your hopes again ... erm ... when you say 'stay in exams' would that be for the whole of the exams, or half the exams?	Practitioner links this back to hopes and clarifies again.
C: Whole of the exam.	
P: Whole of the exam, ok ...	
C: Cause sometimes I can but then ... if I panic, then I come out.	'Sometimes I can'.
P: Ok ...	
C: Well like ... sometimes I'm like panicking but I'm like 'ok', I calm myself in the exam and then sometimes like the invigilators will say to come out cause I'll be panicking too much or I'll say that I can't breathe.	We are perhaps getting a little side tracked here ... The client seems quite chatty about it, which is potentially useful. Practitioner accepts and looks to turn the conversation around to hopes again.

(Continued)

(Continued)

Session transcript	Commentary
P: So sometimes you're able to calm yourself ... in exams yeah? When was the last time you managed to do that? C: In the mocks last week.	Practitioner has picked up on the 'sometimes' in the previous client statement and wants to bring attention to it. It's a bit early to be looking for an Instance, but in this case it's a way of turning the conversation from 'panic' to 'calm'.
P: In the mocks last week ... Ok ... What exams were the mocks that you had last week? C: Every lesson.	Practitioner looking to show an interest in the details here – there may be particular instances where things are better, for use later on.
P: Every lesson, ok ... C: It was like ... Our last mocks before the real thing. P: Ok, and how many of those did you ... well roughly how many did you have first of all? Doesn't have to be exact ...	Practitioner keeping up with the 'Rogers with a twist' reflecting here to keep the client going. Not much of a twist in fact, just reflecting which is good practice at this point to keep the client moving along. This is a trace of the co-creating way in microanalysis where both parties are moving together to put down the next conversational elements.
(They briefly explore how the client managed to stay calm in the exams last week. It seems relevant and the practitioner wants to ground some of these descriptions, possibly to return to later.)	
P: Ok, perfect ... Alright ... Let's just nip back to your best hopes, so far we've got this idea of starting to feel better, which will increase your self-confidence, know that you're actually doing ok and you'll be able to go into exams 'properly' ... this idea of 'properly' and be able to stay in them ... Erm ... Is there anything else ... that you'd like to get from these sessions, that would ... I guess one way of putting it is if erm ... If we fast forwarded to a week's time, fast forward a week, erm ... And you're looking back on the week that's just been, erm, how would you know that this conversation had been useful for you? Had been helpful ...	Practitioner has known all along that they will want to come back to Best Hopes, as they have yet to really get a 'ticket' for the project. Summarising what's known so far ... Asking 'is there anything else?' ... as opposed to 'what else?' is probably good practice here – it is a less presuppositional question, which doesn't assume that there is something else but nonetheless opens the possibility for other angles. Asking for signs of progress within a week is another way to connect a big project with possible small details and signs.
C: I think they'll ... cause then they lead on to ... like if I feel better about myself then I wouldn't want to ... erm ... yeah ... to ... erm ... self-harm.	This is the first we've heard from the client about self-harming. I don't think the practitioner was 'fishing' for the client to talk about it, but it's emerged now at the client's behest. They have mentioned it in the context of not wanting to do it, which is a useful angle from an SF perspective.

Session transcript	Commentary
P: Ok, so you wouldn't want to self-harm, yeah ... and what would ...	
C: Cause ...	
P: Yeah go on ...	
C: Cause I do that when I feel like I'm failing.	
P: Aha, ok ... right ... so are you thinking that, if you started to actually think that you're doing ok ... and staying in exams, growing in self-confidence, that that would actually lead to something different about the self-harm? I mean what difference would it make do you think?	Practitioner neatly constructing a formulation, and then a question which is about alternatives to self-harm. 'What difference would that make?' is a wonderfully open and powerful question when it is directed (as here) onto something useful happening.
C: Well I wouldn't feel as much need to do it because I would believe in myself more.	
P: Ok ... and what would you like to do instead of, you know instead of this self-harming? What would you like to see instead?	Practitioner is going after 'instead' of self-harm. We might note that the client has already mentioned it, and will draw attention to it again below.
C: I don't really understand ...	
P: Erm ... so if you ... if you weren't self-harming ... what do you think that you'd ... you'd be doing instead? ... So when those ... correct me if I'm wrong but you were saying the self-harm is linked to this idea of feeling like a failure ...	
C: I'd be like more proud of myself.	Client already said 'I would believe in myself more', and now that they'd like to be 'more proud of myself'. Practitioner has now picked up on 'believe in myself' and 'more proud' and wants to spread the focus to other perspectives. Starts with a wide-open question about 'who else would notice?'
P: More proud of yourself, yeah ok ... and who would be ... who would be one of the first people to notice these sorts of changes? So if you started to believe in yourself more, be proud of yourself, have greater self-confidence ... who do you think would notice?	
C: Apart from myself?	
P: Yeah, yeah, who else would notice?	Reflecting and leaving the question open rather than taking the very first answer. We can always come back to the parents later.
C: Erm, my parents ...	

(Continued)

(Continued)

Session transcript	Commentary
P: Your parents ...	
C: And the teachers that I talk to.	
P: Yeah ... so which teachers do you talk to?	And another teacher. Let's find out more about that perspective ...
C: Mr R ... erm my art teacher Miss D, ... and Mrs P.	
P: Ok, how do you know Mrs P?	
C: Erm, she was my History teacher last year, but she went off ill so we couldn't have her this year, but I still talk to her now she's back ...	
P: Yeah	Could well be another very useful perspective.
C: Cause she helped me a lot last year ...	
P: Yeah ... so just before we move on, just erm ... start with your parents, what would they ... what would they notice about you that's different if you were able to start feeling proud of yourself, get this self-confidence and belief in yourself. ... What would your parents notice or see that's different?	Practitioner has indeed noted the parents from earlier, and now returns to their view. Again using the client's key words in constructing the question.
C: I don't put myself down as much.	
P: Ok, what would you be doing instead of putting yourself down?	And 'instead' is used again ...
C: Not chucking my work away.	
P: Ah, not chucking your work away, what would you do with your work instead?	And again ...
C: Like submit it or ... like put it up somewhere, cause if I'm proud of my work I put it up in my room.	Aha – this is something the client would be doing with their work. More useful.
P: Ah ...	
C: But I don't do that much because I don't like it.	

Session transcript	Commentary
P: Ok, so one of the ways that your parents would know, oh actually (name) is growing in confidence and belief, is more of your work would be going up in your room and being submitted rather than being thrown away ...	Very neat construction from practitioner who focuses on putting the work up and submitting it, but also acknowledges the throwing away (by putting it last in the sentence)
C: I do submit it in the end; I just have a lot of rubbish that goes before that.	
P: Ok ... alright ... and what about your teachers? If you were able to start getting this belief and self-confidence, what would your teachers notice about you?	Shifting to the teacher's perspectives. And bringing back belief and self-confidence from earlier.
C: I'd speak up more in lessons.	
P: Aha	Aha indeed – this is another new sign of something useful happening – good for building the 'ticket' or common project.
C: Cause that's like, that's why Mrs P started helping me, cause I didn't ever put my hand up ...	
P: Ah ...	
C: And she said she wanted to help me put my hand up once a lesson.	
P: Yeah	
C: Like at first ... and then my mum like told her, like that I struggle with it and stuff.	
P: Ok	
C: So then she kinda helped me along with it more.	
P: Have you been able to do that? Have you been able put your hand up more often?	Practitioner glancing at this Instance ... might have been a bit more presuppositional, asking 'how often have you been able to do that?'. But this conversation is improvised on the fly, and it doesn't make much difference at this point.
C: Sometimes ... like I try to do it at least once a lesson.	
P: Ok ... well we've got quite a list now! Sorry I'm running out of space! Erm, so ... would those be things that you yourself would be pleased about if you saw them? So, if you noticed yourself speaking up more in lessons?	Practitioner starts to sum up the project.

(Continued)

(Continued)

Session transcript	Commentary
C: Yeah.	
P: That would be something that you'd be pleased about ... and if you noticed yourself ... putting a few more things up in your room and submitting work with a bit more confidence ...	
C: A lot of stuff that's been put up in my room was like when I was 14.	
P: Really, ok, so not for a good couple of years.	
C: No ... it would be nice to swap it all around for ...	A nice confirmation from the client that she is ready to do something which could lead to some new work going up!
P: Yeah ... so swap some work around in your room with some more recent, yeah ... fantastic ... so we've got feeling better, so, so just to clarify really ... so if, if our sessions together were helpful, the ways that we'd know is that you'd start to feel better, you'd have this growing self-confidence, belief in yourself, you'd be able to go into exams properly and stay in them, you'd start to feel proud of yourself and that would be shown in actually there's some new, fresh work being put up in your room, err, and also you'd be able to speak up in lessons more as well. So does that sound about right?	Practitioner goes for a full summary of what we have so far about the project.

Well done practitioner! It really is quite a list, and the client's words are nicely kept at the heart of the scene. |
C: [nods]	
P: Ok ... is there anything that I've missed or that you want to add to that list?	A good moment for an 'anything else' question rather than 'what else?'. Give the client a chance to say 'No, nothing else'. Which they do.
C: No, that's about right.	
P: Ok, perfect ... so erm, next question's a slightly funny one *(goes into a miracle question to start building a future description)*	And we have a ticket! It might have been useful to condense all this into a name for the project, but anyway we are off and into the next stage of the session, entering the Future Gallery.

Reflections

This session extract offers a lot of good practice in action. The practitioner starts off by asking for the client's best hopes, and over the course of around 15 minutes takes the client's words and helps them expand them into a workable project based around differences for the client in their everyday life. This practitioner is very skilled at keeping hold of the client's language, offering it back for expansion and confirmation. We see grounding in action (De Jong, Bavelas & Korman, 2013), the three part process mentioned in Chapter 7, where a new element is first mentioned by the client, accepted by the practitioner and finally grounded by the client again. (This is happening through the session, often without clear statements but rather using um-hm type noises and gestures – a full microanalysis transcript would be extremely dense and hard to follow over this length of conversation.)

The practitioner allows themselves to get interested in a couple of Instances of better things already happening to the client. Although this is not strictly part of this Ticket Office conversation, the practitioner may be noting these events and, by mentioning them, let the client know that they are potentially relevant too. They may come into the conversation again in more detail later.

At the end of the transcript, the practitioner sums up the project, and the client agrees that this is what they want to work towards. The ticket is stamped, as it were, and the work begins ... except that this initial phase of the session is very definitely already work. It can be surprising how motivating and encouraging it can be for a client to be setting out on what looks like a useful journey rather than sitting still and worrying about it. The client's view of themselves and their situation has already changed, even though there has been no explicit discussion of what to do.

Key points

- The Ticket Office marks the start of a piece of SF work, where client and practitioner explore the client's best hopes for their work together.
- The 'ticket' is a description of a common project which will be the theme of the work, and of this particular exhibition in the art gallery, where descriptions from the client's life from future, present and past can be viewed.
- The practitioner encourages the client to talk about their best hopes, the differences they will make to themselves and others, in the future.
- The practitioner takes great care to use the client's language to help them expand and build the project definition, acknowledges the client's discomfort in the past and present and keeps a close eye for any words which give a hint of a desired future.
- The client may not always answer the question the first time it is offered, so the practitioner may need patience.

- Concluding this part of the work with a summary and perhaps a name for the project chosen by the client gives the signal to move on to building descriptions in the future (usually), or perhaps the present and past.

References

De Jong, P., Bavelas, J. B., & Korman, H. (2013). An introduction to using microanalysis to observe co-construction in psychotherapy. *Journal of Systemic Therapies, 32*, 18–31.

de Shazer, S. (1988). *Clues: Investigating Solutions in Brief Therapy.* New York, NY: W. W. Norton.

Jackson, P. Z., & McKergow, M. (2002). *The Solutions Focus: The SIMPLE Way to Positive Change* (1st ed.). London: Nicholas Brealey Publishing.

Korman, H. (2004). *The Common Project.* SIKT. Retrieved from www.sikt.nu/wp-content/uploads/2015/06/Creating-a-common-project.pdf

Chapter 10

The Future Gallery

Miracles, parallel worlds and more

Solution Focused (SF) work is often baldly described as 'future-focused'. As we will see in this chapter, discussions about the future play an important role in SF practice. It is perhaps more surprising that this role has grown even more important over the 30 years since Solution Focused Brief Therapy (SFBT) emerged as a distinctive field with the publication of Steve de Shazer's book *Clues: Investigating Solutions in Brief Therapy* (de Shazer, 1988), as we saw in earlier chapters.

In the previous chapter we discussed defining the common project, which is like getting a ticket to proceed to the next stages of the world stretching conversation. In this chapter we will examine how to build detailed descriptions of better futures for the client – life with their best hopes realised. This kind of conversation has changed over the years to assume ever-greater significance in SF work.

In early SFBT this kind of conversation was seen in large part as a prelude to goal-setting and a preparation for the search for relevant exceptions – times when the problem should have happened but didn't, or happened less. These were pointers to times when the client was (perhaps unwittingly) already doing something that helped them to avoid the problem, and therefore could be prescribed as something to 'do more of' to promote more conscious actions towards a life without the burden of the problem.

As SFBT evolved over the years, practitioners seem to have discovered that this description of a better life was more than simply a preparation; it served a significant therapeutic purpose in its own right. At the end of such a conversation, the client is often already coming to new realisations, new understandings and new framings of apparently insignificant everyday events. This is a part of 'stretching the world' of the client, where detailed descriptions and new possibilities come hand-in-hand. In next generation SFBT this is not a preparation for an intervention, it is a key element of the process.

In our art gallery metaphor this is often the second place to be visited after the Ticket Office. The practitioner will often seek to build descriptions of several scenes in the future, rather like different images on the gallery wall. However, this is not necessarily the first place to stop – there are other galleries waiting, like the Instances Gallery with descriptions of times when things have been better. However, it is a common move among practitioners to move to a description of the future early on – perhaps because the future is perceived as more malleable and negotiable than the past, and therefore an easier place to engage in creative thinking.

Breaking the causal link between past and future

Clients arrive burdened by both their past experiences and the thoughts of what future may lie ahead if things continue as they are. By invoking a miracle, the client is asked to consider a future which is unencumbered by past concerns. Miracles are inexplicable – by definition we don't know *how* they happen; we can only see the results. So, wondering about exactly how the transformation was achieved is completely unnecessary, impossible and irrelevant. Steve de Shazer used to observe that a miracle is 'an effect without a cause'. It's not a mysterious cause, but a completely ineffable occurrence – pausing to wonder even for a moment about how it happened is missing the point.

Once the causal link to the past has been broken, the client is liberated to imagine themselves in a better future which is not related to their illness, disorder, pain or problems. This is more than just 'solving the problem', it is thinking on into a life without the problem, or nowadays with the client's best hopes being realised. It can expand out to affect many aspects of everyday life for the client, their families, friends, colleagues, even pets. Many people have described to me that they begin even to feel lighter and become less burdened as the miracle description builds up.

It is not surprising, therefore, that the most common first response to a miracle question is 'I don't know'. Faced at a moment's notice with this vast new world of possibilities, it's only natural for the client to want to take a moment to consider where they are finding themselves. Other responses such as 'Ummmm' or even total silences are very encouraging signs for the practitioner, as we will see later in this chapter. A door is opening, and our clients often want a little time to adjust their eyes to the new light.

I have come across practitioners exploring SFBT for the first time who are worried that asking a miracle question might imply that such a miracle might actually happen, with impossible consequences; the amputee might wish their leg back in place, the widow might wish her husband back alive, and so on. Two points here: first, if the impact of the miracle in based on an actual best hope, this is less likely to occur. Second, even if it does occur, it's not a problem – the conversation can be continued with an exploration of 'what difference would that make to you?'. The amputee might wish to be able to play sport again, to be mobile to visit friends, even to be more able to participate in intimate bedroom activities. All of those are perfectly legitimate hopes that can be explored further. The widow might wish conversation, companionship, someone to take the bins out, and many more things – again, these are all tractable in the context of a miracle description. And of course, the practitioner can acknowledge the overwhelming desire for things to be other than they have been.

Development of the miracle question

Over the years, the art of asking the miracle question, and of encouraging useful and detailed answers, has developed considerably. Many SFBT books, including the most recent edition of the SFBTA's Treatment Manual (SFBTA, 2013) have the impact of the miracle as removing the problem (which keeps the problem in the room, even if peripherally). If we have a project based on best hopes, we can then use a form of words like this:

> 'I am going to ask you a rather strange question.
> The strange question is this:
> After we talk, you will go back to your work (home, school) and you will do whatever you need to do the rest of today, such as taking care of the children, cooking dinner, watching TV, giving the children a bath, and so on.
> It will become time to go to bed.
> And everyone goes to bed.
> And goes to sleep.
> And while you are asleep, a miracle happens and [your best hopes/project come to fruition]!
> But because this happens while you are sleeping, you don't know that the miracle has happened.
> So, when you wake up tomorrow morning, what would be the first tiny sign that will let you know the miracle happened?'

It is worth noting some of the developments seen in this version of the miracle question, compared to the earlier versions mentioned in preceding chapters:

- There is a much longer lead-in to both the question and to the appearance of the miracle. The practitioner starts by announcing that this is a strange question, and perhaps looking for a nod of acceptance or an 'OK' from the client at this point. Sometimes this might be proposed as a 'creative' question, or the client might be asked if they are ready to get a bit creative in the conversation.
- The lead-in then continues with going back to work or home after the session, and everything continuing normally. In my experience this gets the client into the swing of the conversation, and I am watching for nods of acceptance as we go through this piece. Some say that this series of nods or 'yes' responses helps the client into some sort of light trance. Whatever, it seems to get them lined up for the creative jump that is about to come.
- The miracle happens TONIGHT. Not just on some future night, but tonight. My experience is that this is a positive way of bringing everything up very close for the client.

- The practitioner states, at a high level, the impact of the miracle – in the wording from earlier it is that *your best hopes/project come to fruition*. This is vitally important; without such a statement, the client may just expect any old thing from the miracle and become defocused from the issue at hand. If clients emerge from the miracle with vague ideas of having won the lottery and totally changed everything about their lives, we probably haven't been clear enough about the impact of the miracle.
- The last part of the question is very clear about noticing a small change that will be a sign that the miracle has happened/best hopes have been realised. The earlier versions asked, 'what would be different about your life'. Here we are lining up for an even more focused discussion, starting with things that might be noticed when the client wakes up tomorrow.

All these developments are part of bringing the post-problem future up close to the client – both in terms of time (tomorrow) and in terms of detail. While in early SFBT the miracle question was mainly an aid to goal-setting, we can now see the conversation is a key part of 'stretching the world of the client' – exploring a better future in concrete detailed and interactional terms, which by itself expands the salient possibilities for noticing and potential action. Let's look at how it works in practice from this new standpoint.

Suppose ... the most important word

People often think that the 'miracle' is the most important element of the miracle question. I beg to differ. In my view the most important element is the word 'suppose'. This comes at the start of the question, and signals the most important shift which is about to take place in the conversation.

The word 'Suppose' at the start indicates that we are about to move the conversation into an unusual dimension, at least in terms of normal everyday discussion – the world of suppose-land. Suppose-land is a kind of parallel universe – very similar in many ways to the normal everyday world of the client, but with one striking difference; something has happened which has brought the project, the client's best hopes, to fruition. Having crossed the threshold into suppose-land, the client and practitioner are going to explore it, noticing signs that tell the client that this is the different, better world.

The practitioner's aim here is first to help the client stay in suppose-land, and second to explore the tiny details which will stretch their world. The first part can sometimes require some deft footwork from the practitioner. Preparing the ground with the client in terms of asking them whether they are prepared to get a little creative, that there is a strange and unusual question coming, can help a lot here. A strong and clear project also helps – because we can be somewhat confident the client will be interested to take some time to explore it.

Doorway to a parallel world

Phillip Pullman's (1997) literary trilogy *His Dark Materials* is set in a world of a huge number of overlapping parallel universes. These all occupy the same 'space' and lie somehow on top and intertwined, so that for example there are many cities of Oxford sitting together – these Oxfords all have common aspect such as colleges, the river, a suburb called Jericho, even a certain tree with a bench around it. These universes are normally kept apart so that we normal folk can only see the one we are occupying.

The novels feature a Subtle Knife with the power to cut through from one world to another. The wielder of the knife has to search carefully among the 'threads of reality' to find the world they wish to open up, and then cut a hole through which it is possible to step from one world to another. On the far side, in the other world, some things are the same and some are different. The characters can go off to explore the new world, leaving open the hole through which they can subsequently return.

The miracle question and other 'suppose-land' questions work in the same way: the practitioner uses a miracle question or some other form to open the door and invite the client to step through it. Once through it, the aim is to explore the parallel world on the other side for a while, without constantly referring back to the original world or wondering how we got there. The world on the other side has many similarities with the original world – the client will likely have the same family, live in the same place, will be doing many of the same things (perhaps in new ways) ... in the same way as the characters in Pullman's books are still in a similar-but-different Oxford.

And of course it is all in suppose-land. This is an interesting example of creativity which is both profound and rooted in the client's experience. The power of this process comes from sticking with the description, helping the client to expand their description in terms of detail and in terms of other perspectives. The more we stick with it, the more we stretch the world of the client. The miracle is one version of getting clients across the threshold. There are plenty of others to choose from, including

- Something magical has happened overnight
- Someone has waved a magic wand and so when you wake up tomorrow
- Suddenly, you discover that you've reached 10 on the scale (assuming a scale has been set up already)
- Suddenly, there is a time-quake, and you find yourself cast forward into a future where things have developed surprisingly well

There are plenty of other possibilities, and indeed finding ways to make this move that fit with the client's way of talking and thinking is an interesting part of this practice. The key thing is that we are moving into a world where, in some unknowable way, the client's best hopes are realised.

Expanding the description: details and scenes

Having helped the client over the threshold into the parallel universe of suppose-land, we as practitioners want to walk alongside the client and help them notice whatever is important. Of course, what the client notices must come from the client, but there are some key small yet crucial questions which the practitioner can use to expand the description. Here is a basic set of such expander questions:

- What difference would that make?
- What difference would that make to person [M]?
- What would be the first tiny signs that [X] was happening?
- Who else would notice that [X] was happening? What would they notice?
- What would person [M] do when they noticed you doing [X]?
- What might you do in response to that?
- What else?
- What happens next?

These apparently simple questions can be strung together in all kinds of ways to keep the description of the day-after-the-miracle suppose-land world and expanding in the direction of the client's own world and life experience. They can also be used to steer the client back into the world of suppose-land if they wander off somewhere such as the current world where the hopes are unrealised.

The description will often emerge as a series of 'scenes', different pictures in the Future Gallery. These can then each be explored from appropriate multiple perspectives. There is no 'right order' to look at the pictures; it is tempting, but not necessary, to look at them in somewhat chronological order.

It is also tempting for the practitioner to start with what looks like a 'relevant' first scene – the next time the client encounters a potentially problematic situation. However, if we are to help the client stretch their world – their whole world – then we should start at the point at which the client becomes aware of it. This is normally the time they wake up after the miracle. One is never sure quite what signs might start to come into focus for the client as they begin to adjust to this new world – which is why it's always interesting both to ask, and to give the client time to start to get to grips with this new parallel reality.

Case example: Mary and the cuddle (continued)

This case concerns Mary, a woman in her mid-forties who attended BRIEF in London, referred by her GP following depression and the GP's concern at the risk of suicide. We met her in Chapter 9. Having established Mary's hope that she wants to have a sense of peace and hope for the future, and to not be continually dragged back into the past (the project), the practitioner P leads into the following miracle question (after less than five minutes of this first session):

Session Transcript	Commentary
P: If tonight while you are asleep a miracle happened and it didn't get rid of the past, bit it stopped the past messing with your future, but you were asleep when it happened so you didn't know, what is the first thing you'd notice when you woke up tomorrow that began to tell you that you had this sense of peace and acceptance?	Practitioner starts with 'If' rather than 'Suppose' here ... in my view a slightly weaker option but they manage to make it work. The impact of the miracle is stated clearly – in words closely connected with the agreed project.
C: I think I would probably know ... the biggest thing I would know is that I am good enough in who I am. I don't have to prove myself or constantly seek approval from the people who have let me down and brought me to where I am. That I, in my own right, am good enough.	Client starts cautiously to explore the parallel world, with some general high-level thoughts. This is an good start – which the practitioner will now use to start to build the details.
P: So what time are you likely to wake up tomorrow? C: Possibly about seven o'clock. P: Seven o'clock? Okay, so the alarm will just wake you up?	This might look like a rather abrupt question, but it is designed to place the client at a key point in the exploration of the future – at the point where they awake into the parallel world of the miracle.
C: Well I wake ... I don't sleep very well so ... but even regardless of how I sleep I try and get up at the same time.	Note how we immediately get into the details of 'tomorrow morning'.
P: Okay. So seven o'clock you are waking up. What will be the very first sign that you are waking up and getting the sense that you are who you are and... ?	Practitioner is coming back to the moment of waking with a sense that the miracle has happened.
C: I don't know. I can't answer that question at the moment, I don't know. I can just imagine it would be ... I wouldn't feel as heavy hearted and worried.	An interesting moment. Client protests that she doesn't know, practitioner gives her space, and she continues her exploration. This is not unusual in the early stages – remember that she is coming into this parallel world for the first time.
P: Okay. What would you feel instead do you think? C: Possibly excited that it's a new day. P: Okay. C: Hopeful about what it's going to bring.	Practitioner is keen to hear about what it IS like (as opposed to what it isn't like) and so asks what C would experience instead. He matches her verb of 'feel' to go slowly.

(Continued)

(Continued)

Session Transcript	Commentary
P: Okay. So you woke up with a sense of excitement, kind of wondering what the day is going to bring. What difference would that make? Just having that experience?	The first 'what difference would that make' question.
C: Well it's something that I have never felt before, but I would imagine that it's quite a nice positive feeling to have rather than to be filled with dread of what the day is going to throw at you or bring you back into.	Client is getting into the idea that we are exploring something new here.
P: Okay. Is anyone else around? Are you on your own? C: I've got a partner.	Practitioner wants to get towards some other perceptions and so asks about who else is around (so we can look at they might notice).
P: Okay. Will your partner be there when you wake up? C: No.	This is perhaps a surprise – but the practitioner persists at bring the partner into the description about waking up.
P: Okay. Where will your partner be? C: Work.	
P: Work? What time does your partner go? C: Possibly about 5:30am.	
P: Okay. Do you hear him go? C: Depends. Depends on how the early part of the night has gone for me.	
P: If it has gone well, would you hear him go? C: Sometimes.	Again, practitioner reminds Mary that we are talking about the morning after the miracle.
P: How might he know that you are ... even before it was time to get up or what might he notice about you?	Another description-expanding question here – what might he notice?
C: He might notice that I might have slept a bit better perhaps, because I have very, very bad sleep.	

Session Transcript	Commentary
P: How would he have known that you had slept better?	Again bringing more detail to 'slept better'.
C: He probably would not have heard me get up and down so many times in the night or felt me move.	
P: Okay. Would you speak at that time before he went if you were awake?	
C: Yeah.	
P: Okay. What would he notice about you when you spoke?	
C: I don't know, I can't answer that question. I don't know.	These are very detailed questions, much more detailed than normal for looking at a future description. It's not a big surprise that the client is grasping for answers at this point. The practitioner sticks with it.
P: What do you think if you were going to have this miracle happen? ...	
C: I honestly don't know, I don't know.	
P: What do you imagine happened to you or had happened?	
C: I have already said what I thought. I thought ... I have imagined what it would be like. I can't ...	
P: What do you think he would notice about you if you were waking up with this sense of heart for the day?	
C: He would note a difference in me.	Aha. He WOULD notice a difference – but we don't yet know what kind of difference.
P: What is he called?	
C: Pardon?	
P: What's his name?	It's often better for the client to refer to key individuals by their usual name
C: Jeff.	
P: Jeff. So what do you think he would notice? That somehow just that first hint of you waking up?	

(Continued)

(Continued)

Session Transcript	Commentary
C: I don't know. I don't ... how do you expect someone to answer those questions when they have not had any experience of what that feeling might be? How can you ask those direct questions?	More puzzlement here as the client again grapples with the questions.
P: Because they are hard questions to answer. They will take us hopefully where we want to go.	
C: I don't know.	
P: If you are waking up with that sense of hope, that sense of being happy with who you are, that sense of peace, having slept well, what do you think he might notice? Just by the way you say goodbye to him or...?	
C: I have already said how I think I would be as a person and I think he would notice that. You know? That difference.	Once again Mary says that there would be differences for both of them to be aware of.
P: How do you think it would show to him at that fleeting moment, at that time of day?	Practitioner persists in asking about how this difference would show to Jeff.
C: I don't know. Maybe I wouldn't be as tired or feeling like, you know, negative perhaps about the day.	Again, we first get a negatively phrased response – what it wouldn't be like.
P: Okay. What would he notice on your face as you say goodbye to each other?	
C: I don't know. I imagine I might have a smile on my face rather than a worried look.	And yes, here is a noticeable difference – a smile on Mary's face.
P: Okay. Would he be surprised at that or does that sometimes happen?	
C: No, I do try and put on a smile.	This is quite an interesting moment – she has sometimes 'put on a smile' – but this smile might be different?
P: Okay.	
C: Might not always reach the places that I need it to or come from those places, but sometimes I can smile.	
P: Okay, how would he respond to that smile do you think?	

Session Transcript	Commentary
C: I think it would make him really happy.	Another interactional difference popping up here.
P: Yeah? Okay. How would it show that it mattered?	
C: I don't know how he would acknowledge it. I don't know.	
P: Okay. And then maybe another hour of sleep or so and seven o'clock you would wake up. This feeling is still with you, looking forward to the day. You have a sense of peace. What is the kind of routine? What have you got on tomorrow?	Practitioner decides to move on from this rather fleeting moment with Mary slightly awake as Jeff gets up and leaves for work. He moves forward to the next 'scene' in the gallery, which Mary has already referred to – the moment at seven o'clock when she wakes up to properly start her day. Practitioner is still stressing that this is a day with a sense of peace.
C: I get up, I go to the gym.	
P: Okay. What time do you go to the gym?	
C: I probably leave about 8:15am in the morning.	
P: Okay. Do you have breakfast or coffee?	Not wishing to rush ahead to the scene in the gym, practitioner wants to look at what might be signs around breakfast time that we are in the world after the miracle.
C: Yeah, breakfast.	
P: What would you notice as you were having breakfast that told you ... the feelings you want to go...?	
C: I don't know, because the things I do are so ingrained in me. You know? The routine that I have. Even the negative and hurtful emotions are so well practised they become normal feelings. So I am finding it very, very difficult to answer the questions that you are asking me.	
P: Good. You should be, it should be difficult.	Practitioner acknowledging that this is still feeling like heavy going and that's a potentially normal part of the process.
C: Okay.	
P: Because we are going somewhere where you have not been before.	Practitioner reminding client that we are looking into a new world here.
C: Yeah, I don't know.	

(Continued)

(Continued)

Session Transcript	Commentary
P: Which is ... so what do you think you would notice? What would tell you this sense of peace as you were getting tea or coffee? What do you have normally?	
C: I don't know. I think that the biggest thing I would notice about it is I probably wouldn't be as worried about every single little thing.	Notice how Mary answers 'I don't know' before giving a meaningful answer. We can look at the 'I don't know' as a kind of reflex action, not to be taken too seriously to start with.
P: What would be on your mind instead?	Again, looking for what WOULD be happening as opposed to what wouldn't.
C: Maybe excited about seeing people instead of dreading or trying to plan how I could avoid them if I do see them.	
P: Okay. So who might you be likely to see tomorrow?	
C: Just people that go to the gym.	
P: Okay. So who are the people that might be at the gym? Who would you be kind of ... might you be finally be looking forward to seeing rather than... ?	Practitioner looking for names of people here so he can refer to them as real individuals and bring them into the scene at the gym.
C: I have got some people, some really good friends there.	
P: Yeah? Okay, like... ?	
C: My friends Thelma and Beth.	And so practitioner can now start building the next scene – at the gym on the day after the miracle with Thelma and Beth.

So far the practitioner has helped Mary to construct three scenes in the Future Gallery: the time when Jeff gets up and goes to work, the time when she wakes up at 7am, and the scene over coffee before going to the gym. This has taken about eight minutes of dialogue, and we are still only at around 8.15am in the morning in Mary's day – the point being that this is a process of gradual exploration of the parallel world of the day after the miracle, taken quite slowly. In this case, Mary has struggled a little with the level of detail being requested by the practitioner. However, she has kept going and is starting to get more confident in her own abilities to explore this future day.

To see how this confidence continues to grow, we can look at a later part of the same session. Mary has now been to the gym, returned home, had lunch, and read a book. She is now focused on the moment when Jeff returns home from work.

Transcript	Commentary
P: And when does Jeff get home?	Once again, the practitioner is going for detail right away – what time?
C: Usually about five or six o'clock.	
P: Okay. And what would you be feeling then in this sort of half hour or so before he is about to arrive home? What would be telling you then that this miracle was still working for you?	Once again a reminder that we are still exploring the post-miracle world.
C: I would probably be ... instead of locking us both indoors for the evening, maybe thinking about where we could go out just the two of us perhaps for a little walk together or just to do something – I spend too much time indoors.	
P: Where might you think of going for a walk.	Even before her partner gets home the relationship between them, what they do together is changing thus preparing the way for a different interaction.
C: We live quite close to a beach so perhaps along there.	
P: And what is the first thing he would notice when he got home, even before you spoke? What is the very first thing?	Good use of an expander question here – what is the first thing he would notice?
C: I would be ... instead of a worried, stressed, anxious look on my face maybe a smile.	Notice that Mary is now offering the 'what would it be like' version without prompting, a good sign that she is getting into the swing of this part of the session.
P: Okay. And what would be the first thing you would notice about his response even before he spoke?	
C: I think my body language would just be so ... you know normally he has to come looking for me whereas I would imagine that I would be open to go and cuddle him instead. You know? So ...	
P: Would he faint or... ?	
C: Possibly, yeah, absolutely. You might have to have the paramedics on standby, yeah. I think it would be shock, but pleasant shock rather than shock.	Practitioner introduces a humorous touch... Client picks up on the humour and overstatement here, another sign that she is enjoying exploring the new world.

(Continued)

(Continued)

Transcript	Commentary
P: So where would that be? Where would you be cuddling him?	
C: I would imagine that ... because I do almost always hear him pull up. I never go to the door. I let him come in through the door and come find me. Whereas I would probably go find him.	
P: Okay, so that would be a different ...	Practitioner reinforcing the value of what Mary has just said, a useful positive sign.
C: Yeah.	
P: And what would you notice about the way you cuddled him that fitted with this sense of peace and pleasure, of being you?	Another expander question – what would you notice about the cuddle?
C: He describes sometimes that when he asks me for a cuddle ... he said 'When I ask you for a cuddle'; and I do give it to him, he goes 'You are rigid and you almost ... you cuddle me but you are pushing me away'. So I would imagine that it would be a much more natural, open embrace where I felt relaxed and safe enough to do that. Not rigid and tight.	Note how there is now much more detail in Mary's answer which is flowing much more than earlier in the session.
P: And what would you notice about his response to your cuddling and that kind of relaxed... ?	Practitioner is now also in full swing with expanding the description with 'noticing' questions. The whole exploration and description is now proceeding smoothly and in detail.
C: I think that he would be delighted with how it felt to have a cuddle that didn't feel like he was a) having to ask for or b) being pushed away from.	
P: And what would you notice about his arms?	
C: I think they might be quite tight around me and probably hold me for longer than normal.	
P: Okay. And what would you notice about how you handled that?	

Transcript	Commentary
C: I think it would be quite difficult because you get so rehearsed in how you do things. Whether that be good or bad, that's how you are. So I think it would be quite a new experience to have that.	
P: And if you are feeling like hugging him?	
C: Not wanting to let go either rather than wanting to break that embrace.	
P: Okay.	A little time is then spent on the post-cuddle moment and then on to the next scene.
C: Because at the moment it's like 'Okay, cuddle, quick, out of the way'. Whereas to actually enjoy the embrace and feel it rather than just do it and break away from it.	

This description of the cuddle takes about three minutes, considerably longer than the event itself is likely to be. During it a visible change takes place on the client's face, in her tone of voice, which suggests that the description is evoking some sort of felt experience. This is not an 'accidental' description. Such detail does not come without careful scene-setting which helps place the client's future within her everyday routines.

Key points

- The creative envisioning of a better life in SFBT has moved from an optional element to a key part of the process.
- The purpose is directly therapeutic – 'stretching the world' by exploring in detail the experience of a better future.
- The most important word in the miracle question is not the miracle – it is 'suppose'. Everything after that happens in suppose-land.
- Suppose-land, the world of the day after the miracle, is like a parallel universe for the client, where many things are quite similar and some are rather different.
- The miracle question or other future questions cut a hole through into this parallel universe, through which the client and practitioner can step to explore.
- Once through into the parallel universe, the practitioner's role is to expand the client's descriptions of detail from their own and relevant other perspectives.

- None of this is about HOW to reach the world after the miracle – it is about exploring it once it's there. The client may, of course, be starting to form ideas for potential action as the conversation progresses.

References

de Shazer, S. (1988). *Clues: Investigating Solutions in Brief Therapy*. New York, NY: W. W. Norton.
Pullman, P. (1997). *The Subtle Knife* (His Dark Materials, Vol. 2). New York, NY: Scholastic.
SFBTA. (2013). *Solution Focused Therapy Treatment Manual for Working with Individuals*. 2nd version (2013). Retrieved from http://sfbta.org/PDFs/researchDownloads/fileDownloader.asp?fname=SFBT_Revised_Treatment_Manual_2013.pdf

Chapter 11

The Instances Gallery

Instances connected to the better future

It has often been said that Solution Focused Brief Therapy (SFBT) and related practices are very future focused. This is indeed the case, as we have seen from the previous two chapters about the Ticket Office (best hopes for the future) and the Future Gallery (exploring a better future in tiny interactional detail). However, the past and present also have a role to play.

The powerful contribution of the 'solution focused (SF) past' – elements which have already happened and support and connect with the preferred future descriptions – has sometimes been undervalued. It has perhaps gone from being the central tenet of early SF work to being the unglamorous ugly sibling alongside the sparkling beauty of the day after the miracle. It is a very flexible component of our work; when I am working with organisations the people are quite accustomed to looking to the future but are much less used to seeking ideas about what's working in the past.

In this chapter we will explore how descriptions of instances – events in the past and the present – can play a key role in SF work. One important way into this can be using scales, but there are also other ways to bring focus on potentially overlooked events which can play a key role in stretching the world of the client to bring new possibilities for action to the fore. The use of scaling is not new; the way we can use them to produce world-stretching detail is more of an extension to practice.

Using scales as a powerful starting point

'On a scale from 1–10' has become almost as synonymous with SFBT work as the miracle question. Rather like the miracle question, it was a relatively late arrival on the SF scene. Steve de Shazer told me (Norman, McKergow & Clarke, 1997) that he learned about using scales from watching Insoo work, and that Insoo had picked it up from the way their clients at the BFTC drop-in therapy clinic were talking anyway. It's certainly the case that the idea of placing things on a 10-point scale was out there anyway in the late 1970s, and probably before. It forms a basic assumption for the Blake Edwards movie *10* starring Dudley Moore and Bo Derek; Moore's character is in the (disrespectful by modern standards) habit of rating girls he sees in the street on a 10 scale. He sees Bo Derek's character and immediately rates her as an 11 – setting up the romantic comedy that follows.

Berg and de Shazer developed scaling into a more sophisticated concept in the early 1990s, culminating in one of the real classics of the SF literature, 'Making Numbers Talk' (Berg & de Shazer, 1993). This paper was reprinted in InterAction in 2012 and is really worth a look online. Romping through a summary of how language works in various philosophical traditions, they end up with a post-structural view, of which Wittgenstein would have approved, that the meaning of a word (or number) is freshly negotiated in use between the interlocutors in each setting. The purpose is not to do with the numbers but rather with noticing small distinctions and differences.

This is a key breakthrough. When we ask a scaling question, the client responds with a number – say '3'. We know nothing at all about what this means, other than it's lower than 10 and higher than 1. So we have to find out, by asking more questions. (Of course, we are really helping the client find out what *they* mean, and hear what they themselves say.) This is nothing to do with mathematics or the usual logic of numerical relations. So, 5 is not 'halfway there' (no matter what the client might say). One person's '6' might be less good than another person's '2'. A team's answers of 3, 3, 4, 6 do not add up to an average of 4 (whatever arithmetic might tell us); they are four different scales for four different people.

These numbers are not really the secret of scaling. They are starting points for a piece of conversation. What is curious is how easily and clearly most clients can put themselves on a scale, and how having done so they are quite content to accept the consequences; that they are not at 10 (yet) and they are also not at the bottom of the scale. This latter point, whether the scale starts with a 0 or a 1, is one of the great bar-room conversations among SF practitioners; some prefer 0, some prefer 1. It seems to be of little consequence in practice, though psychiatrist Dr Alasdair Macdonald tells me he uses 0–10 for patients with severe mental disorder in case offering them 1–10 appears too optimistic at the start. Some countries use other scales or numbers; the norm in Vietnam is 1 as top and 10 as the lowest condition. It is not unknown to start with a negative number and move upwards.

This all puts SF scales into a different category to all the many psychological rating scales that are out there – see for example (picked largely at random from hundreds of examples) the eating disorder questionnaire ED-15 (Tatham et al., 2015). These instruments usually come with labels saying 'only to be used by psychological professionals' and have much more detailed questions with descriptions about what each number is supposed to mean. The scales are designed to be comparable when used across different clients or populations. This is not the case with SF scales at all. The numbers mean what the client says they mean, there are no descriptors other than those created by the client and practitioner in the conversation, and those meanings very likely evaporate at the end of the session. (We may find the scale being used again in later sessions ... but by then it's not really the same scale.)

Setting up an SF scale

One thing is important in setting up a scale; the ends must be defined. If you fail to do this, the question is broadly meaningless. So, 'on a scale from 1–10, where are you?' will be answered by the client, but with their own scale – which you are not privy to! Practitioners learn to set up a scale by defining the end points:

> Let's imagine a scale from 1–10, where 10 is [X] and 1 is [Y]. (Looking at client for confirmatory nodding or accepting.) Where would you say you are on this scale right now?

The 10 point is always used as the better position. [Y] can be defined as 'none of that is happening' or similar. *Both* need to be there for this question to really make sense. In introductory sessions I always get asked 'what if they say 1 (or 0)?' This happens extremely rarely in practice, but here's the answer; ask about how come they are coping and keeping going with things so tough. What is helping? Some people have been known to set the scale so that the bottom point is clearly not applicable, for example '1 is things are so bad you didn't get out of bed this morning'. And we know they got out of bed, so it can't be a 1. This doesn't stop the occasional client saying it anyway, which usually means they haven't really thought about it, or you didn't set the scale up well enough.

Another point to note is at the end of the question: 'right now'. I find it helpful to make clear that this is what we're talking about initially – even if the conversation will shift into the past quite quickly. It encourages the client to take a little inward look and answer instinctively about where they are at this moment. Whatever they say will be a useful start to the next section of the conversation.

Of course, simply using a scale doesn't make a conversation solution focused. The next question is what defines that. A (non-SF) colleague is prone to asking 'why aren't you at 10? What's stopping you?'. He does this with good intentions, of attempting to motivate the client by encouraging them to look at themselves and try harder to overcome the barriers. That's not our way, even if it occasionally has some effect. The next question after an SF scale is 'how come you are that high and not lower?'.

Progress scale/miracle scale

This is perhaps the most often used scale in SFBT work. The day after the miracle, or the day described in the Future Gallery, is 10. 1 is the opposite – none of that is happening at all. Where would you say you are right now?

Of course, clients may take a moment to think about it. As with the miracle question, just wait. Don't ask again, let them figure it out. If it's a new question for them (and it usually is, particularly with ideas about hopes, projects and future descriptions that you've just been talking about). They may well want a moment to think about it and sum it up.

Then we can follow up with 'how come you are that high and not lower?' or some variant. Then the fun starts; we may get all kinds of answers. Some of them may be about 'right now', others can be about something that happened in the (usually relatively recent) past. Many practitioners like to build up a list first and then dive in to expanding them and stretching the world of the client yet further. Others go with the first instance offered and unpack it, and then come back to look for more things. Once again we are using the description-building questions in various combinations; the only difference is that they are now phrased appropriately for the past:

- How did you do that?
- What difference did that make?
- What difference did that make to person [M]?
- What were be the first tiny signs that [X] was happening?
- Who else noticed [X] was happening? What did they notice?
- What did person [M] do when they noticed you doing [X]?
- What did you do in response to that?
- What else?
- What happened next?

As with the Future Gallery, these description-building questions help build up a detailed picture of the instance with the client at the heart of it, with other perspectives and participants brought in as appropriate. See the case example towards the end of the chapter for an illustration of how this can happen in practice.

Other points on the progress scale

In the first instance, we start with where the client says they are *right now*. Once this has been explored, it is possible to begin to look at different points on the scale:

What's the highest you've ever been on this scale?
This is a broad question. It asks the client to think a way back in time and look for events or experiences which were 'better'. It can be a little intimidating for the client though, and bearing in mind our preference for small and accessible details, some practitioners prefer this option:

What's the highest you're been recently on this scale?
Again, this asks the client to sort through their recent experiences and find one which stands out in some relevant way. As usual this can take some time, so

wait while they think. Then you can together build a detailed and interactional description of those moments, how everyone was involved, what they noticed, and so on. As always, focus on building the detail and let the client sort out the relevant links for themselves.

What would be 'good enough'?

Curiously, most clients don't actually find they need to reach 10 on the scale to be satisfied and move on. Another point on the scale can be labelled as 'good enough' – at least for this thing not to be an issue any more and take its place in the everyday ups and downs of life. I often hear '8' in answer to this question, but of course I don't know what that means. We don't always explore it with the client, but it can be useful for the client to hear themselves says this – it seems to take the pressure off somehow and bring more focus onto the present and immediate future.

What would be the first signs you'd reached (N + 1) on the scale?

This is a very useful question indeed. We will meet it again in the Gift Shop section at the end of the session. Of course, this isn't about the past but about the near future. Notice for now that it isn't 'what could you do to get to (N+1) on the scale'; we are working here with signs, which connect to possibilities for action. The client will decide on their actions for themselves.

Other forms of scale

The SF scale is a marvellously flexible thing – many aspects of a client's life and experience can be brought into the conversation in a focused way starting with a number. Here are a few of the more common possibilities, with some ideas about how to use them. These are not all relevant to the Instances Gallery, and we will meet them in detail further on the session.

Different aspects of the miracle/future

When different aspects of the future or day after the miracle appear, it is possible (and sometimes desirable) to create separate scales for each aspect. For example, if the client is seeing themselves as getting out more and eating less, there could be a scale for each with different numbers and question sequences, building descriptions of both. I don't normally use this unless it seems that taking the whole miracle picture as one piece is causing some kind of tension or conflict for the client. Sometimes things that should be dealt with separately are put together; other times things that should be dealt with together are separated.

One situation from my own work where this tactic often comes into play is when I am working with a workplace team or organisation. There may be ten to 20 people in the room, and suggesting that they group up around particular aspects of their future picture both helps people engage with something they want to work on and also helps to spread the work around. I find that I can easily take all the groups through the same scaling questions and processes at the same time; the questions are the same, but the discussions are of course different.

Different perceptions

It's possible (though not usual) to ask the client where they think other people might put them on the scale. The scale has to be suitable of course, so if there was a scale about 'ready to return to school' (where the client wanted to return to school) the practitioner could ask about where the teacher or parent might put the client on the scale. This is then followed up with the usual routine about how come it's that high and not lower, what else, and so on. The point is to bring other legitimate positions into the conversation and perhaps encourage the client to see things from others' point of view.

This is *not* the same as asking the client to place other people on the scale. To ask 'where would you put [hated authority figure] on the scale?' would make no sense because it's not their scale. This would also invite blaming and accusatory discussions, where we are seeking to sidestep in favour of more solution focused dialogue.

Confidence scale

I find myself reaching for confidence scales on quite a few occasions. They are more associated with the Present Gallery and the Gift Shop but can be a good starting point for Instance descriptions and instances too. Rather than progress, the scale is about the client's confidence: of making progress, of doing what they hope to do, of successfully tackling their challenge or project. In setting up the scale the practitioner has to choose one of these options, in order to define the scale clearly.

The great thing about a confidence scale is that it can bring many different and interlinking aspects together in a single scale, which can always be discussed in terms of right here, right now. This is particularly good for projects which are under way and will likely take some time to bring to fruition. If the client is at 9 on the confidence scale, we can start asking about what helps them to be there and not lower, which might well bring forth descriptions from the past and present. This can be a prelude to stopping therapy; if the client knows what they are planning to do and are confident that it will help them, then they are probably taking back control of their lives and feeling able to live under their own steam, without professional help. We will look more at confidence scales in the forthcoming chapter on the Gift Shop.

On-track scale

An on-track scale is a variant of the confidence scale described earlier. Something is hoped for in the client's future. On a scale of 1–10, how on-track are they that this will happen where 10 is 'totally on-track' and 1 is nowhere? The advantage, as with a confidence scale, is that the various future uncertainties can be brought into the here and now. I may not know whether I will get into college, achieve a happy and stable marriage, or publish my novel but I *can* know today how on-track I am. The follow-ups are the same, how come you are that high and not lower, what else, what else and so on, with the possibility of building descriptions based on any of the responses.

Scaling without numbers

The genius of SF scaling is that even though we know nothing about what each number means to the client, we *can* know that 5 is better than 4. The purpose of a scale is to help the client create distinctions about small differences or changes. This has long been a key aspect of brief therapy, and the scale achieves it neatly and practically. So there are alternatives to using numbers in scaling, but they have to achieve the same end – to be open in meaning and yet to also have clear gradations about what is better.

These tactics tend to be used with children and others who may struggle with easily using numbers. Perhaps the simplest tactic is to have a line on a piece of paper with 'better' at one end and 'worse' at the other end, or even smiley and frowny faces. The client simply marks a point on the line about where they are now, and the conversation ensues. (The client can even be asked to draw the line for themselves, which is both involving and fits with our wish not to take control from the client if we can possibly avoid it.) Other marks can be put on the scale for 'a bit better' (like N + 1), good enough, where you were last Tuesday when things went better than usual, and so on.

Pictures of ladders can be used, with the rungs marking the points on the scale. Space in a room can be used, with one wall being the preferred future and the facing wall being 'as bad as things can possibly be'; people are invited to stand where they see things and engage in stepping forward and back to explore the differences. (I use this with teams quite a lot; it's engaging for people to move around, and any clear distinctions between different people are immediately clear and can form the basis of further exploration. If the boss thinks we are at 8 and most team members think it's a 3, then some interesting and fruitful discussions lie ahead.)

Almost anything can be used at the basis for a scale as long as:

- The end points are somehow defined.
- We are clear which end is 'better'.
- The clients make their own choices about where to put themselves.
- Everyone remembers that the scaling number is not an end in itself but rather the start of a piece of work about describing useful instances in the past (and the present) before moving on to the future.

Case example: Jack feeling properly heard

The client, Jack, is a 17-year-old school student. There have been tensions at home; Mum died two years ago, and it appears that Dad is uncomfortable with the client's identity and how he chooses to represent himself through feminine clothing. These factors do not appear much in the transcript – another example of how SF work takes focus away from the problem and onto other things. The client's best hopes are to 'feel properly heard'. The practitioner has helped the client to create a future description based on the day after the miracle where these best hopes were realised, including better interactions with Dad and sister. About 35 minutes into the 50-minute session, the practitioner finishes the future descriptions and moves onto exploring the past and present with a scale:

Transcript	Commentary
P: So I'm just going to ask you another question, so, that miracle day that we just described, say that was 10 on the scale, and 0 was the opposite of that. Where you put yourself on the scale?	
C: I, I'd probably go – ah, it's a bit difficult – I'd probably go six, I think.	Practitioner waits while the client grapples with the question and gives space, rather than jumping in to 'help'.
P: OK, so what makes you six and not a five or lower?	
C: I think that we're, uh, sort of steering towards a 10 a bit more, because there are perhaps days when my sister is feeling a bit better. And I guess, therefore, both me and my dad are feeling better because that's a big worry of ours.	This is quite a vague initial answer, which the practitioner wisely accepts and lets the client go on.
P: Mm.	Part of grounding the client's words. This practitioner makes quite frequent responses along these lines.
C: So we're able to relax and stick around and things like that, and ...	
P: Mm.	
C: There are days like that, you know.	
P: Mmm. So what's different on those days, Jack?	Practitioner has heard that there are some days which are better, and wants to explore the differences on those days.
C: Well, I think that my ... well, fundamentally, I think my sister's feeling a bit better herself.	'Sister feeling a bit better'.

Transcript	Commentary
P: Mm.	
C: And me and dad are able to relax and not have to worry ...	'Me and Dad'.
P: Mm.	
C: – for her. Um –	
P: Yeah.	The exchanges at this point overlap considerably, with the practitioner making moves to ground the client's words and encourage the client to continue.
C: – and just know that she's feeling happier –	
P: Yeah.	
C: – herself, and –	
P: Mm. C: – you know, just be a bit more relaxed, I think.	
P: Mm. Do you know what's different for her on those days?	
C: Not [sighs] – no. I think that's what I'm trying to sort of –	Practitioner lets the client grapple with things here, and doesn't accept the 'No' too quickly ...
P: Mm.	
C: – speak to her and work out, I think, at the moment. I, yeah, I don't know.	
P: Mm.	
C: And plus, I've known that it's just – I've just sort of heard this kind of general thing that it's got worse and it's got better.	Client acknowledges that there are better days, which is worth noting, even though there is yet to be more detail.
P: Mm, OK.	
C: But I haven't known what's perhaps been going on.	
P: Mm.	
C: Mm, you know, I've done my best to help and that kind of thing.	Aha! So given some space, the client says he's been doing something.

(Continued)

(Continued)

Transcript	Commentary
P: Mm.	
C: And she, you know, they can tell me when they're ready.	
P: And still on those days when your sister's feeling a bit better and you've described that you and your dad can joke around a bit together, so tell me about that.	The first focused question for some time. Practitioner has noted the client's words about the sister feeling a bit better, and client and Dad able to relax. Jack and his Dad 'joking around' was mentioned during the Future conversation. P is now asking for more details ...
C: I think, you know, it's just this, it's a, it's, a sense of ease kind of thing -	
P: Mm.	
C: – and it's just nice. You know, like yesterday when Max came round, um, he's got a Beetle, as he's sort of – he's gone out and bought that, and he was just –	(Max is a friend of Jack's who has just got a car, and talked with Jack's Dad about it.)
P: Cool.	
C: He was just talking about that, and I was interested because he was telling Max about all these different things and I'd never heard of it before.	This is all part of the 'sense of ease' that the client was talking about ... 'he' is the father here ... 'Things I never heard before'.
P: Yeah [laughs].	
C: And I was just really interested to hear all these different things about how, you know, how an elderly lady owned it at one point and all this stuff, all these different things that I was quite interested about.	
P: Yeah.	
C: Um, and I could just see that he was proud of it and we were just quite happy to sort of share that, I guess.	'Proud of it'.
P: Yeah, yeah, yeah.	
C: It just felt nice to sort of, you know, see something that he was really proud about, I think.	

Transcript	Commentary
P: Yeah, yeah. So seeing something that he was proud of, and hearing things that you hadn't heard before and –	Practitioner re-offered client's words with an open invitation to continue.
C: Yeah.	
P: Yeah. And what difference did that make to you?	Another 'what difference did it make' question, to connect this interaction with Dad, Max and the car to the client.
C: That just made me feel a little bit, a lit – a little bit closer, I think.	
P: Mm.	Practitioner is again encouraging the client to keep going, even though we don't really know yet where it might lead.
C: To get into that. And –	
P: Mm.	
C: – just that sort of pleasant feeling of just we were able to share things, I think, and just –	
P: Mm.	
C: – again, that positive sort of feeling.	
P: Mm.	
C: I think all of these things sort of lead back to that, just the sort of nice air at home, I suppose.	'A nice air at home'.
P: Yeah, so a nice air at home, yeah. Yeah. So, so what else makes you that six and not lower, do you think?	Practitioner summarises by using the last relevant phrase and asks 'what else?' to look for other instances.
C: I suppose we're not, um – I suppose that I think all of us have got a way to deal with things, I think –	
P: Mm.	
C: – perhaps me and dad more so than my sister. But we've got some kind of method or some kind of person that we can talk to, that we can deal with things.	'Some kind of method ... person we can talk to ...'
P: Mm.	

(Continued)

(Continued)

Transcript	Commentary
C: And I think the fact that we're able to do that, even if we don't talk to each other about it –	
P: Mm.	
C: – we're able to sort of keep on going and –	
P: Mm.	
C: – not necessarily – not, not let it affect, but, um, not – I don't know how to say it – not sort of overtly worry -	
P: Mm	
C: – in the way the other person – um –	
P: So you've got other ways, you know, people to talk to and to – yeah.	Practitioner offers back the 'ways, people to talk to'.
C: Ways to cope, I suppose.	'Ways to cope'.
P: Ways to cope, mm. OK.	Grounding ...
C: Yeah.	Grounded.

What strikes me about this quite short passage is the way in which the practitioner gives the client lots of space to explore and think aloud, while they keep on offering verbal acceptance and grounding moves along the way. The client is somewhat hesitant, which is quite normal as they are thinking through past events in a new way and with a new context of connection to 'feeling properly heard'. The practitioner is patient, listens for key words from the client, offers them back and keeps the space open for the client to add and extend. On this occasion the client was producing quite a lot of detail without a lot of digging; on another occasion the practitioner might have to do a bit more focusing with the short description-building questions like 'what difference did that make?', 'what else?' and so on.

At this point of course, we don't know what this will all add up to for the client. Taking a world-stretching perspective, it's unlikely we will know all that much until next time (or the client calls to say things are better and they don't need to come any more). The session is a few minutes away from ending, and we will see how it concludes later in the book.

Key points

- The Instances Gallery contains descriptions of events in the past and present which connect and support the client's hopes, project and preferred future.
- A scale from 1–10 (or 0–10) is a good way into this piece of work; the client almost always tells themselves that things are not at their lowest ebb, and so can seek examples of events which seem to be helping.
- The value of scales is not in the number per se (which is very personal and contextual to the client) but in the conversation that follows.
- These events may well be small, momentary, even fleeting, but they can be expanded using description-building questions into more attractive and relevant experiences.
- Different points on the scale can be interesting to explore; where are you now, when things were better in the past, the best it's ever been, 'good enough' for this not to be a problem any more.
- Different kinds of scale can be used, including separate scales for aspects of the future, different people's perceptions, confidence and on-trackness.
- Scales don't need to use numbers, as long as the ends are identified; everyone knows where 'better' lies, and the client makes their own choice about where they are.

References

Berg, I. K., & de Shazer, S. (1993). Making numbers talk: Language in therapy. In S. Friedman (Ed.), *The New Language of Change: Constructive Collaboration in Psychotherapy* (pp. 5–24). New York, NY: Guilford Press. Retrieved from http://sfwork.com/resources/interaction/06Berg_de-shazer.pdf

Norman, H., McKergow, M., & Clarke, J. A. (1997). Paradox is a muddle: An interview with Steve de Shazer. *Rapport, 34,* 41–49. Retrieved from http://sfwork.com/paradox-is-a-muddle

Tatham, M., Turner, H., Mountford, V. A., et al. (3 more authors). (2015). Development, psychometric properties and preliminary clinical validation of a brief, session-by-session measure of eating disorder cognitions and behaviors: The ED-15. *International Journal of Eating Disorders.* ISSN 0276–3478. https://doi.org/10.1002/eat.22430

Chapter 12

The Gift Shop
What to take away?

The final element of the Solution Focused Brief Therapy (SFBT) art gallery comes as the client and practitioner are about to leave at the end of the session. Here the client has the opportunity to look back at the experience, take stock and decide what, if anything, they wish to take away as a reminder of the conversation. In the SF art gallery as in life, the experience of participating cannot be un-experienced. We say that 'change is happening all the time' and so it is perhaps inevitable that the client will leave changed in some way. However, if the experience has so far been useful and relevant, it's quite possible that the change could be enhanced by the client taking with them something they can use in the days to come to positively remember the experience and build on it: 'presents in the present' if you like.

This means bringing the focus of the conversation to the present and the very near future. The client may well have been on a temporal journey, from forming their project in the ticket office, descriptions of a better future (perhaps miraculously so) and scenes from the past and present which may have taken on new levels of detail and relevance. As the end of the session draws near, the client will begin to prepare to step out into their stretched world and experience it anew. This will happen anyway, and yet the practitioner can also help to prepare them for the next steps in various ways.

From tasks to summaries

The changing face of SF practice can be seen most clearly in the way the session is brought to a close. In the early days, practitioners took their cue from previous brief therapy traditions from the Mental Research Institute (MRI) (Weakland, Fisch, Watzlawick & Bodin, 1974), which in turn drew on family therapy methods (Satir, 1964). The therapist in the room was part of a larger team of practitioners, who were watching proceedings from behind a one-way mirror (they could see the clients and therapist but could not themselves be seen). The idea was that these external observers could see things from a different perspective to the therapist in the room, and could add in their own ideas for lines to take, questions to ask, and interventions to make. At the end of the session the therapist would consult with the team behind the mirror and together they would arrive at an end-of-session message including a task for the clients.

In the MRI approach this was quite a challenge; the task would be based around the client stopping doing what they had been trying to do, which seemed counter-intuitive and so required a 'sales job' to be accepted. It was usually designed to break or a least interrupt the patterns of behaviour which led to problems, as in the squirt-gun-fight-in-the-garage we saw from the young Steve de Shazer in his early work (de Shazer, 1975).

In the early days of the Brief Family Therapy Center (BFTC), de Shazer and Berg moved to embrace a co-operation model of working with clients (de Shazer, 1982). They saw their first job as not to second-guess the clients but to build co-operation with them. One way to do this was to observe the session (still from behind the mirror) for what clients were doing that could be complimented, and then offer these compliments before giving the task. This had a powerful effect as an intervention in its own right; the clients were inclined to accept the compliments with nods and cries of 'Yes!', which set them into a better mood to accept the task which followed. In the early stages this might have been the Formula First Session task, asking clients to notice what they wanted to keep in their lives (itself a powerful redirection of attention).

The role of compliments

The power of compliments is one of the longest-running distinctive elements of SFBT and is still with us although in a somewhat different form. This is unsurprising; in all walks of life offering a *sincere* expression of appreciation is a powerful move. In order to do it, one has to first pay attention to the other long enough to notice something about them that is worth mentioning, and then to formulate it in such a way as to both be accepted and to shed a little new light on what may have been a tough struggle for the client so far. In my work with managers and leaders, where the norm has been for supervisors to spot and correct errors rather than be impressed, it can make a significant difference on its own. Indeed, some companies in Japan have based entire change programmes on using 'OK-messages' as they call them (Aoki, 2006).

Frank Thomas (2016) has surveyed the differing uses of compliments in SFBT. For many years compliments were used directly by practitioners to introduce language around strengths, useful qualities, personal resources, co-operation with others and so on. These are offered by the practitioner as a formulation (in microanalysis terms), a statement of their own view which they hope the client will accept and can therefore be grounded in the conversation. A typical compliment might look like:

PRACTITIONER: 'Well, I've been thinking about what you've said, and it seems to me that you are being very tenacious. You've been working away at this for months and yet you haven't given up – on the contrary you are even more determined to do something'.

CLIENT: 'Mm–hm ... yes ... thank you'.

The client has not said anything about 'tenacious' or 'determined', but now these words are part of the story. This simple move has all kinds of effects. The client perhaps starts to see themselves differently. They may also respond physiologically; the broaden–and–build research of Barbara Fredrickson (2001) shows a correlation between positive emotions, relaxation and openness to thinking about problems in new ways. It is important to note that in SF work we are not talking explicitly about 'positive emotions' but rather about our perceptions of the client as a resourceful person. However, many clients would say that speaking about their lives in an SF way helps them to feel better, whatever that may mean. Also recall that the power of compliments was arrived at empirically by the BFTC team two decades before Fredrickson, as part of a very different programme of pragmatic inquiry.

Some SFBT practitioners (Korman, Korman & Miller, 2020) have been connecting their complimenting practice to the work of Carol Dweck (2006). Briefly, Dweck found that people adopting a 'growth mindset', where intelligence and ability were buildable, tended to make more effort to help themselves than those with a 'fixed mindset', where these things are set at birth. Those with a fixed mindset see success as the product of their natural ability, while effort and continuing application is more important from a growth mindset perspective. Following this thinking, complimenting clients for effort rather than success – for hard work, things tried, persistence, patience – may well result in more impact than merely complimenting the client's achievements and successes.

Other practitioners have steered away from this direct complimenting. Another way to bring the power of appreciation into the conversation is to ask the client to self-compliment, ask them what the conversation has told them about themselves, or even ask them what a trusted and respected other (grandparent/mentor/old friend, for example) might have to say about them. The conversation can get very slow at this point – these are not easy or customary matters, and we can expect the client to perhaps become reflective. As ever, giving space and being patient can pay dividends, particularly as they can start coming to conclusions that often are different from what has been talked about earlier.

Yet another form of complimenting is indirect compliments. The very act of taking the client's words seriously, being impressed with progress (even if it might seem very small to an outsider), and asking the client not-knowing questions about how they did that and what everyone else noticed, is in itself a kind of affirmation of the client, their abilities and their power to enhance their lives. The kind of appreciative summaries we see in next-generation SFBT are often in this fashion.

Appreciative summaries

Compliments and appreciation are still very much part of the SF scene as it develops. The way these aspects are used, however, is changing. First of all, as we are now seeing the whole conversation as 'the intervention', there is no explicit need for the client to be assigned a task. There is therefore no need either to get them into a receptive state for the task they will not receive, and therefore also no need for a determined series of compliments at the end of the session. However, the co-operative approach is still very much in use, and so the practitioner is still listening for things to appreciate about both the client as a person, and what they have been doing that seems worthy of mention.

So, rather than a series of complimenting statements or formulations, we might see the practitioner creating 'appreciative summaries' at different points in the session. These will be based foremost on the client's key words, offered back perhaps to further ground them as important, and can be useful to draw things together as we move from one description to another, or one gallery to another. They are given from a stance of appreciation, and so there is still considerable room for conveying that the practitioner is not only merely 'accepting' this language but sees the client as someone who is capable of building their life in their hoped-for direction, and has the personal resources to go about it. This stance is a key part of SF practice. It often forms a backdrop to the conversation; it would not make sense to be asking about better futures and useful instances if one thought the client had no hope of making progress. However, at times it can come to the fore with the practitioner openly being impressed with the client, their hopes and their efforts. Remember, we are not trying to 'join the dots' for the client but to sum things up so that key elements may be remembered to form the basis for new possibilities.

Tiny signs of progress

Another possible take-away from the session is additional thoughts about tiny signs of progress. We can hope that the conversation has been filled with talk of small details, in descriptions of the Future and Instances galleries and indeed in the Ticket Office ('what might be a tiny sign in the next week or so that our work has been useful to you?'). If it has, the world of the client may be stretched enough for there to already be new possibilities for action and engagement. There is another important chance to build on this at the end of the session: tiny signs that would be noticeable in the next few days. These signs can occasionally become part of a new angle or priority for the client, as well as building on what has gone before.

One point higher

One very neat and useful way to do this is to have a short conversation about N+1 on the scale – one point higher. You will recall that we probably set up a scale from 1–10 (or 0–10) as part of the Instances Gallery, in our search for instances from the past. Most commonly we used a progress or miracle scale, where 10 represents the day after the miracle or the descriptions of a better future, and 1 is the opposite with none of it happening at all. The client places themselves on the scale at a number we can call N (it might be 3, 6, 1, 8 or anything else). A discussion has followed about how come it's that high and not lower, when things have been better in the past, and so on (as discussed in the previous chapter). This conversation can be extended into the near future by asking:

> 'What would be the first tiny signs you would notice that would tell you you'd got to (N + 1) on the scale?'

This looks like a simple question, but it's very precisely worded. First it is pre-suppositional – the question is very definitely not about whether there would be signs, but simply what they would be. Second, it asks for signs, things the client would notice, and not steps they would take. These signs may be of them taking action, or they may be things they would notice – that's up to the client. Third, it asks for *tiny* signs – directing the client's attention to the small and accessible rather than the large and distant. And fourth, it is about signs of (N + 1), not just of 'better'.

Steps, signs or neither?

It took me a while to figure the distinction between the next steps for the client, and tiny signs that things were improving. At the start of my SF career I was keen to make sure the client was taking something away to do, even if they had chosen that thing for themselves rather than me giving them a task to do it. From the stance of world-stretching, I can see more clearly how this process works; we are priming the client to respond differently and doing so in a way which leaves them still in charge of their own actions. This value of client autonomy is deeply held in SF circles, and we will discuss it further in the final chapter. What they will perhaps do after the session will seem quite natural to them – these are now 'normal' actions in a stretched world rather than unusual and difficult actions in the world of the problem.

We can look at the options for looking at what happens next on a spectrum, from directive towards suggestive:

* Practitioner tells client what to do (for example, have a squirt-gun fight when the problem seems to be arising)
* Practitioner suggests to client in general terms what they might do ('carry on doing what works' or 'notice when things seem a little better')
* Practitioner asks client what they think their next steps might be (a 'coaching' approach)

- Practitioner asks client about tiny signs of progress (which focus on the very near future but may not be actions)
- Practitioner asks client about confidence of progress (of which more in what follows)
- Practitioner doesn't mention anything at all, expecting that the previous work in the session will be sufficient.

I have seen all these options in use, and they are all (apart from the first one) part of the current SF repertoire. Recent developments have seen practitioners moving down this spectrum towards more minimal options. The final option is an interesting one to be explored and researched. One view is that if the level of detail discussed has already been sufficiently small, the client will already have many possibilities for action and so asking about them is at best superfluous, and at worst distrustful and disrespectful; why do we need to be satisfying ourselves about the client's life, about which they are the experts?

In my own background field of organisational work, clients are very relaxed about discussing next steps. It is a normal part of organisational culture, to the point where if people haven't agreed actions they may get the idea that they don't need to do anything. We want people to find new ways to think and act. From a world-stretching perspective they have done the groundwork for this during the session, and the fruits of it may start to be apparent there and then or may begin to appear later when the client walks out and experiences their newly stretched world. There is nothing to say that an action discussed in the session is any more or less important than one which appears the following day. It might be said that 'next step' conversations are more to do with the practitioner's expectations than the client's future.

One aspect of SF work which has been around for years and is agreed among those from all areas of the tradition is that if a follow-up session happens, it does *not* feature discussions about 'did you do the actions?'. This strand would be consistent with some kind of accountability of the client towards the practitioner, and a detailed responsibility of the practitioner about the client. We are not here to hold the client to account if they didn't do the action; we are much more interested in what they experienced that connects to a better life (in a stretched world). There is thus no need to agree next steps for this purpose. We will see more about follow-up conversations in the next chapter.

Confidence scales about the future

We have already seen how scales can be used to create distinctions about all kinds of things. We have already seen how a miracle or progress scale can be used to develop descriptions of past instances, and to look at tiny signs of progress. Another type of scale looks at the client's confidence that they will be able to do something. This is not, of course, anything to do with what precisely they will do. It could be seen as another way of building the client's potential for action and helping all parties ensure that nothing vital has been left unexplored at the end of the session.

BRIEF's Evan George (2017) has written cogently about three different ways to use confidence scales in this context:

*   Confidence of being able to make progress on your best hopes (scale of 1–10, followed by discussion of what is helping to be that high). This can be particularly useful at the end of a first session.
*   Confidence of maintaining the changes you have made (scale of 1–10, again followed by discussion about what helps things to be that high, and perhaps even higher). This can be useful when therapy is coming to an end.
*   Confidence of maintaining change and of reaching 'good enough'. This concept of 'good enough' can be a useful way to gauge progress, in terms not of reaching a 10 but rather in the client's own experience at the moment.

As ever with SF scales, the number is not very relevant (although one might want to go slower with someone who rates their confidence of making progress as a 3, as compared to a 9). The value comes in the following step, 'how come it's that high and not lower?'. And (of course) 'what else?'.

If signs of progress have been hard to find

A low number on a confidence scale, or slow to minimal responses from the client about details of a better future, instances or signs of progress, are not reasons to give up. Sometimes the world-stretching takes time and effort, and it's not fair to expect it all to be in place at the end of the first session (though sometimes things can progress remarkably quickly). If the client still appears to be unsure of the details of 'better', it's probably time to go slow. One SF saying which goes all the way back to the BFTC days is 'don't be more keen on change than your client'. If the client gets the idea you are trying to drag them forward, they will probably resist you – even if, in the end, they want to go in that direction! Offering space to the client to think, keeping most of our weight in the circle of acknowledgement (about how tough things have been and how it's been difficult for the client up to now), and also looking for tiny hints about what the client wants to be better, are all useful strategies.

If such doubts and uncertainty remain at the end of the session, there are at least two options:

Ask the client to notice when things are better

The practitioner encourages the client to look out for anything they experience over the coming days which seems to be better in some way – indeed, in any way. The conversation so far may well have had more impact on the world of the client than they realise while still sitting in the practitioner's chair. The real test is about how they see things and respond to events outside, faced with the rich stimuli of everyday life. Assuming they wish to come back for another session, anything they report can be used as new starting points for world-stretching descriptions and new possibilities.

Ask the client to think more about what they want in their lives

If even noticing when things are better seems like a step too far, the practitioner can ask the client to think more about what they want (and may want to keep) in their lives, and what 'better' might entail for themselves and those around them. This might result in reports about 'better' instances at the next session, which can be expanded. It could also lead to the formulation of a new project and a new ticket, redefining the work and effectively making a new start next time. As a striking alternative, the 'worst-case' scenario method proposed by John Henden (2008) can bring a new angle,

Offering choice about future sessions and possibilities

In the old days of psychodynamic therapy, regular attendance of the client over months and even years was seen as a prerequisite for effective treatment. In the brief therapy tradition we take a very different view; we think each session may be the last, and so we want to achieve as much as possible for the client in that time. As we saw in Chapter 1, the ethics of brief therapy demand that we do not waste the client's time, and the client is best placed to judge when treatment should be concluded.

The way in which sessions are brought to an end is therefore different from some other traditions of practice. We do not assume that another session will happen. We ask the client whether they would like one. (There may be other considerations such as a limit to the number of sessions and mandates from other authorities for treatment – these should be dealt with at the start of the session, not the end.)

If we have been listening carefully to the client, their hopes and their experiences, we might hope that they wish to continue. If they don't, it may well be a cause for gentle celebration; it's not unusual for clients to feel sufficiently rebalanced to be able to carry on their lives without professional help. (Sometimes this comes in the form of a cancelled second session rather than an immediate realisation.)

Some practitioners like to use short questionnaires like the Session Rating Scale (SRS) (Duncan et al., 2003) to gather feedback after sessions. This fits well with the idea that SF practitioners are researchers-in-action and should be keeping tabs on their own effectiveness. It is not infallible (there are examples of clients leaving a session less than satisfied and nonetheless returning with surprising progress to report), but it is at least one way to be mindful of the impact of one's practice.

In keeping with the idea of offering choice and power to the client, we prefer to let them choose wherever possible how long they wish to wait before returning. Of course this will also depend on practicalities such as available appointments. An interesting development around the world in recent times has been the growth in drop-in therapy clinics, where people can simply walk in off the street and see someone (Young & Jebreen, 2019). This fits the brief therapy ethos very well; the starting assumption is of a single session, not a series. And of course, if people want to return they can always drop-in again.

Case example: Jack feeling properly heard (continued)

We pick up the case from the previous chapter with Jack, the young man experiencing family tensions with his father. The practitioner P has been building a description of instances where the client had experienced events relating to their best hopes of 'feeling properly heard'. This transcript picks up immediately from that in Chapter 11.

Transcript	Commentary
P: So we kind of looked at the scale and being 10 that miracle day, so that, that, that's, you know, waking up and...	Practitioner bridged from the Instances Gallery to the Gift Shop with an appreciative summary of the previous piece of description-building and re-establishes the progress scale which they will use again to look for tiny signs of progress.
C: Yeah.	
P: – feeling more confident and, and open to talk to dad and having a meal together, you know. And you described what difference that would make and what would be happening. So if you were to move up the scale a little bit closer to that when we talk again, what will you be telling me that's been different?	Practitioner uses an interesting way to introduce the idea of tiny signs in the future: if you were to move up the scale a little bit when we talk again, what will you be telling me that's been different? (Practitioner could be accused of presupposing another session, but they aren't really; it's more of a way of putting the client a little way into the future, in the here-and-now of the conversation.)
C: I think even just thinking now, it probably would be something like just making a dinner for everybody and we'd all kind of sit down at the same time, because that does happen – we all do end up sitting round together. And I suppose I probably would make a meal and get my sister involved in making it as well or –	

Transcript	Commentary
P: Mm. So you'd make a meal and get your sister involved in it as well, yeah.	Grounding making a meal and getting sister involved as well.
C: Yeah.	And grounded.
P: Mm.	
C: Just, yeah, take that weight off dad to do it all the time, and –	
P: Mm, yeah.	
C: Yeah, I think just something, something like that –	
P: Mm.	
C: – would I think, in a weird way, bring everybody together.	
P: Mm. So, having a meal together would, in a weird way, bring people together. And if you were able to do that, what difference would that make to that hope of yours, you know, that sort of hope of feeling more confident and open to, to talk to dad about your identity?	Practitioner summarises using client's word and asks about the difference that would make, linking back to the original ticket office project of feeling properly heard (which involved the client's identity).
C: We would get just a little bit closer, you know, and I feel that doing that kind of thing and bringing us all closer together as family –	
P: Mm.	
C: – would sort of take steps towards being able to share if we weren't doing so good.	
P: Mm.	
C: Being able to share more vulnerable parts of ourselves, um –	
P: Mm.	Client very firmly grounds the idea of 'share more vulnerable parts'.
C: Yeah, I think that will probably be it, being able to share more vulnerable parts, and then I'd feel more comfortable –	Client is taking their time here and going slowly. Practitioner shows patience and gentle encouragement.

(Continued)

(Continued)

Transcript	Commentary

P: Mm.

C: – to share that vulnerable part of myself –

P: Mm.

C: – that we haven't necessarily talked about –

P: Mm.

C: – in depth.

P: Mm. So having that meal together, having that opportunity to be together, just talk about stuff would also – would lead or give opportunity for you to talk about those more vulnerable, those parts, yeah. OK. So, now we'll sort of draw the session to a close –

Practitioner summarises again, once more including client's newly grounded words.

C: Of course, yeah.

P: – if that's OK. So I just want to ask you, Jack, what have you noticed about yourself in our conversation that we've had today that's been useful? If you were to compliment yourself based on our conversation today, what would you say?

Practitioner doesn't offer compliments but rather asks client to self-compliment.

C: I don't know. It's funny, I think I've noticed that [sighs] – it's funny just thinking about it and thinking about it as a sort of a whole – I kind of just thought about it as I've had this block of speaking to dad. Um, but thinking about it like this and thinking you can just – doing a meal might get us a little bit towards that.

The client's initial 'I don't know' doesn't mean that ... it gives them a moment to think. Practitioner wisely lets the 'I don't know' ride.

Client is drawing the session together for themselves.

So there are now new possibilities for action, it seems. The client's world has been stretched.

P: Mm.

C: Um, I think it's nice to see that I, you know, I can almost think of a path through it and not just view it as a big wall.

P: Mm.

Transcript	Commentary
C: I can just think of it as a sort of smaller chunks to get there, I think. And being able to sort of stop and being able to just see that, yeah. I think stop – and able to just see that it isn't a wall.	
P: Mm.	
C: It can be sort of a longer journey, I suppose.	
P: Mm. So being able to stop and to see that it isn't a wall and that you can break it down into smaller – yeah.	Once again, practitioner summarising using client's words about the wall and breaking it down.
C: Sort of divide it, yeah.	
P: Yeah, OK. And what difference would noticing that make to you?	And another description-building 'what difference would noticing that make to you?'
C: It'll, I guess, give me more of a, a knowledge to think like this perhaps, if things happen in the future –	
P: Mm.	
C: – not necessarily look at it as a wall, but think of it – there is a little path, but you've just got to sort of think of what the first thing might be.	
P: Mm-hmm.	
C: To backtrack all the way ... what is the first thing?	Client is telling themselves that progress is about a step at a time, which coincidentally fits with SF focus of small steps from here.
P: Yeah.	
C: What's the second thing, you know?	
P: Mm. So when we talk again and, and I ask you what's been better, what will you be telling me?	Practitioner asks client to sum up for themselves.
C: I think I will say I've done a meal.	Client sounding more confident here.
P: You've done a meal, yeah [laughs].	

(Continued)

(Continued)

Transcript	Commentary
	And more detail comes about how the meal can happen and how it can play a part in the bigger picture.
C: Yeah, and I think my sister would have helped with it, and we all sort of would have – the two of us will have a bit of a chat and try to get dad involved, I suppose.	
P: Mm.	
C: We'd all sat down and just had a bit of chat, I think is a –	
P: Mm.	
C: And whether we lead onto watching a movie together or, certainly, who knows, but –	(The idea of watching a movie together emerged during Future Gallery descriptions earlier in the session.)
P: Mm.	
C: – even just having that opportunity of all – for all three of us to – sit down together and just chat –	
P: Mm.	
C: I think that will sort of I think lead to other things, I suppose.	Client is seeing the possibility of preparing a meal together and a chat as a step forward rather than as the 'solution', which again fits well with the SF outlook that 'change is happening all the time'.
P: Mm, yeah, so the opportunity to sit and chat and have a meal together could lead to other things.	Practitioner summarises.
C: Mm.	
P: Yeah, mm, OK. Gonna leave it there, if that's OK, yeah?	And winds up.
C: That's fine, yeah, yeah.	
P: Yeah, OK.	

Key points

•   Ending an SF session has evolved over the years and continues to evolve with giving even more power, choice and responsibility to the client.

- Asking for signs of progress, rather than next steps, brings small and short-term details into the conversation as well as leaving open many possibilities for the client.
- Rather than taking a break to compile and offer a list of compliments, the practitioner can summarise appreciatively and ask the client to self-compliment.
- Confidence scales can help the client to feel more secure that they have options and options for the future.
- If signs of progress are hard to find, encouraging the client to notice moments when they experience life as a little better can keep things going. Alternatively ask the client to consider further what they want in their lives and begin with a new project next time.
- Offer the possibility of a follow-up session rather than insisting or expecting it. Every session can be the last, and it's broadly up to the client.

References

Aoki, Y. (2006). *Solution Focused Practical Management*. Tokyo: Kawade-Shobo Shinsha.

de Shazer, S. (1975). Brief therapy: Two's company. *Family Process, 14*, 79–93.

de Shazer, S. (1982). *Patterns of Brief Family Therapy*. New York, NY: Guilford Press.

Duncan, B. L., Miller, S. D., Sparks, J. A., Claud, D. A., Reynolds, L. R., Brown, J., & Johnson, L. D. (2003). The Session Rating Scale: Preliminary psychometric properties of a "working" alliance measure. *Journal of Brief Therapy, 3*(1), 3–12.

Dweck, C. S. (2006). *Mindset: The New Psychology of Success*. New York, NY: Random House.

Fredrickson, B. L. (2001). The role of positive emotions in positive psychology: The broaden-and-build theory of positive emotions. *The American Psychologist, 56*(3), 218–226. https://doi.org/10.1037//0003-066x.56.3.218

George, E. (2017). *Scaling Up Our Practice*. Retrieved from www.facebook.com/BRIEF. SolutionFocus/posts/10155063623559976?pnref=story

Henden, J. (2008). *Preventing Suicide: The Solution-Focused Approach*. Hoboken, NJ: J. Wiley.

Korman, H. J., Korman, J. M., & Miller, S. D. (2020). Effort-focused interviewing. *Journal of Systemic Therapies, 39*(1), 35–48. https://doi.org/10.1521/jsyt.2020.39.1.35

Satir, V. (1964). *Conjoint Family Therapy: A Guide to Theory and Technique*. Palo Alto, CA: Science and Behavior Books.

Thomas, F. N. (2016). Complimenting in solution-focused brief therapy. *Journal of Solution Focused Brief Therapy, 2*(1), 1–22.

Weakland, J., Fisch, R., Watzlawick, P., & Bodin, A. (1974). Brief therapy: Focused problem resolution. *Family Process, 13*(2), 141–168.

Young, K., & Jebreen, J. (2019). Recognizing single-session therapy as psychotherapy. *Journal of Systemic Therapies, 38*(4), 31–44. https://doi.org/10.1521/jsyt.2019.38.4.31

Chapter 13

Revisiting the gallery
Follow-on sessions

A lot of Solution Focused Brief Therapy (SFBT) books focus on first sessions. This is understandable. After all, that is often where the main action
happens and the trademark methods such as miracle questions and scales
are deployed. And sometimes one session is enough. However, often there
will be follow-up sessions. In this chapter we will look at these conversations from a world-stretching perspective, which adds to a broader view of
what is going on when we ask the simple and classic SF follow-up question
'What's better?'.

What's better?

This follow-up starter question is so simple and stark that some new practitioners find it quite un-nerving. What if nothing is better? What if things are even
worse? What if it's all my fault?

Relax. The client has been making their own choices and living their
own life since you saw them last. What you were part of was stretching their
world – building their affordances, their opportunities for relevant action. Sitting in the room as that initial conversation unfolds, it's impossible to tell how
it's really going – apparently unmoved and reluctant clients can come back
with tales of their lives transformed, while others who seemed happy and
enthusiastic can return in less favourable mood. We just don't know – so we
have to ask. And wait.

Note that this is *not* 'did you do the actions?'. It may look like it at first sight,
but it isn't. For one, in next generation SF work there are often no actions
to ask about. And even if the client talked about what they might do in the
first session, that doesn't matter. This is not a game of holding to account, or
catching the client out, or accusing them of fecklessness. What we want is to
talk about 'in what ways has your stretched world shown up?'. Any actions
may well have become irrelevant in the swirl of what has happened since the
previous session.

What's happening with 'what's better?'

This is a deliberately wide-open question. It presupposes a considerable amount:

- That the client knows what 'what' refers to – their lives, particularly connected to the project discussed last time
- That something (at least) is better, and perhaps more than one thing at that.

Within that, it can be taken to ask about anything in the client's life. It could be things that the client left the last session thinking about. It might be unexpected things that happened, apparently (or even actually) at random. These things could be big or small. They could be the result of terrific striving by the client, or no apparent effort at all. We don't care. What's better? Any experiences of better become Instances to be expanded and explored, as we saw in the chapter on the Instances Gallery.

From the world-stretching perspective, this is an invitation for the client to say how they have experienced this stretched world, which is now their new normal world. What have they noticed, what has suggested itself as interesting or useful, which affordances have appeared, or seemed more attractive or noticeable? In the world-stretching view, we cannot know at the end of the session exactly how the stretched world will look and feel to the client (and thus to those around them). The wide open 'what else?' question starts to explore that.

Often clients will have something to say. Great – we can expand and build on whatever it is, using our description-building questions and tiny micro-analysis encouragements, as discussed in the Instances Gallery chapter. What they are talking about are, of course, now Instances of events in the past that support progress with their project. The near future has moved into the recent past; the experience of the client holds it all together.

Love it or list it?

The client offers their first example of 'better' and the practitioner how has a choice. They can 'love it' and explore the details of the first thing. Or they can (metaphorically or on paper) 'list it', asking 'what else?' for more things that are better. The idea is to keep up the flow of the client's thinking at this early stage; the first example can be revisited for exploration and expansion later. This is down to the preferences of the practitioner in the situation – I prefer to list, and then go back. And there are also opportunities for appreciative summarising, as the client recalls several different things that are better. (*Love It Or List It* is also a popular UK property-hunting television show, by the way.)

The idea of using lists has gained useful currency in some quarters. If clients are asked to list (say) 23 things that are better, they will strive to reach the target (as long as it's presented cogently and with some supporting grounds for optimism, i.e. the client has already started to list things themselves). They may reach 23 (and be slightly triumphant). They may sweat their way to 16, 17, 18, protesting all the while that there are no more (except that there often are). This is world-stretching in action once again. The 'stretch' may feel like hard work to the client and is all the more valuable for that. The role of the practitioner is to wait expectantly, note down and help to ground each aspect as it comes, to be appreciative, be impressed that the client has managed to notice so many things, and ask 'what else?'. The use of practitioners' expectations has been part of our work since the Brief Family Therapy Center (BFTC) days in the mid-1980s, when de Shazer and Berg were drawing on the work of Robert Rosenthal (1966).

Use your EARS

How to expand on 'what's better' is captured in another long-standing piece of SF wisdom attributed to Insoo Kim Berg (De Jong & Berg, 1998) – the EARS protocol. This memorable and usable framework is justifiably widely used. In its original form it stands for:

- E – Elicit what's better
- A – Amplify by asking detailed questions about how this came about, how the client did it, remembered it, knew that it was time to do it, and so on
- R – Reinforce by offering a compliment about the successes and strengths which have been shown, and
- S – Start over, finding another thing that's better and doing it again.

Insoo obviously preferred loving each thing that's better rather than listing them. With the next generation world-stretching view, we can still use EARS, with slightly altered definitions:

- E – Elicit what's better
- A – Amplify by building the detailed description from the client's and other perspective, using our description-building questions. These include:

  - How did you do that?
  - What difference did that make?
  - What difference did that make to person [Y]?
  - What were the first tiny signs that [X] was happening?
  - Who else noticed [X] was happening? What did they notice?
  - What did person [Y] do when they noticed you doing [X]?
  - What did you do in response to that?
  - What happened next?

- R – Reinforce using the client's words, ensuring that they are well grounded in the conversation, and summarise appreciatively
- S – Start over with another example.

Of course, all this detailed description continues to stretch the world of the client, expanding and firming up developments since the last session. This process might look like a simple monitoring exercise, but it's not; it's a full-strength continuation of the processes we were using in the first session.

What if ... nothing seems to be better

This is always the concern of novice practitioners. It does not happen all that often. However, it is as well to be equipped with some options.

Wait ...

Sometimes people offer a rather rapid and glib 'Nothing!' response to the question of what's better. This is often the equivalent of saying 'I haven't thought about it', or 'I'm not ready' or even 'why am I here again?'. The first thing to do is look expectant and wait. Nod a little. Ready your pen and paper. Don't take it as an answer. Wait for another response.

If the response is still 'nothing', we can start working with it. Don't protest, but remind the client of the project you started working on together – the name, the key differences. Ask again what they have noticed since you last met – stressing that even tiny details could be relevant and useful. Wait again.

If still 'nothing', suggest some key relevant moments from the intervening period – going to work, seeing the parents, going to the shops, evenings with the spouse, whatever relates to the hopes and future descriptions. Gently ask in a more focused way what they noticed at these times. We are working very much in the Circle of Acknowledgement here (as discussed in Chapter 9) – give plenty of space, and don't leap too fast on any tiny signs of progress. List them and keep waiting.

Coping

If there is still no response, one tactic is to switch the focus from what's better to how the client is coping and keeping going. Again, we are firmly in acknowledging territory here, so give plenty of space and acknowledge whatever emerges. Resist the urge (for now) to leap on anything as an Instance to be pursued – just note it and wait. Asking 'what else?' can also be useful here.

Sometimes coping experiences and strategies can be a way into building progress. At other times they can be ways to handle unexpected developments – even positive ones. Life is, in many ways, quite a lot about coping with what comes and feeling able to carry on anyway. That's normal for most of us, most of the time.

If useful things do emerge, this can be another opportunity for appreciative summarising, being patient and present with the client and seeing what may come next.

Returning to the project definition

If nothing is better and little is helping the client to cope, another option can be to return to the Ticket Office. The client described their best hopes for the work and the differences this would make in the first session. Sometimes things shift around in the intervening period – after all, we assume as a starting point that change is happening all the time. If things seem really stuck, one option is to go back to the project and restart from the client's new best hopes, given their experience. This is rarely necessary, but it is a good option to have to reach for if all seems messy and confused. It might even be that talking isn't the best option in this particular case; seeing a medic or social services might be alternatives.

Grounds for optimism

Another track is to ask the clients about how come they think that progress is possible, with this project. One of the variants of SFBT practice, the Bruges model (de Shazer & Isebaert, 2003) revisits a distinction that first appeared in the Mental Research Institute's work in the 1970s (Watzlawick, Weakland & Fisch, 1974) about the difference between a problem (which can be worked with) and a limitation (which is not itself solvable, but must rather be worked around).

To give a simple example, there are 24 hours in a day. The client may wish there were more hours in the day, but there aren't. That's a limitation. Of course that is not the end of the story; what difference would it make if there *were* extra hours in the day? Helping the client use their time better is a perfectly workable project but adding extra hours to the day is not. Not all projects are equally workable. If the client has some grounds for optimism that progress is possible, then that may help in redefining the project.

'Doing something different'

We first met the three 'golden rules' of SF work in Chapter 3:

1   If it ain't broke, don't fix it.
2   Once you know what works, do more of it.
3   Stop doing what doesn't work and do something different.

The third rule, a key element of MRI model brief therapy, is rarely used in SFBT practice. However, it sits there as a kind of backstop, something to use in the rare cases that the usual practices in rules 1 and 2 fail to yield anything at all.

In my experience such cases are rare, and even rarer since I brought more focus to detailed description-building and world-stretching. At one point in my career I recorded many coaching sessions with clients in the expectation that one day the usual things would have no impact and I would get to brilliantly improvise something novel. This never happened. As a result, I am much less interested in alternative strategies. Some do exist which don't involve straying outside the SF norms; here are three to work with if you really need them.

What has worked for other people in a similar situation?

A starting point of SF work is that every case is different (Jackson & McKergow, 2002). However, there may be useful ideas in the experience of others, particularly if they are credible to the client. This could be positioned as a project for the client, to go and explore the stories of others. There may be local support groups where such people hang out. There may be books and online resources/forums where people are discussing these things. There is a distinction between telling the client what to do and pointing them at potentially useful resources. The key things is that it's the client who gets to choose whether to get involved, and what to make of it. We don't want to force things on the client, but we do want to expand their horizons and possibilities. Some ideas 'fit' well for some clients and not for others, an idea going back to the work of Milton Erickson in the 1950s (see Chapter 2).

Change to another modality or method

Some practitioners work with SF alongside other modalities such as hypnotherapy, transactional analysis, NLP, gestalt and so on. Personally, I think that doing SF really well requires setting any other ideas aside while I focus on this client, their language and their experience. However, SFBT is not the only thing that works. So, if after perhaps three sessions things are really going nowhere using SFBT ideas, another option might be to try something else. I would suggest this to the client rather than simply imposing it and get them alongside in doing something different. Mark Beyebach (2014) reports work by his colleague Herrero de Vega showing that if the client is still at less than 3 on the progress scale after three sessions, the case can be considered stuck and open to new options. He recommends re-scaling in each session, even if there is not time to work on the scale, to give feedback to the practitioner.

I would also take the case to supervision. Sometimes other practitioners can see things in different ways, which can be helpful either in continuing this case or in learning for the future. The SF approach can also be used for effective supervision (Thomas, 2013), although this is a different and wider application than the standard client work we've been describing here. I have found great value in peer supervision groups over the years; these can also connect SF practitioners from different areas of expertise, with counsellors and coaches working together.

Change to another practitioner

Alongside changing to another modality, it is worth considering an even more dramatic shift; changing the practitioner. You may decide that things aren't going anywhere with this client, and when you catch yourself thinking that, it's probably time to move on. We don't have the right to waste the client's time. It is quite ethical and proper to refer the client on to someone else. We can involve the client in this move, seek their thoughts (they may want us to carry on, in which case we can explore what has been helpful so far), and ask them about what they think might be helpful. I would say that if nothing is happening at all after five or six sessions, it may be best for everyone to move on.

Ending the process

As brief therapists and practitioners, we will be hoping for many successful ends to treatment and client relationships. Steve de Shazer always said that SFBT should take 'as many sessions as necessary, and not one more', and that still holds good today. (This does not necessarily mean that there cannot be a continuing relationship – in my work as an organisational coach I am sometimes contracted to work with a manager for say six sessions – but each will very likely be on a different project.)

Treatment ends when the client feels able to carry on under their own steam, without our support. All along we have been giving the client as much choice as possible, leaving them to live their lives and notice useful differences. The transition from doing this as part of a continuing conversation with us, to doing it alone, is a very modest one. Indeed, at the end of what may turn out to be the last session the client may not yet know that they will be able to carry on without further support.

Many practitioners like to offer the client a session 'in the bank', the possibility to return at any point in the future if they feel they would like to. This gives the client a safety net, which they may hold onto for months or even years before using. Many never use it at all; the possibility of another session is enough to keep going. On other occasions the client may phone or email to cancel a planned session if they feel they are doing well enough not to need it. Others may (rudely) simply not show up.

This is not the anguished wrench of a parent whose child is leaving home, a divorcing couple parting or even the death of a loved one. All along we have been seeking the healthy adult within (in the words of Bill O'Hanlon) and working with them as far as possible as equals. The client-practitioner relationship is more like a taxi-driver or coffee server than a long-term commitment, and the end of treatment may well be a relief to the client – their problems are dissolving. We will explore more about what makes SFBT different in the next chapter about aesthetics in action.

Case example: Jack feeling properly heard (follow-up)

This is part of the follow-up session to the case with Jack, the young man we've been following in the last two chapters. His project was about 'feeling properly heard' at home, where there had been tensions with his father. He had talked about making dinner, perhaps with his sister, for his father (his mother died some time ago), as part of building more connection. We pick up at the very start of the second session.

Transcript	Commentary
P: So, this is our follow-up session; this is, uh, a second session to the session that we had a couple of weeks ago. So, Jack, what, what's been better since I saw you last?	Practitioner straight into 'what's better?'. Not asking about anything specific, this is a wide open question.
C: I think immediately, um, I've definitely noticed a change and I've felt a bit more open to talk about, well, how I'm feeling, I guess, and how I'm feeling about other people in the house, um, and just be a bit more open to talk about feelings in general, I suppose.	Client starts slowly and a little uncertainly here, which is very normal. This is very likely the first time they've talked about these experiences in this way.
P: Mm.	Practitioner listening and gently encouraging ...
C: And that hasn't felt that what I sort of previously mentioned as a kind of – like a wall kind of thing to talk about feelings. There hasn't been that –	
P: Oh [laughs].	Practitioner gently 'surprised', noting something new from the client.
C: – as much, at least, it's felt like a bit of – quite a bit of a change, to be honest.	
P: Mm-hmm, wow. So more open to talk about feelings -	Offering back 'talk about feelings' and adding 'more open'.
C: Yeah.	

(Continued)

(Continued)

Transcript	Commentary
P: – has been quite a bit of a change, yeah?	
C: Mm, even, you know, talking about, um, identity, which was something that was a bit sort of unheard of me doing.	Talking about his identity was a key thing for the client in the first session.
P: Yeah.	
C: It has sort of come up and, um, it's just that made me feel a lot more comfortable, I think -	'It has just sort of come up' ... This is not at all an unusual way that things get reported in SF follow-ups. The client didn't seem to really strive to bring it up (though it's important), but it came up anyway – perhaps in the stretched world there are new possibilities?
P: Mm-hmm.	
C: – at home. Um –	
P: Mm.	
C: Yeah, it's just been a lot more comfortable, I think.	
P: Yeah, so a lot more comfortable.	Offering back 'a lot more comfortable'.
C: Mm.	Grounded.
P: I'm really interested to hear how this happened, so –	Now the practitioner starts to explore and expand the detail. They are going for the 'love it' strategy of taking the first moment, rather than 'list it' be looking for more better moments right now.
C: Yeah.	
P: – when did you first notice this change and, and what happened? How did it change?	'When did you first notice?' Not 'what did you do' – very much about description building.
C: Yeah. Well, I suppose it was kind of my sister came to me to talk about how she was doing. And it got to a point where I thought, oh, I just kinda need to just kind of go for it and try and talk to dad in whatever capacity I can, just to sort of try and sort of bridge up a bit of this gap that we've got between everybody. Um, in doing that, I just sort of told, you know, told dad how she was feeling –	
P: Mm.	

Transcript	Commentary
C: – um, and how I was feeling about perhaps how she was.	
P: Mm.	
C: Um, and I just sort of said about I was, you know, how I was, um, trying to help her with that, trying to just talk through it with her, um, trying to talk to both dad and my sister. And it's a different kind of way of – for me, I think it's a different way that I hadn't approached before.	There seems (unsurprisingly) to be a complex set of relationships between client, sister and father. Practitioner lets client talk in his own words.

(From this point the Mm's and Yeah's are mostly removed in the interests of readability and space. They continued to occur in the dialogue.) |
| P: So what did you do? Tell me exactly. So you had this conversation with your sister – and she had come to you to tell you how she was feeling. So how did the...? Where were you and how did the conversation come together with dad and your sister? | Practitioner again asking for more details in the realm of concrete, observable and specific.

Practitioner also feeling their way slightly here, being tentative to encourage client to step in and be clearer if he can. |
C: Well, yeah, I think, so as, as it does quite a lot of the time, it kind of – my sister just wanted a bit of a rant and a bit of a brain dump, you know. Because that's how it is sometimes, and so she did. And I just kind of listened. I listened to that and just sort of took it all in and then just sort of started to ask her questions, perhaps – to get to – I don't know – where – not where her problem lies, but sort of exploring things a bit more with her – as to how, as to perhaps why and things that were making her feel this way.	
P: Mm.	*(Practitioner is continuing to encourage the client with Mm's through this section.)*
C: Um, and I kind of chatted with her for a bit and just sort of got my mind a bit more – just clear as to what she – how she was feeling. And I thought, you know, I, I said to her, I think I want to go and speak to dad now. And I did – [laughs], don't know what sort of came over me – but I did.	
P: Oh!	Again, practitioner notes a little surprise at something new appearing in the dialogue.

(Continued)

(Continued)

Transcript	Commentary
C: [Laughs] Um, but yeah, I just sort of sat down and asked if she'd mind if we had a bit of a chat. And it was a bit like yeah, that's fine. Um, and it was just like we were able to sort of bridge that gap. And to be honest, I suppose we were – we almost felt like we had this kind of thing, because we were both a bit nervous to speak to each other in a way. It sort of felt like that. Um, and I think we just wanted to be – the two of us wanted to be on the same page really.	'able to bridge that gap'.
P: Yeah. So how did you bridge that gap? What was it happening in that moment that had changed?	Practitioner offers back the phrase 'bridge that gap' for more detail.
C: Well, I was sort of – I [pause], I don't know, I was just kind of acknowledging that suddenly it felt like there, there was this gap perhaps between – in the family that we had, we'd just sort of of – whilst we are trying to help, you know, my sister out – there's still this kind of gap perhaps which just isn't – feelings aren't perhaps talked about as much.	
P: Mm.	
C: Um, and I think for me, it was just being able to acknowledge that and tell that to dad and just sort of get it out to him ...	
P: You said that to dad?	Practitioner recognises something that the client said was important to him in the last session and wants to make sure it isn't passed over.
C: Mm.	
P: Yeah.	
C: I think. And I was stressing that it's none of our problem, it's not a problem, it's just how things have gone, and we just kind of need to be mindful of that and – just sort of – I don't know – have these more open – not be afraid to have these open conversations, because we all want to help each other. And, um, you know, I just – I-I-I – what I said is I'm trying different things, that I've been talking	Client is still exploring these words with himself and naturally stumbles from time to time. Practitioner listens patiently and encouragingly.

Transcript	Commentary
these through, these methods that I've been taught, which is a bit of a different way that I've done in the past, you know.	
P: Mm-hmm.	
C: And I felt like I'm getting somewhere, um, and so I said to that to dad. I just want to – him to know that I am trying to do things as well, I suppose.	
P: And, how did he respond?	Practitioner looking for interactional detail – what did dad do in response?
C: He was, he was sort of, to start with, um, I don't know. It was, he was just sort of [sighs] perhaps focusing on the issue of naturally you, you know – focusing on the issue that perhaps my sister thinks negatively.	Client again exploring the experience for himself and thinking out loud.
P: Mm.	
C: But as I was sort of getting there, I felt like I'm just sort of speaking. You know, I'm trying to focus a bit more on the solution and not – I'm just trying to speak in a more positive manner.	
P: Mm.	
C: Um, he said just, you know, try whatever works for you and, well, naturally, you know, the end goal for all of us is that we all, you know, are all feeling good. Um, so he's sort of saying if that works for you and you find that works, then just go for it. I still see there was a bit of doubt, you know, but I-I – it felt like it has been working, so I am gonna try, you know, try to keep doing that.	
P: Mm. So what have you noticed that's different about you, do you think?	Practitioner brings descriptive focus back to client – self-noticing.
C: Well, first off, I think we've just been talking more. We've just been, you know, we've had a couple of dinners together and, um, you know – we had a dinner the other night, which was really nice,	

(Continued)

(Continued)

Transcript	Commentary
one of my favourite meals I haven't had for absolutely ages, you know, long, long time. But, um, we were just sat around and chatted for a bit, and – that was actually after, um – there was quite a moment at home where, um, sort of got home and my sister just sort of – it got a bit much for her. I think she just literally let it out.	
P: Mm.	
C: And I think dad did the same. Um, in a way, for me, I said to dad after it all sort of finished, that in a way that felt like a step for me – because she had opened up and said what the issue was to dad.	
P: Right.	Practitioner continues to gently encourage client to keep going, with nods and occasional words.
C: And so she'd known it, and just sort of hidden it away a bit. But she'd sort of just kind of – you know, even if she hadn't touched on a big part of it, she's just let some of it out. Um, so we're on the same page, all of us.	
P: Mm, yeah.	
C: And immediately then, you know, she went up to her room and laid in bed, um, and usually when that happens, I can't get her out of bed. But that day, I was able to go up there and have a bit of a chat with her. Um, and I was able to get her out of bed – which was novel, you know.	
P: So what was different, do you think? What was it that enabled you to get her out of bed?	Again, practitioner shifts onto what how client has been able to notice and act differently.
C: It was a more [sighs] – it wasn't me kind of saying ... I suppose it wasn't me – I think actually, to be honest, it wasn't me focusing on the problem.	
P: Mm.	

Transcript	Commentary
C: And I think it was me sort of – I guess just [sighs], oh, I don't know, it was – it just felt a more, more positive way of speaking.	
P: Mm.	
C: And I was sort of saying to her that, you know, it might not feel like that to you, but I'm really proud of you for just being able to go and let that out.	
P: Mm, yeah. So saying to her that you were really proud of her for letting that out, yeah.	Grounding 'really proud of her for letting that out'
C: Yeah.	And grounded.

The earlier dialogue has taken around ten minutes. The conversation continues for about another 20 minutes, covering more details about how these interactions between client, sister and dad played out around the dinner. It turns out that dad made the dinner for them all, and that the act of sitting down together more often has opened up opportunities for more and different conversations in the family. The session concluded without any specific actions, plans or even things to be noticing stated by either party. The client was able to carry on with his life with better family relationships and has become more able to express his identity both with the family and with friends. He feels properly heard, at least sufficiently, and this is no longer an overbearing concern.

Key points

- Follow–up sessions in SFBT consist of further expanding the client's descriptions of scenes in their lives which support their best hopes coming into action, stretching their world still further.
- The session starts with 'what's better?' to ask the client to start to talk about these scenes, which are treated as Instances in the Instances Gallery and expanded as such.
- The practitioner has a choice of 'love it' (expand each scene in turn) or 'list it' (starting by getting the titles of several scenes and then going back to expand them in turn).
- Expanding the descriptions can be done using the EARS protocol.

- If nothing seems to be better initially, the practitioner has choices to wait, ask again, give space, and perhaps ask about key moments which may have happened.
- If there is still nothing to work with, the practitioner can look at how the client is coping, go back to the project definition and look at how come the client thinks progress might be possible.
- If after several sessions there is still no progress (and this is very rare), there are further options to 'do something different':

  - Have the client explore what has helped others in a similar situation – pointing to resources, support groups, online information etc.
  - Change the modality and try a completely different method.
  - Change the practitioners – refer on to someone else.

References

Beyebach, M. (2014). Change factors in solution-focused brief therapy: A review of the Salamanca studies. *Journal of Systemic Therapies*, *33*(1), 62–77.

De Jong, P., & Berg, I. K. (1998). *Interviewing for Solutions*. Pacific Grove, CA: Brooks/Cole.

de Shazer, S., & Isebaert, L. (2003). The Bruges model. *Journal of Family Psychotherapy*, *14*(4), 43–52. doi:10.1300/J085v14n04_04

Jackson, P. Z., & McKergow, M. (2002). *The Solutions Focus: The SIMPLE Way to Positive Change* (2nd ed., 2007). London: Nicholas Brealey Publishing.

Rosenthal, R. (1966). *Experimenter Effects in Behavioral Research*. New York: Appleton-Century-Crofts.

Thomas, F. N. (2013). *Solution-Focused Supervision: A Resource-Oriented Approach to Developing Clinical Expertise*. New York, NY: Springer-Verlag.

Watzlawick, P., Weakland. J., & Fisch, R. (1974). *Change: Principles of Problem Formation and Problem Resolution*. New York, NY: W. W. Norton.

A Solution Focused aesthetic

Chapter 14

The SF aesthetic
What is beautiful and why

This book has examined the origins and development of Solution Focused Brief Therapy (SFBT) and the spread of the Solution Focused (SF) approach into many fields over the past three or four decades. The current book has set out to show SF work in a new light, through the lens of 'stretching the world' of the client. I hope that having a friendly, plausible and (I think) accurate story about what we do will help others appreciate it and become more interested.

SFBT is not merely another therapy, it is a different *kind* of therapeutic practice. That could be why so many practitioners from other traditions look puzzled when they discover what we do and don't do. The difference between this work (and perhaps other forms in the brief therapy tradition) and the popular view of what constitutes 'proper' counselling and therapy is stark. These are like two different aesthetics: sets of values and priorities.

I was immediately and passionately engaged with SF work when I first discovered it in 1993, for reasons that were not completely clear to me at the time. Over the past three decades or so, I have continued in this commitment, and have come to realise that these aesthetic aspects are particularly important to me. This chapter is an overview of why I personally love SF practice.

What is an 'aesthetic'?

Looking at the dictionary (Lexico.com, 2019), we find definitions of 'aesthetic' in the following terms:

> Adjective: *Concerned with beauty or the appreciation of beauty.*
>
> > Example usage: *'the pictures give great aesthetic pleasure'*
>
> Noun: *A set of principles underlying the work of a particular artist or artistic movement.*
>
> > Example usage: *'the Cubist aesthetic'*

The term originates from the Greek word *aisthētikos*, meaning 'perception connected with the senses'. Although sensory perception is clearly important, the idea of aesthetics means more than this. David Hume, 18th-century Edinburgh philosopher and a good cook as well, wrote that delicacy of taste is not merely 'the ability to detect all the ingredients in a composition' but also our sensitivity 'to pains as well as pleasures, which escape the rest of mankind' (Hume, 1987. p. 5). This is about considered affective and emotional responses as well as sensory distinctions.

German philosopher Immanuel Kant (1790/2000) built on Hume's work by pointing out that aesthetic judgements have two elements: subjectivity and universality. There is always a subjective component to a claim of beauty, which is (as all agree) in the eye of the beholder. Kant points out that there is also a claim in such judgement of universality; it is based on logical and observable criteria. Others ought to share our judgement (though they may not). Claims of beauty are more than simply subjective relativism; they convey more than that. The aesthetics presented here are offered in that spirit.

Aesthetics in art

One way into this topic is through the world of art. For centuries, artists strove to produce renditions of (say) landscapes which were detailed, clear and representational. Look at Canaletto's famous paintings of Venice for a fine example, or the British artist Thomas Gainsborough. In these cases the artists made extensive preparatory sketches and then worked up a final highly detailed artwork in their studios, constructing the composition to be pleasing (aesthetically) rather than a snapshot of a particular moment. Even today, the results are sensational.

In the second half of the 19th-century painters started to explore with greater vigour what happened when they ventured out and worked *en plein air*, in the open air at the location. Painters such as John Constable and JMW Turner had begun to explore this in the early 19th century, but it was taken to new extremes by painters such as Claude Monet, Pierre-August Renoir, Alfred Sisley and others in the early 1860s. Their work focused on light and the immediacy of the moment. It was being routinely rejected from the Salon de Paris, the accepted leading curated art show which favoured painters of the classical style.

Emperor Napoleon III saw the rejected works and decreed that the public should be allowed to judge for themselves. As a result, a 'Salon de Refusés', an exhibition of the refused, was organised. While many came to laugh, this exhibition was a key rallying point for those keen on the new 'impressionist' aesthetic which took its name from Monet's *Impression, Sunrise*. As has often been the case through history, the name came as an insult from a critic that Monet's work was at best a sketch, nothing like a finished work.

The impressionist aesthetic is much more about capturing an 'impression' of a moment in time; the brushwork is bigger and bolder, the effect more spontaneous. If we look at an impressionist painting with a classical aesthetic, we see what the critics saw – unfinished, incomplete daubs of little lasting consequence. If we look at Caravaggio and Gainsborough with an impressionist aesthetic, we see stylised, overworked 'perfection' which says little about the artist's (or the viewer's) response.

An alternative paradigm

Both of these aesthetics are interesting and valuable. What I am pointing to here is the way that an alternative paradigm, a new way of looking at things, can be seen through the aesthetic lens; what makes something beautiful? What is valued, prized, admired, noticed, applauded? It's something to do with what makes you go 'Yes!!' and what makes you go 'Blurghhh!'. In this chapter I will seek to explore what makes me cry 'Yes!' in my SF work, and thereby shed a little more light on what it means to work in an SF aesthetic.

What follows is what I love and value about SF practice. The list is not complete, of course, and it's a personal one. I hope that many SF practitioners may find a recognition and a resonance in at least some of these items.

Brevity

SF was originally called Solution Focused Brief Therapy for a reason – it's brief! The original version of interactional brief therapy emerged from the Brief Therapy Centre of the Mental Research Institute, Palo Alto, is still around and uses a ten session framework as its basis (Segal, 1991). At the time (in the 1960s and 1970s) this was startlingly brief, compared to the years of weekly treatment considered normal by practitioners trained in the expectations of the psychodynamic tradition.

When Steve de Shazer and Insoo Kim Berg moved from hanging around MRI to setting up their own centre in Milwaukee in the late 1970s and early 1980s, they wanted to build on this work and developed the idea that brief therapy should be 'as brief as possible, and not one session more' (de Shazer, in his Foreword to Dolan, 1991). This is quite a step onwards from even a ten session basis – every session could be the last, and is carried out with this possibility in mind. The choice of continuing is at least partly with the client; we will return to this aspect of power sharing later.

The very idea that therapy can be effective at all in one or two sessions is still considered outlandish by some, and second-rate by others. Workers in the psychoanalytic tradition developed the concept of the 'flight into health', where the client's claims that they are suddenly and completely cured is seen as a defensive reaction to the treatment, and therefore a sign of the need for even more therapy. This can be seen as a kind of Catch-22 bind; if the client says they are better, they need more treatment. And if they say they aren't better, then of course they need more treatment!

Why is brevity an important end in itself? It helps the client get on with their life sooner, and it frees up the practitioner to help new clients. The advantages of this are particularly clear when resources are limited, as in the UK National Health Service (NHS). According to the 2013 report *We Still Need To Talk* (MIND, 2013), over one in ten people had been waiting over a year to see a therapist, and approximately 50% had waited more than three months. Although things have reportedly improved in the intervening years, there is obviously a direct link between efficient treatment and shorter waiting times. It remains a mystery to me why the popular view of longer equals better still seems to hold so much sway.

Another benefit of brevity is that a short treatment will mean that the client is back living their own life sooner. The goal of SF is, to echo an old aphorism sometimes attributed to Edna St. Vincent Millay, to return the client to a life of 'one damn thing after another'. This is everyday life as we know it – not a flawless and effortless glide but a series of ups and downs, handled by the client without professional help.

Brevity is not a simple matter of a small number of sessions or a limited time. It's about the work being as brief as possible – subject to a satisfactory conclusion, or onward referral. This is not to say that every person only has one problem in their lives. As an SF coach to business leaders, I sometimes get contracted for a series of sessions. I don't consider this to be outside the brief aesthetic, as we are not using the ten sessions to tackle a single issue. Each conversation is usually about a new issue, something that's fresh on the client's mind, or perhaps reflects a developing situation that we've discussed before. And the client can decide that they've had enough of a topic, or indeed enough of me – which leads us onto the next aspect of an SF aesthetic, the valuing of client autonomy.

Client autonomy

In the normal everyday world, people get to make decisions about their own lives; what to do, who to be with, where to go. These decisions are never the only factor in determining what happens. There are always other contexts and forces at work. One of my favourite quotes is from biologist Steven Rose (1997) who, paraphrasing Karl Marx, observed that 'we create our own futures, but not in circumstances of our own choosing' (Rose, Lifelines, p. 309). It is worth pausing to consider that in therapeutic work it has been normal for practitioners to take decisions for, and sometimes in spite of, their clients.

This comes from an old version of the basic doctor/patient relationship, where in decades gone by the doctor's word was law; the patient's role being to be grateful recipient of the doctor's expertise. Of course, if about to undergo brain surgery, then we would want someone with expertise in charge of it, and we would listen seriously to their advice. The risk is that this relationship can become unbalanced, one-sided and potentially abusive. If the doctor becomes an unchallengeable authority figure, the risks of over-long treatments and dis-empowered clients are clear. The same happens all too easily in organisational consulting, where the consultant ends up calling the shots (and often extending their contracts).

The SF position has been that, broadly, it is the client who makes many of the decisions. What are their hopes from therapy? What are they going to do about it? When are things good enough to stop coming? In everyday life these questions are clearly for us as individuals. In the therapy world, however, it can be seen as a paradigm-busting revolution. While the conventional doctor/patient relationship can be characterised as parent/child (in the Transactional Analysis tradition, see for example Berne, 1958), the SF worker/client relationship is much more adult/adult. Both have responsibilities, both have parts to play, both have priorities, and these are to be kept as balanced as feasible.

Of course, client autonomy is not automatic and over-riding in all circumstances. If the client seems to be putting themselves, or others, at risk then clearly the practitioner has some choices to make. Should they inform others? Should they instigate safeguarding processes? These are matters of professional judgement for the practitioner and are not to be underestimated. Outside constraints — for example court orders, probation agreements or other matters of law, impinge on the client's freedom of action. These can be taken into account in various ways with the client's autonomy bounded rather than removed. In all these situations, the limits on client autonomy are seen as topics for discussion and ideally agreement with the client in terms of the next steps to be taken.

There is an interface here with brevity as discussed earlier. The client's autonomy includes their choice to decide when the treatment is over, or that they wish to see someone else. SF has found a healthy home in the world of coaching over the past couple of decades. One reason for this may be that SF therapy looks more like coaching than many other forms of practice. Coaching clients are not usually seen as vulnerable people needing protection — rather, they are informed individuals who are making their own decisions about seeking support. The International Coach Federation (2019) defines coaching as 'partnering with clients in a thought-provoking and creative process that inspires them to maximize their personal and professional potential'.

The focus on partnering with clients seems to me to be a clear fit with the aesthetics of SF. When we ask the miracle question, the space is open. We are offering the client freedom to choose. As we wait, we are in way demanding (respectfully and carefully) that they take that freedom.

Radical acceptance

If we are viewing the client as making their own decisions, then we should also think very carefully about trying to argue with them. This skill of not arguing is sometimes called 'radical acceptance' (de Shazer, 1997). de Shazer argued in the same article that 'The client's answer needs to be accepted fully and literally' (p. 378), which is an art rather than a science, and which is

> difficult for many people. It requires a lot of self discipline and a good deal of close listening. It is not easy to give up making judgments about how high the [scaling] number should be or how unreasonable and unrealistic the initial response to the miracle might be.
>
> (p. 378)

The 'initial' response to a question is key here. One of the concerns I come across from people learning SF is that their clients may seek something impossible from the miracle; the amputee seeking the return of their lost limb, or the bereaved child wanting their parent to come back. And yes, it can be unsettling in some way when this happens. It is also a very obvious and heartfelt wish and can therefore be accepted quite easily. Who wouldn't want these things? The key point is that accepting doesn't mean blindly agreeing and moving on. It can look like nodding gently, exhaling and waiting; waiting is often a good strategy, to allow the client to continue their thinking. It can look like quietly saying 'Yes, of course' and pausing to see what comes next. What comes next – sometimes after a very considerable silence – might be something like 'I'd be visiting my friends more' or 'I'd be happier going to school'. These are more tractable and can be picked up and expanded in the conversation.

Radical acceptance comes down to not arguing with the client, even when to do so would be quite normal and acceptable. de Shazer shared this outlook with his long-term mentor and friend John Weakland. In a joint interview from 1994 (Hoyt, 2001) de Shazer speaks about taking the client seriously, whatever they say about their situation.

> A client tells you they've got a problem, then they've got a problem and you'd better take it seriously. You'd also better take it seriously if they tell you they ain't got a problem ... someone sent him because he drinks too much. He says he doesn't drink too much and it's not a problem. Leave it alone. Take it seriously.
>
> (p. 21)

Of course, there are other ways to take this kind of conversation forward without arguing with the client, such as asking about how come the referrer sent then along. And as the conversation develops, the client's view of what they want may well develop and change. But if we don't take them seriously to start with, an argument immediately ensues, enabling the practitioner to label the client as 'resistant' or 'in denial' which contributes little to progress and much to continuing stuckness.

'Reading between the lines' is a distraction; listening very carefully to the lines and formulating appropriate responses is the name of the game. Radically accepting, not arguing with our clients and not reading between the lines leads to another key element of the SF aesthetic; staying at the surface.

Staying at the surface

In more traditional methods of therapy, counselling and allied practices, it is quite normal to see the client's behaviour as the outward manifestation of some kind of hidden internal causal mechanism. There are various forms of these hidden mechanisms, ranging from emotional to neuroscientific to ancient experience. The therapist's task is to go deep to discover these causes and assist the client to deal with them. Indeed, they may claim to be the first to notice these causes which the client must then address in order to satisfy their practitioner.

In SF work, as I have written before (McKergow & Korman, 2009), we step around these potential questions by looking not for causes and explanations, but at the 'inbetween' – the interaction of the client with their environments, including other people. Sometimes newcomers don't notice initially that SF questions are always framed from the point of view of an active person (often the client, but sometimes others in the client's world) and their interactions rather than 'internal' drivers. 'What would be the first tiny signs you noticed that things were getting slightly better?' is a typical example. It is not inviting them to introspect, to speculate over their feelings or other causal matters. We seek to focus our clients' attention towards the outside, towards the world and towards what's better in the past, present and future (Jackson & McKergow, 2002).

Workers in the brief therapy tradition strive to take mental health out of the clients' heads and into their interactions with others. It's an easy assumption to think that mental illness is lurking within the client's body or brain, and therefore diagnosis accompanied by either internal reflection or drugs are required to cure it. I am not anti-drugs by any means, but I am not in favour of putting people on drugs when they can be helped by a few sessions of conversation. The sessions may even help the clients use their medication more effectively (Panayotov, Strahilov & Anichkina, 2011). The new work I presented in Chapter 6, and discussed initially in McKergow (2019), shows how an enactive view can bring a truly integrative perspective to these matters.

It's interesting to notice how client autonomy and radical acceptance sit happily alongside staying at the surface. These are all important parts which add up to a dramatic new take on what it means to be human.

Valuing small differences

This final, part of the SF aesthetic is slightly different to the others – the value we place on small differences, detailed descriptions and tiny as opposed to huge signs. It is normal and logical to assume that large changes to the client's life and circumstances will require big plans, big efforts, total commitment, and utter transformation. One part of this is why it is assumed that long treatments must always be superior to short ones, despite evidence to the contrary. Small signs of progress are very valuable, the potential forerunners of more change, and signs that the client is on the way to a good enough life, where they feel able to tackle things under their own steam.

From my very first SF training workshop (with Jane Lethem of the then Brief Therapy Practice in 1994), the idea has been present that small changes in one area of the client's life can expand both through natural processes and a ripple effect into other areas of life. It's not hard to see how slightly better relations at home can spill over into more confidence at work, more openness to relations with children and parents, less stress, more time to enjoy life and so on.

This kind of connectedness fits well with both Buddhist philosophy, in which Steve de Shazer was interested (see for example de Shazer, 1994, p. 9), and also with the science of complexity (see for example Waldrop, 1993), which emerged in the early 1990s. I discovered both SF and complexity at the same time, and made some initial connections of my own. Complexity shows how novel and unpredictable outcomes can emerge from small differences in unplanned and unexpected ways.

Sometimes when I have worked with people from other traditions, I have noticed that while they may be happy to discuss better in big picture, abstract noun, $5,000 word terms, they can become very nervous when I start asking about tiny details. One very experienced facilitator complained that they thought I was forcing people into action by doing this. Well, as long as that's what they are paying me for, I make no apology! It is certainly interesting and under-discussed how talk about tiny details seems to lead smoothly and quickly to new possibilities for action. The idea that SF work stretches the world of the client is all about this being a natural and compelling opening of possibilities.

Looking backwards and forwards

At the end of this book, this is a good moment to look back at where we've come from and to look forward at what might come next. Let's start by looking back.

Therapeutic practice

SFBT is a different *kind* of approach to most. If we take these five aspects of an SF aesthetic, we can see a very telling contrast from the classical psychotherapeutic norm (Table 14.1).

Note that none of these is about miracle questions, contracts, scaling, compliments and so on as such. These techniques seem to me to be more like corollaries of the aesthetic, natural ways of working which follow from these basics.

There may well be a clue here about how come SF gets such short shrift from those accustomed to a more classical/traditional way of working. In the same way that Monet and Matisse were laughed at by the Parisian art audience, so SF is seen as risible by those accustomed to valuing length and depth. And there are also practical difficulties; practitioners accustomed to long and lucrative engagements may not see why they should change.

Table 14.1 Comparing the classical therapeutic and SF aesthetics.

Classical therapy aesthetic	SF aesthetic
Long treatments are necessary	Brevity – as brief as possible – is desirable
Power is with the practitioner	Client autonomy is to be respected wherever possible
Read between the lines	Radical acceptance
Go deep	Stay at the surface
Valuing large and dramatic transformations	Valuing small differences

SF practitioners

If SF practice can look odd to those looking from outside, it can also present difficulties to those working within the tradition. Some take their practice very seriously, and seek to use the principles throughout their work, their working lives and even beyond. This can create problems for what purports to be a maturing field. Not-knowing can be to extreme and unhelpful levels; folk refuse to say anything at all about what they do, merely reflecting questions and dodging any form of open debate. This extreme lack of curiosity about our practice, as opposed to our clients, has made building connection with the academic and professional worlds much harder. It looks like inclusivity, but actually it's one-up-man-ship masquerading as humility.

Others value appreciation and consensus and would apparently rather have a united practitioner community than any debate about what we do and why it makes sense. Yes, we accept whatever our clients say (as a starting point), but that's not the same as accepting any old nonsense as 'solution-focused' simply because someone says it is and it would be rude to disagree. Steve de Shazer, with his five books, 76 chapters and articles, was not one to suffer fools gladly. I would welcome developing the field with rational (and appreciative) experimentation and discussion rather than treating any new idea with a mix of bafflement and reluctance.

Future research and exploration

This book has offered a new way to look at SF work as stretching the world of the client. There are sound reasons for proposing this from both practical and conceptual stances. It opens the door to further questions for exploration:

- How does detailed language connect with the generation of affordances?
- What is the experience of clients in the period after an SF session? How is it to be in a stretched world?
- How can the practitioner know that they are making progress in the session rather than waiting until the follow-up?
- And most importantly, how is the idea of stretching the world received by practitioners, clients, health professionals and the public? I intend it to

offer a plausible and acceptable way to explain what we do, to aid wider use of SF approaches. My initial work suggests that people 'get it' quickly and easily and become more interested in the approach.

Conclusion

We started from the idea that 'change is happening all the time'. It seems odd that practitioners can embrace this with their clients, get perturbed when their field starts to move on. I come back to the five defining qualities of SFBT mentioned at the start of this book:

- Effective
- Efficient
- Ethical/respectful
- Energising
- Elegant.

If it does that, only better, then I'm in. This shift to a new paradigm got me interested back in 1993 and has kept me at it for all the years since. For a new way of things to be more elegant is precious enough. For the new way to be more efficient as well is truly extraordinary. If SF delivers brief, respectful, humane treatment and progress at work, at school, in the hospital and the therapy room, then we owe it to everyone to go on.

Key points

- SFBT practice is a new *kind* of treatment compared to traditional views of therapy, counselling etc.
- It can be viewed as a new aesthetic, a term coming from the art world to describe a new paradigm and way of looking.
- I propose five key values of the SF aesthetic:

  - Efficiency
  - Client autonomy
  - Radical acceptance
  - Staying at the surface
  - Valuing small differences.

- These values stand in stark contrast to older views of what treatment should look like, which may explain the lack of acceptance and interest from other practitioners.
- Overplayed, these values have sometimes led to unhelpful misunderstandings within the practitioner community.
- SF practice deserves to become much more widely used and accepted, if effective and rapid treatment is a prime goal.

References

Berne, E. (1958). Transactional analysis: A new and effective method of group therapy. *The American Journal of Psychotherapy*, *12*(4), 735–743.

de Shazer, S. (1994). *Words Were Originally Magic*. New York, NY: W. W. Norton.

de Shazer, S. (1997). Commentary: Radical acceptance. *Families, Systems, & Health*, *15*(4), 375–378. http://dx.doi.org/10.1037/h0090136

Dolan, Y. M. (1991). *Resolving Sexual Abuse: Solution-Focused Therapy and Ericksonian Hypnosis for Adult Survivors*. New York, NY: W. W. Norton.

Hoyt, M. F. (2001). On the importance of keeping it simple and taking the client seriously: A conversation with Steve de Shazer and John Weakland. In M. F. Hoyt (Ed.), *Conversations with Brief Therapy Experts*. London: Routledge. Retrieved from http://web.uvic.ca/psyc/bavelas/De%20Shazer_Weakland%20interview.pdf

Hume, D. (1987). *Essays Moral, Political, Literary*. Indianapolis: Literary Fund.

International Coach Federation. (2019). *Definition of Coaching*. Retrieved from https://coachfederation.org/about

Jackson, P. Z., & McKergow, M. (2002). *The Solutions Focus* (2nd rev. ed., 2007). London: Nicholas Brealey Publishing.

Kant, I. (1790/2000). *Critique of the Power of Judgment (Kritik der Urteilskraft)*. (Trans. Paul Guyer & Eric Matthews). Cambridge: Cambridge University Press.

Lexico.com. (2019). *Aesthetic*. Retrieved from www.lexico.com/en/definition/aesthetic

McKergow, M. (2019). Stretching the world: A friendly explanation of SF practice. In K. Dierolf, D. Hogan, S. van der Hoorn, & S. Wignaraja (Eds.), *Solution Focused Practice around the World* (pp. 50–56). London: Routledge.

McKergow, M. W., & Korman, H. (2009). Inbetween: Neither inside nor outside: The radical simplicity of solution-focused brief therapy. *Journal of Systemic Therapies*, *28*(2), 34–49.

MIND. (2013). *We still Need to Talk: A Report on Access to Talking Therapies*. Retrieved from www.mind.org.uk/media-a/4248/we-still-need-to-talk_report.pdf

Panayotov, P. A., Strahilov, B. E., & Anichkina, A. Y. (2011). Solution-focused brief therapy and medication adherence with schizophrenic patients. In C. Franklin, T. Trepper, E. McCollum, & W. Gingerich (Eds.), *Solution-Focused Brief Therapy. A Handbook of Evidence-Based Practice* (pp. 196–202). Oxford: Oxford University Press.

Rose, S. P. R. (1997). *Lifelines: Life beyond the Gene*. New York: Oxford University Press.

Segal, L. (1991). Brief therapy: The MRI approach. In A. S. Gurman & D. P. Kniskern (Eds.), *Handbook of Family Therapy* (Vol. 2, pp. 171–199). Philadelphia, PA: Brunner/Mazel.

Waldrop, M. (1993). *Complexity: The Emerging Science at the Edge of Order and Chaos*. New York: Pocket Books.

Index

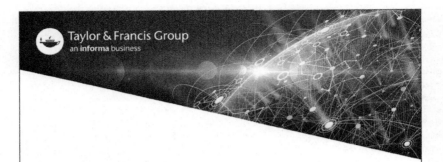

Printed in Great Britain
by Amazon